The Complete Book of Business Forms and Agreements

Cliff Roberson, LLM, Ph.D.
University of Houston, Victoria

McGraw-Hill, Inc.
New York San Francisco Washington, D.C. Auckland Bogotá
Caracas Lisbon London Madrid Mexico City Milan
Montreal New Delhi San Juan Singapore
Sydney Tokyo Toronto

Library of Congress Cataloging-in-Publication Data

Roberson, Cliff.
    The complete book of business forms and agreements / Cliff
Roberson.
        p.   cm.
    Includes index.
    ISBN 0-07-911611-6 (book : acid free paper/disk set) :   —
ISBN 0-07-053116-1 (book : acid free paper).—ISBN 0-07-852677-9
(disk)
    1. Commercial law—United States—Forms. 2. Contracts—United
States—Forms. 3. Small business—United States—Forms. I. Title.
KF886.R63 1994
346.73'-07'0269—dc20
[347.30670269]   93-24204
                                                       CIP

1 2 3 4 5 6 7 8 9 0 DOH/DOH 9 9 8 7 6 5 4 3

PN 0-07-053116-1
PART OF
ISBN 0-07-911611-6

*The sponsoring editor for this book was David Conti, the editing supervisor was
Fred Dahl, and the production supervisor was Donald Schmidt. This book was
set in Palatino by Inkwell Publishing Services.*

Printed and bound by R.R. Donnelley & Sons Company.

This publication is designed to provide accurate and authoritative information in regard to the subject matter covered. It is sold with the understanding
that the publisher is not engaged in rendering legal, accounting, or other
professional service. If legal advice or other expert assistance is required, the
services of a competent professional person should be sought.
            —from a declaration of principles jointly adopted by a committee
                of the American Bar Association and a committee of Publishers

 This book is printed on recycled, acid-free paper containing
a minimum of 50% recycled de-inked fiber.

Contents

Chapter 1   Using Forms / 1

Chapter 2   Personnel / 5

Chapter 3   Real Estate Forms and Agreements / 95

Chapter 4   Leases and Rental Forms and Agreements / **131**

Chapter 5 Credit and Collection Forms and Agreements / 179

Chapter 6 Assignments / 229

Chapter 7   Sales Forms and Agreements / 281

Chapter 8   Sale of Business Assets / 325

Chapter 9   Corporate Forms and Agreements / 355

Chapter 10 Independent Contractors and Subcontractors / **393**

Chapter 11   Loans and Security Forms and Agreements / 407

Chapter 12   Partnership Forms and Agreements / 443

Chapter 13   Powers of Attorney / 461

Chapter 14   Professional Services / 481

Chapter 15 Bankruptcy / 501

Legal Glossary / 511

Index / 517

Preface

This book is a collection of forms, agreements, and contracts that I have developed in my 20-plus years of law practice. Included also are discussions on the legal aspects of doing business. As we get older, we learn to work smarter, not harder. One way to do this is to have a library of forms to cover the various situations that generally occur in the conduct of running a business. It is my goal to provide you with a general discussion of the legal issues and with the most complete set of forms available so that you will have them ready for use in almost any situation.

It is commonly said, "Why reinvent the wheel?" Businesses should adhere to this maxim. Each day businesspeople face situations in which the use of standard forms can assist them in putting the necessary agreements, contracts, or intentions in writing. Having the right form provides everyone with a paper record of the contents of any agreement, contract, or statement of intention. Using a library of standard forms obviates the need to reinvent the wheel.

Each chapter begins with a discussion of the legal issues, followed by a collection of legal and business forms or agreements, or both, related to those issues. Each of the forms has been reviewed or written by an attorney. Depending on the complexity of the situation it covers, you may wish to have your attorney review the completed form. The cost to have a lawyer review a completed form is substantially less than the cost of having it prepared from scratch. In case of doubt, consult an attorney regarding the proper use of any specific form.

Chapter 1 contains general instructions and guidelines for using standard forms. It also contains general principles for using forms.

The other chapters are divided by subject matter. The separate chapters are arranged to facilitate the identification and completion of the appropriate form within each subject area.

Cliff Roberson

How to Use the Disk

The disk that comes with this book is easy to use.

If you own an IBM personal computer (PC, AT, etc.) or an IBM compatible and use MS/DOS (Microsoft Disk Operating System), you can make use of this disk. The disk itself is 3.5-in., double-sided, high-density.

Getting started is simple. After turning on your computer (and you have "C:>" prompt in DOS), insert the disk into the 3.5-in. drive (usually called the b: drive, but it could also be a:). Type:

    md c:\forms

This will create a directory called "Forms" on your hard drive. Then type:

    c: [Enter]
    cd\forms [Enter]
    copy b:\forms*.* c:\forms   [Enter]

You will see files being copied from the disk to the hard drive. You can now store the floppy disk as a backup.

When you run your word processing program, these files may be loaded from the "Forms" directory. Note that the filenames are "forms2-," "forms3-," and so on. Any form found in Chap. 2 of the book will be found in the file entitled "forms2-." Chapter 3 forms will be in "forms3-," and so on.

You may want to organize your files differently (perhaps create a separate file for each form), or select only some of the files for storage on your computer's hard drive. Having all the forms available on the hard drive makes it easier for you to tailor them to your needs—and keeps the original disk safe if you mistakenly delete something.

The forms have been saved in ASCII, so that they can imported into most or all word processors. To call up a form on your screen from the floppy disk or the hard drive, access the directory name, and then type the filename.

For example, suppose you want to access something from the file FORMS2- in the book. For floppy disk users, the pathname is b:\forms\forms2-. For hard disk users, it is c:\forms\forms2-.

If your word processor contains default margins, the letter should appear on the screen with line wraps at those margins. If your word processor does not contain default margins, the lines of the letter may run off the right edge of the screen. If so, simply define the margins you want, and the line wraps should be adjusted accordingly.

The Complete
Book of
Business Forms
and Agreements

Chapter 1

Using Forms

This chapter introduces the forms and agreements in the book and explains the general rules and principles for completing and using them.

In the text, the term *form* is used in the broad sense to include all types of standard agreements, form letters, and so on. The terms *contract* and *agreement* are often used interchangeably. For the most part, the two terms *are* interchangeable. A contract is a binding agreement. In some cases, however, an agreement may not be binding, in which case it is not a contract. In this book, only binding agreements are discussed. A nonbinding agreement is merely an unenforceable promise to do something. For example, a promise to have lunch with a friend is not an enforceable agreement. The courts would probably consider it to be only a social engagement. An agreement to meet with an attorney for lunch to discuss a problem that you are facing may be a binding agreement, however, because the principal purpose of the lunch is business. Accordingly, the attorney probably could bill you for the time if you did not keep the promised appointment.

The advantages of using standard forms include the following:

- *Preventing disputes.* A written agreement that spells out each party's rights and duties is the best method of preventing disputes.
- *Avoiding lawsuits.* By using written agreements, each party is forced to recognize what the agreements really provide. Written agreements help to prevent the types of misunderstandings that usually end up in court.
- *Reducing legal fees.* The forms in this book may often be used to eliminate the need for the assistance of an attorney.

1

- *Improving accuracy.* By using the standard forms you are less likely to make a mistake in the agreement or to leave out a key provision.
- *Improving records.* The use of written agreements helps to provide proof of your activities, which therefore help you to avoid tax and other difficulties in establishing a record.
- *Increasing efficiency.* It is easier and more efficient to complete a standard form than to attempt to draft one from scratch.

General Rules

In building and using a library of standard forms, certain general rules should be followed. Accordingly, the most important general rules are highlighted and numbered throughout the book. Consider them as cardinal rules to be violated only with caution.

Rule 1

Read the selected form carefully. After you have tentatively selected the correct form, read it carefully. Are there any terms, statements, or other materials in the form that do not correspond to the purpose you intend? If so, delete the inappropriate parts or statements. Too often business persons in a hurry select the apparently correct form and use it without carefully examining it. After you have completed the form, reread it. Does it make sense? If not, seek professional advice.

Rule 2

If there is any phrase or statement in the form that you do not understand, don't use the form. People often use a standard form that is apparently what they need for a transaction without fully understanding all parts of the form. This is a dangerous practice and can lead to expensive litigation later. If you don't understand a part of the form, find out what it means or delete it before you use the form.

Rule 3

Ensure that the complete terms of the transaction are in the form. Too often, we use a form as a record of a transaction but do not include the verbal understandings by the parties of essential aspects of the transaction. Omission of the verbal understandings is dangerous. *All* important aspects of the transaction, including the verbal ones, should be contained in the form. The general law in most states is that the parties to a written agreement may not bring in evidence of verbal agreements that contradict the terms of the written agreement. This principle, known as the *Parol Evidence Rule*, has caused many problems when all the terms of an agreement are not reduced to writing and signed by both parties.

Rule 4   *Date all forms on the date they are executed.* Any form that is the record of an agreement or contract should be dated as of the date that the parties complete and sign it. If the form applies to a transaction that is to be completed in the future, the form should still be dated on the date that it is completed and signed. In addition, it should contain a performance date or completion date. As a general rule, contracts are considered as valid and binding on the date that they are signed. It is assumed that any contract that is dated was signed on the date indicated on the contract.

Rule 5   *If the standard form does not fit the transaction, modify it.* No forms are set in concrete. If the selected form does not fit your requirements, tailor it to fit the situation. Some legal forms must meet certain requirements. For example, notice to a tenant that rent is past due usually requires a statement of the exact amount of rent that is actually past due. If you are concerned about deleting or changing a portion of a form, obtain legal advice. Obtaining legal assistance at the time the contract is entered into or the notice given is more economical than obtaining it when a problem arises.

Rule 6   *Build your own library of forms by keeping a file of the forms you use.* Although this book contains one of the most complete sets of forms available, you should also start your own library, because your forms are designed for your particular business. Develop a filing method to prevent the need to hunt through a stack of forms. One method is to make an extra copy of each form that you use and file it in a forms folder. To make forms easier to locate, it is often helpful to build an index of forms by key words.

Signing Agreements

If an agreement is to be binding on you in your personal capacity, then you may just sign your name to the contract. If, however, you are signing on behalf of your corporation or partnership, make sure that your signature indicates that you are signing on the basis of your authority as an officer of the business. Failure to do so may make you personally liable on the contract. Note the two following examples in which the individual is signing only in the capacity of an officer of the business:

Example by a corporate officer

ABC, Inc.
By:
_____
William J. Smith, President

Example by partnership officer

ABC, A General Partnership
By:
_____
William J. Smith, Partner

If it is required that the agreement be signed before a notary public (i.e., acknowledged), then do not sign the agreement until you are in the presence of the notary. If the contract is to be completed by mail and you sign the contract first, sign two copies and mail both to the other party. Request that the other party sign one of the copies and return it to you. This procedure provides both parties with a signed copy of the agreement. If you want the other party to sign first, then send two unsigned copies and ask the other party to sign both copies and return them to you. When you receive both copies, sign one and return it to the other party, keeping one copy for yourself.

If last-minute changes are made to the agreement, you may write them in. In which case, make sure the change is readable and is initialed by all parties to the contract.

Using an Attorney

No book involving business agreements could possibly cover every situation involving the complex world of business. This book is designed to give you help with the simpler, more straightforward transactions. If the agreement is complex or involves large sums of money, have it reviewed by your attorney before you sign it. The book cannot replace your attorney, but it can help you to reduce your legal fees.

Chapter 2

Personnel

This chapter contains a brief overview of personnel law, followed by personnel forms, agreements, and form letters concerning personnel matters. Personnel practices are a potential source of costly civil litigation for any company. It is essential that the company have written personnel policies and rules.

General Rules

Companies should adopt and follow certain golden rules to reduce their liability in the personnel area.

Rule 1   Have written rule and policies. Ensure that they are followed.

Rule 2   Apply all rules and policies uniformly. Do not discriminate in applying the rules and policies.

Rule 3   Keep detailed records on all important personnel decisions, especially the hiring and firing of employees.

Rule 4   Do not provide references on present or former employees. Only confirm details of their employment and position held.

Rule 5   Keep detailed records on employee performance of duty.

Hiring Employees

Common sense and an honest desire to be fair call eliminate many of the legal problems normally associated with hiring or not hiring employees. Because of the equal opportunity requirements, the decision to hire should be based on a comparison of individual applicants' ability, experience, and qualifications for the job. Even unintentional discrimination can cause the employer legal problems. For example, placing an employment ad in the local newspaper for a recent high school graduate can be construed as discrimination based on age. The words "recent high school graduate" could be taken to mean that you want only young people to apply. Therefore, it would discriminate against older persons.

Although employers are not required to restructure their employment practices to maximize the number of members of a minority or other protected group they hire, they are required to provide equal employment opportunity to all.

The protected classifications in employment practices are those based on age, sex, race, religion, and national origin. In addition, with the recent passage of the Americans With Disabilities Act, there are protections based on physical status (i.e., the handicapped). The other important federal laws pertaining to equal employment opportunity include the following:

- The Civil Rights Act of 1964 (Title VII), which prohibits discrimination on the basis of race, creed, color, sex, or national origin. Title VII has been amended several times; the most important was the Civil Rights Act of 1991.
- The Equal Employment Opportunity Act, which established the Equal Employment Opportunity Commission (EEOC).
- The Equal Pay Act, which requires equal pay to men and women doing equal work.
- The Age Discrimination Act, which prohibits age discrimination against persons between the ages of 40 and 72.
- The National Labor Relations Act, which prohibits discrimination by labor unions.

Interviewing Applicants

To prevent any questions regarding unintentional discrimination in the screening process, certain interview questions should not be asked of applicants. Some of the more common improper questions are the following:

- Where were your parents born?
- Do you have grandparents or other relatives living in a foreign country?
- Where did your ancestors come from?

(These first three questions are not job-related and would tend to indicate the national origin of the applicant.)

- Do you attend church?
- What church do you attend?
- Do you believe in abortion?
- Who is your pastor?

(These four questions can indicate the religious beliefs of the applicant.)

- Do you expect to have any children (if asked of a woman)?
- If you go to work, who will watch your children?
- What does your spouse do?

(These last three questions can be considered as indicating a sexual bias.)

Checking References

The firm of Robert Half (a national employment agency) has conducted extensive research regarding the checking of references of job applicants. The following list includes some of the points that they recommend in screening employment applicants:

- Start checking references as soon as possible.
- Ignore written references provided by the candidate.
- Seek additional references not previously mentioned by the applicant.
- Call former employers.
- Get references by phone, not in writing. People tend to be reluctant to provide negative information in writing.
- Start reading the résumés from the end to the front. People tend to put the less flattering information at the end of the résumé.
- Be wary of résumés without fixed dates of employment.
- Verify the accuracy of the résumé.

Physical Handicaps

The Americans With Disabilities Act prohibits an employer from discriminating against an employee or prospective employee who is physically handicapped unless the handicap could impair job performance or create a danger to other employees. In a recent California case (*Raytheon* v. *California Fair Employment & Housing Commission*), the court held that an employer could not discharge an employee solely because he had Acquired Immune Deficiency Syndrome (AIDS). The court stated that AIDS is a physical handicap because it is a condition that affects the body and at some point will impair functioning of the body. The fact that the condition may not currently be disabling does not prevent including AIDS in the definition of physical handicap. The court noted that at the time of the firing the information available to Raytheon indicated that AIDS was not transmissible in the workplace and that the employee was fit to return to his job.

Immigration Law Requirements

Employers are required to verify that all employees hired after November 6, 1986, are U.S. citizens or aliens authorized to work in this country. Failure to make a good faith effort to comply will subject the employer to civil penalties. *Note:* It is illegal to discriminate in employment on the basis of citizenship status and national origin. Also, employers should not fire or fail to hire any person on the basis of foreign appearance, language, or name.

Employers are required to complete an INS I–9 form on each new employee within three business days of the hiring. Any questions about completing the form or other questions about the requirement should be directed to the nearest U.S. Immigration and Naturalization Service office.

Firing Employees

Employers can reduce their liability for wrongful termination of employees by following certain practices. Some of the actions recommended to reduce an employer's liability in this regard are the following:

- Avoid any derogatory remarks when terminating an employee.
- Do not give written reasons for the termination, even if requested to do so by the employee.

- Rather than firing employees, when possible assist them in finding new jobs.
- Make and retain documentation for your firing decision.
- Establish standards regarding layoffs and terminations.
- Fire employees at the first of the week. Most employees are fired on Fridays. Accordingly, they have the weekend to brood about it. If individuals are fired during the first part of the week, many of them will begin looking for other work the next day. In most cases it is best to provide only general reasons for dismissal. Reasons that are too specific may cause problems if the employee can establish some error in the alleged reasons. If, however, the employee is under contract that requires specific reasons for dismissal, those reasons should be delineated.

Resignations

When an employee wishes to leave the company, the human resources department should prepare a letter similar to the one shown in Form 2–57 and have the employee sign it. Notice that in the letter the employee acknowledges an obligation to return all company property and to protect the company's trade secrets. The employee also states that the termination is voluntary.

Employee Relations

Maintaining high standards in dealing with employees and expecting similar treatment from them benefit the company by reducing absenteeism, employee turnover, and employee misconduct.

Four workplace factors contribute to good or bad employee relations, as follows:

- *Opportunity*. Are employees provided an equal opportunity to advance in the company? Are promotions based on merit, and do the promotions create the impression of fairness?
- *Differential association*. Differential association is a behavior theory that contends that the influence of those persons with whom we associate determines to a great extent our own behavior. If some employees are unhappy with management or company

actions, their perceptions tend to cause other employees with whom they associate also to be unhappy.

- *Managerial attitude.* If a company's managers have a poor attitude, the employees will likely also have a poor attitude. For good employee relations, the managers must set the example.

- *Job satisfaction.* Job satisfaction helps to create good employee relations. Employees who are not satisfied with their jobs seldom promote positive employee/employer relationships.

Occupational Safety and Health Act

The Occupational Safety and Health Act (OSHA) is a broad statute designed to protect all employees except those specially protected by other legislation. The general theme of OSHA is that the employer has a duty to provide a place of employment free from recognized hazards that are likely to cause death or serious bodily harm. The Occupational Safety and Health Administration (also referred to as OSHA) administers the act. Employers should obtain two handbooks from their regional OSHA office: the *OSHA Handbook for Small Businesses* and *Record-keeping Requirements Under the Occupational Safety and Health Act of 1970.* Some of the general provisions of OSHA include the following:

- All identifiable hazards are covered by the act.
- It is unlawful to fire a person because the person refuses to do work that the employee reasonably believes exposes him or her to immediate and substantial risk of bodily injury.
- Most employers are required to keep extensive records regarding employee injuries, deaths, and use of protective equipment.
- Employers with fewer than 10 employees are exempt from OSHA recordkeeping requirements.

Note: Many states have state OSHA agencies with similar responsibilities.

Dealing with Labor Unions

The labor policy of the United States as set forth in the major labor relations acts includes the following aims:

- To promote industrial peace between employers and employees by use of the collective bargaining process.
- To promote the self-organization of employees.
- To place restraints on certain unethical labor practices.
- To encourage the use of conciliation and mediation services in labor disputes.
- To provide for cooling-off periods in labor disputes that threaten the health and welfare of the nation.

As noted, employees have a right to organize and to form labor unions. The general rules for dealing with labor unions include the following:

- It is an unfair labor practice to interfere with, restrain, or coerce employees in their efforts to form a labor union.
- An employer is not permitted to show favoritism in cases involving two or more competing labor unions.
- Promising additional benefits to those employees who do not join a labor union is illegal.
- An employer cannot change employee benefits in an attempt to prevent or influence a union election.
- Management has a duty to bargain in good faith with a labor union that is certified to represent company employees.
- The employer may inform employees that unionization will reduce the company's flexibility in the management of employees and the operation of the company.
- The employer may in a nondiscriminatory manner bar off-duty employees from soliciting on company property.
- When bargaining with recognized unions, management must bargain in good faith over wages, hours, terms, and conditions of employment.
- Management is not required to bargain with unions regarding management decisions that deal with policy and long-range planning decisions.

Right-to-Work Laws

Many states have enacted right-to-work laws that prohibit union or agency shop agreements. These agreements are contracts between the employer and the union that either require all employees join the union or, if an employee chooses not to join the union, that the employee still be required to pay union dues.

Providing References on Former Employees

Employers have been sued for giving references on former employees. For example, in one case a former employer was sued by a doctor for libel and back pay because the doctor's prospective employer was informed that the doctor was discharged "for cause." The court held that the doctor may have been libeled by the statement that the firing was for cause. In another case, an insurance company was sued for informing a prospective employer that the job applicant was fired from his former job because of a dispute over a travel expense claim.

Giving only favorable information regarding a former employee can also cause trouble. In one case, an employee was fired after he was implicated in a rape case. The former employer provided a very favorable recommendation for the former employee and did not mention the rape charges. The second employer later sued the first employer for the false favorable recommendation after the second employer had to pay damages to another employee who was raped by the employee.

The safest policy for an employer to follow is to provide only a statement of fact that the former employee was employed from one date to another, without any comment regarding the quality of the employment or whether the individual was fired or left voluntarily.

Unfair Competition

An employer can take three steps to prevent exemployees from providing secret trade information to a competitor:

1. Limit access to only those employees who need to know.
2. Educate employees about the importance of protecting company secrets.
3. Require employees to sign a restrictive agreement with provisions that protect the business.

Keeping Clients

One problem most companies have is the stealing of clients by former employees. Many employees feel that when they move to a new business, they can take their clients (i.e., the company's clients) with them. One way to prevent this is to include in any employment agreement a promise that on termination of employment, an employee will not solicit or pursue any clients of the employer. In most states, as long as the restrictions are reasonable as to time and distance, the restrictions can be enforced in a breach of contract suit.

Company Secrets

An important asset of a business is its secrets. Business secrets can include price lists, blueprints, programs, plans, availability of supplies, and other information necessary to run a business. Some protection is received from patents, copyrights, and trademark law, but other valuable business secrets are not so protected. To combat the practice of unethical businesspersons who use commercial espionage to their own advantage, many states have adopted some form of the Uniform Trade Secrets Act, which protects a business' ownership of business and trade secrets. Courts have the power to prevent competitors from using illegally obtained secret information. To take advantage of the protection of the Act, the business owner should take the following steps:

- Clearly mark essential documents "Confidential—to be shown only to authorized persons."
- Restrict access of secret information to only those employees who need to know the information.
- Make only a limited number of copies of the documents containing secret information, and safeguard the location and distribution of those documents.
- Require all employees to sign secrecy agreements.
- Counsel all new employees on the importance of company trade secrets.
- Counsel all departing employees on their obligation to honor the secrecy agreements.

If you do not have an employment contract with employees, you may use a separate agreement. In this case, have the employee sign the agreement as a condition of employment. Execute the agreement in duplicate. Keep one copy and give one copy to the employee. Check local laws to see if any additional requirements are necessary to protect yourself from unfair competition.

If you do not have a contract and a former employee has unfairly provided other businesses with your trade secrets, check with a local attorney to see if you have a cause of action based on an implied contract. Many states recognize in any employment situation an implied agreement that an employee will not engage in unfair competition after leaving the company.

Personnel Records

Title VI of the Civil Rights Act and the Wage–Hour Law requires that certain records be kept on each employee. *Note:* There may be additional record-keeping requirements placed on you by state law. Federal record keeping includes those required by the EEOC and the Wage–Hour Law.

The EEOC requires that applications for employment be retained for at least six months. *Note:* One court concluded that the failure to retain the applications for the six-month period could be considered as evidence of illegal discrimination. Because of the frequency of litigation in this area, I recommend that you retain all employment applications for at least three years.

The Wage–Hour Law requires that records on employees be maintained and kept for three years. The data required under this law include the following:

The name and home address of each employee.

The sex, occupation, and age of each employee under 19 years of age.

The hour and day of week that the work week begins.

Hours worked each day and total hours worked each week.

Record of overtime pay.

All deductions and additions to wages.

Wages paid each pay period and date of payment.

Inform employees of the records being kept on them and of their right to inspect their individual records for accuracy. Employees also have a right to know how the records will be used when promotions, retention, and the like are being considered. *Note:* Individual employee records are confidential; release them only on a need-to-know basis. Before releasing any confidential information on an employee, ascertain the legality of releasing the requested data.

Forms in This Chapter

- FORM 2–1: CONFIRMATION OF EMPLOYMENT. Confirms an employment offer that has been made orally to an applicant.

- FORM 2–2: EMPLOYMENT AGREEMENT. An employment contract and a written record of an employment agreement between an employer and an employee.

- FORM 2–3: SUMMARY OF EMPLOYMENT TERMS. Used when there are no written employment contracts. Provides a record of the employment terms under which the employee was hired.

- FORM 2–4: PART-TIME/TEMPORARY EMPLOYMENT AGREEMENT. A written record of a part-time or temporary employment agreement between an employer and an employee. Also serves as a notice to employees that their employment position is only part-time or temporary.

- FORM 2–5: EMPLOYEE WARNING NOTICE. Notifies an employee that unless the employee takes corrective action, the employee will be dismissed. Provides a written record of the warning.

- FORM 2–6: EMPLOYEE NOTICE OF DISMISSAL. Notifies an employee of his or her dismissal. Provides written record of the dismissal.

- FORM 2–7: NOTICE OF NIGHT WORK. Notifies new employees that they are hired with the understanding that they are subject to being assigned night work.

- FORM 2–8: SALES REPRESENTATIVE AGREEMENT. An agreement between a business owner and sales representative.

- FORM 2–9: INVENTIONS AND PATENTS AGREEMENT. A record of the agreement between an employee and employer regarding inventions and patents that may be developed on company time.

- FORM 2–10: NONCOMPETITION AGREEMENT (ACCOUNTS). Protects customer accounts after an employee has left the business. Prevents an ex-employee from attempting to steal the accounts of the business.

- FORM 2–11: NONCOMPETITION AGREEMENT (AREA). Protects geographic areas after an employee has left the business.

- FORM 2–12: NONDISCLOSURE OF TRADE SECRETS. Protects the employer from the disclosure of trade secrets.

- FORM 2–13: EMPLOYEE STATEMENT REGARDING CONFIDENTIAL DATA. Used by the employer when an employee who is subject to a confidentiality agreement terminates employment.

- FORM 2–14: NOTICE OF CONFIDENTIALITY AGREEMENT. Notifies other companies that their new employee is under a confidentiality agreement with your company. It is important that this notice not be sent unless you have a signed statement from the former employee permitting such notification.

- FORM 2–15: DECLARATION REGARDING CONFLICT OF INTEREST. Records an employee's declaration of no conflict of interest.

- FORM 2–16: AGREEMENT TO INDEMNIFY EMPLOYER. Records an agreement by the employee to indemnify the employer for willful violations of federal or state law and injuries caused by negligence or willful actions of the employee.

- FORM 2–17: CONSENT TO RELEASE CONFIDENTIAL INFORMATION. A record of an employee's consent to release confidential information.

- FORM 2–18: RECORD RETENTION CHECKLIST. Ensures that the appropriate records are kept for the required length of time.

- FORM 2–19: CHANGE OF PERSONNEL DATA. An employee notification to human resources department of a change in the employee's personal data.

- FORM 2–20: CHANGE OF STATUS. Notifies human resources department of a change in employee status within the company.

- FORM 2–21: ORIENTATION CHECKLIST. A checklist for new employee orientation and a record of the orientation.

- FORM 2–22: NEW EMPLOYEE CHECKLIST. Ensures that all necessary charts and records are prepared for new employees.

- FORM 2–23: PAY RATE HISTORY. A record of the pay rate history on an employee.

- FORM 2–24: EMPLOYEE TIME SHEET. A record of employees' time sheet.

- FORM 2–25: WEEKLY TIME SHEET. A record of hours worked each week by employees.

- FORM 2–26: DAILY TIME SHEET. A record of the daily time for employees.

- FORM 2–27: WEEKLY WORK SCHEDULE. A posting record of the weekly work schedule of employees.

- FORM 2–28: FLEXTIME SCHEDULE. Used by those employees who are on flextime to record their work hours.

- FORM 2–29: OVERTIME AUTHORIZATION. A record of overtime authorization.

- FORM 2–30: REQUEST FOR COMPENSATORY TIME OFF. An employee's request for compensatory time off.

- FORM 2–31: PHYSICIAN'S REPORT. Verification that an employee is receiving medical care during a prolonged absence.

- FORM 2–32: INJURY REPORT. A report and record of an injury to an employee.

- FORM 2–33: SUPERVISOR'S REPORT OF INJURY. A supervisor's written report of an injury to an employee.

- FORM 2–34: RECORD OF INJURY REPORTS. A log of all injury reports.

- FORM 2–35: REPORT OF ABSENCE FOR MILITARY DUTY. A report of an employee's absence for military duty.

- FORM 2–36: REQUEST FOR TRANSFER. An employee's request for transfer to a different department or position within the company.

- FORM 2–37: GRIEVANCE REPORT. An employee's report of a grievance.

- FORM 2–38: SALARY REVIEW REQUEST. An employee's request for a salary review.

- FORM 2–39: RECEIPT FOR COMPANY PROPERTY. Acknowledgment by an employee of having received company property.

- FORM 2–40: EMPLOYEE PERFORMANCE RATING (SUMMARY). A summary rating of an employee's performance of duties.

- FORM 2–41: EMPLOYEE PERFORMANCE RATING (NARRATIVE). An annotated rating of an employee's performance of duties.

- FORM 2–42: GENERAL PERFORMANCE SUMMARY. A summary record of an employee's performance.

- FORM 2–43: PERFORMANCE ANALYSIS WORKSHEET. Provides information by employee that may be considered by the supervisor in completing the performance review.

- FORM 2–44: EMPLOYEE RESPONSE TO PERFORMANCE REVIEW. An employee's response to a performance review.

- FORM 2–45: LETTER OF COMMENDATION. Acknowledgment of an employee's performance of duty.

- FORM 2–46: FIRST WARNING NOTICE. An warning to an employee of violations of company rules and policies. A written record of the warning, which may be needed if further actions are taken against the employee.

- FORM 2–47: SUBSEQUENT WARNING NOTICE. A warning to an employee who has already received a first warning. A written record of the warning, which may be needed if further actions are taken against the employee.

- FORM 2–48: REPORT OF MISCONDUCT. Reports acts of misconduct or violations of company policy.

- FORM 2–49: ACKNOWLEDGMENT OF WORK RULES. Establishes that an employee has been informed of the work rules and understands that he or she may be fired for failure to abide by the rules. Also places a duty on an employee to report rules violations by other employees.

- FORM 2–50: NOTICE OF PROBATION. Notifies an employee of being placed on probation for either unsatisfactory performance of duty or for misconduct.

- FORM 2–51: NOTICE OF EXTENDED PROBATION. Notifies an employee of the extension of a probation period.

- FORM 2–52: TRAINING EVALUATION FORM. An evaluation by an employee of the company's training programs.

- FORM 2–53: NOTICE OF DISMISSAL. Notifies an employee that the employee is being dismissed.

- FORM 2–54: NOTICE OF DISMISSAL FOR VIOLATION OF WORK RULES. Notifies an employee that the employee is being dismissed for violation of work rules.

- FORM 2–55: NOTICE OF DISMISSAL FOR EXCESSIVE ABSENCES. Notifies an employee that the employee is being dismissed for excessive absences.

- FORM 2–56: NOTICE OF DISMISSAL FOR EXTENDED ABSENCE. Notifies an employee that the employee is being dismissed for a continued unauthorized absence.

- FORM 2–57: RESIGNATION. Used by an employee to resign from the company.

- FORM 2–58: EXIT INTERVIEW. A checklist for and written record of exit interviews.

- FORM 2–59: SAMPLE CONTRACT PROVISIONS TO PROTECT YOUR BUSINESS. Sample contract employment provisions that may be included to protect your business.

- FORM 2–60: CHECKOUT RECORD. Ensures that an exiting employee has completed the company's checkout procedures.

- FORM 2–61: TERMINATION REPORT. A record of the termination of each former employee.

- FORM 2–62: ACCRUED BENEFITS STATEMENT. Provides the employee with a statement of accrued benefits. Can also be used as a final statement for terminated employees.

- FORM 2–63: REPLY TO REFERENCE REQUEST. A reply by your company to another employer's request for a reference on a former employee.

- FORM 2–64: TELEPHONE REFERENCE LOG. Logs your company's telephone requests for references on prospective employees.

- FORM 2–65: SKELETON INTERVIEW. Questions on which to base interviews of middle-level employees.

- FORM 2–66: SAMPLE SEXUAL HARASSMENT POLICY.[1] Helpful in establishing a sexual harassment policy.

---

[1]For additional information on sexual harassment, see Petrocelli and Repa, *Sexual Harassment on the Job* (Berkeley, Calif.: Nolo Press, 1992).

- FORM 2–67: SAMPLE SEXUAL HARASSMENT COMPLAINT. Records important dates, facts, names. Flags important follow-up procedures.

- FORM 2–68: APPLICANT CHECKLIST. A summary record of applicants for an employment position.

- FORM 2–69: MEDICAL CONSENT. Applicant's consent for company to obtain an applicant's medical records.

- FORM 2–70: EXPENSE REIMBURSEMENT CONTRACT. Establishes a contract for reimbursement of employee expenses.

- FORM 2–71: EMPLOYEE EXPENSE REPORT. Documents employee expenses.

- FORM 2–72: REQUEST UNDER FREEDOM OF INFORMATION ACT. Request information from the federal government under the Freedom of Information Act.

2–1

CONFIRMATION OF EMPLOYMENT

[date]
[your name,
address]

Re: Confirmation of Employment

To: _____ [name of new employee]

This memorandum is to confirm our offer to you of a position with our company as [position]. The employment is to commence on [date] and will continue at the pleasure of the company.

Your starting salary will be [state employment terms]. The following fringe and other benefits are provided in connection with your employment:

[list fringe benefits such as insurance, vacation, etc.]

This employment is an at-will employment that may be terminated without cause on two weeks notice. Termination for cause may be made at any time without notice or payment in lieu of notice of good cause. Only the president of the company has the authority to modify the terms of your employment.

Your hours of employment are [state normal working hours]. You may be required to work additional hours for which you will be paid at the overtime rate of pay. All overtime must be approved in advance by your supervisor.

Your normal lunch hour will be from _____ to _____. In addition, you have a right to two _____ minute coffee breaks each full working day.

Your primary duties include the below listed duties. Other duties may be assigned to you by your supervisor.

[list primary duties]

By accepting employment, you agree not to disclose any confidential information regarding this company, any persons employed by this company, or our clients that you may learn in the course of your employment to anyone outside of this company during and after your term of employment.

If you have any questions regarding the information contained in this memorandum or regarding the position please contact [list name and telephone number of contact]. If you accept the employment subject to the above terms, please sign one copy of this memorandum and return to our offices not later than [date].

Welcome to our company.

[signed by president or other officer]

Employment on the terms set forth above are accepted.

Dated: _____   _____

                                                    signature of new employee

EMPLOYMENT AGREEMENT

This employment agreement hereby entered into between [name of employer], the Employer, and [name of employee], the Employee.

Employer and Employee agree as follows:

The Employer agrees to employ Employee and the Employee agrees to work for the Employer in the following position [insert position title here] for an indefinite period of time. The employment will commence on [date].

The duties and responsibilities of the Employee shall include:

[list primary duties and responsibilities here]

Both parties agree that the above list of duties and responsibilities are not exhaustive and may be changed, modified, or increased at the discretion of the Employer.

The Employee's normal work hours and work days are as follows:

[include work schedule at this point]

The above work schedule is subject to modification at the discretion of the Employer. The Employee is entitled to _____ weeks of vacation each calendar year after _____ months of employment. Scheduling of vacation is subject to reasonable control by the Employer.

The agreement shall be governed by the laws of the State of _____.

By accepting employment, you agree not to disclose any confidential information regarding this company, any persons employed by this company, or our clients learned in the course of your employment to anyone outside of this company during and after your term of employment.

This employment is an at-will employment that may be terminated without cause on two weeks notice. Termination for cause may be made at any time without notice or payment in lieu of notice of good cause. Only the president of the company has the authority to modify the terms of your employment.

The Employee starting salary will be _____. Except for increases in salary provided at the discretion of the Employer, the terms of this agreement remain in effect until amended in writing and signed by both parties.

Dated this _____ day of _____ 19_____.

_____   _____
Employer   Employee

2-3 SUMMARY OF EMPLOYMENT TERMS

Date: _____

To: _____

We want to take this opportunity to welcome you to our company and to summarize the employment terms that we have agreed on.

1. Position:
2. Primary duties:
3. Starting salary:
4. Benefits:
    a. health insurance:
        eligibility:
        cost to you:
    b. vacation eligibility:
    c. pension or profit sharing plans:
    d. other benefits:
5. Starting date of employment:
6. Normal working hours:
7. This employment is at will and may be terminated by either party without cause.
8. Employer reserves the right to change or modify terms of employment or benefits.
9. Other terms or conditions:

If the foregoing summary does not accurately state the agreed employment terms and conditions, please notify me immediately.

Once again, welcome to the company.

Sincerely,

2–4 PART-TIME/TEMPORARY EMPLOYMENT AGREEMENT

This employment agreement hereby entered into between [name of employer], the Employer, and [name of employee], the Employee.

Employer and Employee agree as follows:

The Employer agrees to employ Employee in a part-time/temporary status, and the Employee agrees to work for the Employer in the following position [insert position title here] in a part-time/temporary status. The employment will commence on [date].

The duties and responsibilities of the Employee shall include:

[list primary duties and responsibilities here]

Both parties agree that the foregoing list of duties and responsibilities are not exhaustive and may be changed, modified, or increased at the discretion of the Employer.

The Employee's work schedule will vary according to the needs of the Employer.

As a part-time/temporary Employee, the Employee is not eligible to participate in any fringe benefits or retirement programs.

The Employee understands that the part-time/temporary status does not entitle Employee to any special consideration for permanent or full-time employment.

The agreement shall be governed by the laws of the State of _____.

By accepting employment, you agree not to disclose any confidential information regarding this company, any persons employed by this company, or our clients learned in the course of your employment to anyone outside of this company during and after your term of employment.

This employment is an at-will employment that may be terminated without cause and without advance notice. Only the president of the company has the authority to modify the terms of your employment.

The Employee starting salary will be _____ per hour. Except for increases in salary provided at the discretion of the Employer, the terms of this agreement remain in effect until amended in writing and signed by the Employer.

Dated this _____ day of _____ 19_____.

_____   _____
Employer   Employee

2-5   EMPLOYEE WARNING NOTICE

[company name]

To: [name of problem employee]

    This memorandum is to document our discussion of this date regarding your performance of duty. At the meeting, certain unsatisfactory aspects of your employment performance were pointed out to you. The problems discussed included:

[list problems here]

    Unless the above problems are resolved and your overall performance of duty improves, it is the intention of the company to terminate your employment relationship with this company. I will provide you with assistance needed to improve your performance and meet our expectations of company employees in your type of position.

_____

[signed by company official]

    I hereby acknowledge that I have received the above warning.

Dated: _____   _____

                                     [problem employee]

2-6 EMPLOYEE NOTICE OF DISMISSAL

[company name,
address]

Date: _____

To: [name of employee being dismissed]

I regret to inform you that your employment with this company is terminated effective immediately.

Please vacate the premises immediately with your personal possessions. You may pick up your final employment check at the personnel office.

Sincerely,

_____
[signed by company official]

_____
[title]

2-7

NOTICE OF NIGHT WORK[2]

Date:

To: [new employee]

This notice is to advise you that night work may be necessary to meet present or future production requirements. Accordingly, all new employees are hired with the understanding that they are available and willing to work nights.

a. Is there any reason that you would be unavailable or unable to work the night shift?

b. If assigned to night work, do you have the necessary transportation?

_____

[signed by company officer]

I acknowledge that the offer of employment is contingent upon my being willing and able to work at night if needed.

_____

[signed by new employee]

---

[2]If employee is unable to work nights because of a disability, the Americans With Disabilities Act requires that the employer attempt to make a reasonable accommodation for the employee.

2-8

SALES REPRESENTATIVE AGREEMENT

The following agreement between [business], hereinafter referred to as the Company and [sales representative], hereinafter referred to as the Agent, is entered into between the parties on the date indicated below.

The Agent agrees:

1. to sell the company's products or merchandise in the following geographic areas: [list areas to be covered by agent at this point];
2. to comply with all Company policies;
3. to represent and state accurately the products to the customers;
4. to promptly submit all orders to the sales manager;
5. not to represent a competitive product line during the life of this agreement;
6. to make weekly contacts with the sales manager;
7. to return all Company materials, products, samples, etc. at the end of this agreement; and
8. to give at least 30 days' written notice prior to terminating this agreement.

The Company agrees:

1. to pay the following commissions to the agent:
   [include commission schedule at this point]
2. to provide the Agent with the following equipment and materials:
   [list equipment and materials to be provided]
3. to give 30 days notice before terminating this agreement; and

This agreement shall constitute (an exclusive) (nonexclusive) sales territory for the agent.

Dated: _____

_____   _____
Company Officer   Sales Representative

2-9 INVENTIONS AND PATENTS AGREEMENT

This agreement between [company name], the Company and [employee], the Employee, is entered into and effective on the date noted below.

In consideration of the employment of the Employee and the payment of wages, salary, and other benefits by Employer, Employee agrees as follows:

1. will have access to confidential secrets and equipment of the Employer.

2. not to use the information or knowledge obtained for himself or others.

3. not to take any such material or data from the Company facilities except as required by his duties to the Company.

4. to return all materials, supplies, and equipment upon request of the Employer and on termination of the employment.

5. not to disclose or publish any trade secret or confidential information of the Company's or of any other party to whom the Company owes an obligation of confidence at any time during the employment or after termination of employment.

6. to assign to the Company the Employee's rights, title, and interest in and to any inventions and improvements that are related to the activities of the company, or that are suggested by or the result of any tasks, duties, or work done for or on behalf of the company or on company time. This assignment shall be without benefit of additional compensation.

7. to promptly furnish Employer with a complete record of any and all inventions and improvements that Employee developed, conceived, made, or first disclosed during the period of this employment.

8. to give Employer timely notice of any prior employment agreements or patent rights that may conflict with the interests of the Company.

9. to notify the Employer if the Employee accepts employment with any business organization that is in competition with the Company. Such notice shall be in writing and within 30 days of such activity.

This agreement shall supersede the terms of any other agreement or understanding between the Employee and Employer if the prior agreement or understanding is in conflict with any terms of this agreement.

Dated:

_____   _____
Employer   Employee

2-10   NONCOMPETITION AGREEMENT (ACCOUNTS)

For good consideration and to induce [business name] to employ [employee name], the undersigned Employee agrees that (he)(she) will not directly compete with the [business name] during the period that the Employee is employed with the business and for five years after employment ceases.

The Employee acknowledges that during the course of Employee's employment with the Company the Employee will have access to records containing the names and addresses of customers of the Company and this agreement is therefore necessary to protect the Company's interest.

The term "compete" includes soliciting on behalf of any party other than the [business name] the business of any customer or account of the company existing during the period of employment wherein such solicitation involves a product or service that is similar to or in competition with the present or future products or services of the company.

This agreement shall be binding upon and inure to the benefit of the parties, their successors, and personal representatives.

Dated:

_____   _____
Company Officer   Sales Representative

2-11 NONCOMPETITION AGREEMENT (AREA)

For good consideration and to induce [business name] to employ [employee name], the undersigned Employee agrees that (he)(she) will not directly compete with the [business name] during the period that the Employee is employed with the Business and for five years after employment ceases.

The Employee acknowledges that during the course of Employee's employment with the Company the Employee will have access to records containing the customer names, trade secrets, and other confidential information of the Company and that this agreement is therefore necessary to protect the Company's interest.

The term "compete" includes the owning, operating, consulting, or employment by any company or entity engaged is a business similar to or in competition with the Company.

It is provided, however, that this agreement not to compete shall apply only to a radius of 50 miles from the present location of the Company.

This agreement shall be binding upon and inure to the benefit of the parties, their successors, and personal representatives.

Dated:

_____   _____
Company Officer   Sales Representative

2-12 NONDISCLOSURE OF TRADE SECRETS

Date:

As part consideration for being employed by [name of employer], the employer, the undersigned employee agrees and acknowledges:

1. That during my course of employment trade secrets of the employer may be disclosed to me. Trade secrets include, but are not limited to, technical information regarding products and services, business information such as customer lists, pricing data, sources of supplies or materials, production data, merchandising plans, and accounts.
2. I will not either during or at any time after termination of employment with employer use for myself or others, or disclose to others any trade secrets, confidential information, or any other confidential or sensitive data of the employer.
3. On the termination of my employment with the employer, I will immediately return all documents, supplies, equipment, lists, etc. that belong to the employer.
4. The employer may notify any future or prospective employer of the existence of this agreement.
5. This agreement shall be binding upon and inure to the benefit of the parties, their successors, and personal representatives.

Dated:

_____   _____
Company Officer   Employee

2-13 EMPLOYEE STATEMENT REGARDING CONFIDENTIAL DATA

I hereby acknowledge that I have received all salary and compensation due me during my employment with [name of company].

I also certify that during my course of employment I have not done or permitted any of the following:

1. Disclosure of any trade secrets or other confidential data of the company.
2. Retained any copies of any documents, materials, or drawings that are of a confidential nature.

I acknowledge that I am obligated not to disclose any of the company's trade secrets or any other confidential or sensitive data regarding the company. In addition, I acknowledge that the company has the right to inform my new employer or prospective employer of my obligation not to disclose any of [name of company]'s trade secrets or confidential data.

Dated:

_____

Signature of departing employee

2-14 NOTICE OF CONFIDENTIALITY AGREEMENT

Date: _____

To: [company to which notice is being sent]

Regarding: [name of former employee]

We have been informed that the above named person, who was previously employed by our company, is now employed by your company.

The purpose of this notice is to inform you that the individual during his/her employment with our company entered into an agreement regarding the protection of trade secrets and other confidential information. Accordingly, the individual is under a continuing obligation to our company relative to trade secrets or other confidential information.

It is not our desire to prevent the individual from exercising his/her acquired skills or general skills. We are interested only in protection of our company's confidential information. I am sure that you understand our position, and your cooperation is greatly appreciated.

A copy of this letter is also being sent to the individual named above.

Sincerely,

2–15   DECLARATION REGARDING CONFLICT OF INTEREST

Date:

[company name]
[employee name]

I have received a copy of the company's policy on conflicts of interest. I have read and understand the policies on conflicts of interest. I hereby declare that to the best of my knowledge I nor any member of my immediate family has any conflict between our personal affairs and the proper performance of my responsibilities for the company that would constitute a violation of the company's policies. I also declare that I will continue to maintain my affairs in accordance with the company's policy on conflicts of interest.

_____

Employee signature

2–16   AGREEMENT TO INDEMNIFY EMPLOYER

Date: _____

As part consideration for my employment with [name of company], I hereby agree to fully indemnify and make harmless the company from any claim by a third party claiming neglect or wrongdoing on my part. In addition, I agree to fully indemnify and make harmless the company for any loss or expense caused or incurred as the result of any violation of federal, state, or local law, or federal or state regulation within the scope of my employment with the company. Exempted from this indemnity are any such claims for which the company is adequately insured and or any liability to which the company or any other employee shares responsibility.

This agreement shall be binding upon and inure to the benefit of the employer, its successors, and personal representatives.

Signed this _____ day of _____ 19_____.

_____

Employee

2–17 CONSENT TO RELEASE CONFIDENTIAL INFORMATION

Date: _____

To: [employee]

    A request for release of confidential information has been received from [name of requesting person, agency, or company].

    Please initial each of the items below for which you consent to the release of information regarding those data:

_____ Salary
_____ Dates of employment
_____ Whether you worked under any other names
_____ Reasons for separation
_____ Position and duties
_____ Part-time or full-time employment
_____ Name of your supervisor
_____ Other information: _____

Please return to the human resources department.

Date: _____   _____
                                Employee

2-18 RECORD RETENTION CHECKLIST

The following records should be kept permanently:

Corporate records and minutes
Real estate titles and mortgages
Partnership agreements
Federal and state tax returns
Insurance records
Tax reports
Audit reports
Cash receipts journals
Inventory journals
Social Security returns
Equipment records
Long-term contract agreements
Employee injury reports and investigations

The following records should be kept for seven years:

Expired leases
Canceled checks
Canceled payroll checks
Bank deposit records
General tax records
Purchase contracts
Bank statements
Payroll journals
Sales journals
Accounts receivable ledgers
General correspondence
Uncollectible accounts records

The following records should be kept for three years:

Employment records not listed above
Employment applications
Bank deposit slips
Shipping invoices

2-19 CHANGE OF PERSONNEL DATA

Employee name: _____ Employee number: _____

Department: _____ Social Security number: _____

Effective date of change: _____

Please change my personnel records as indicated below:

Name change: _____

New address: _____

New telephone number: _____

Change in number of dependents _____

Name of dependent being added or dropped _____

Other Changes: _____

_____

Date submitted: _____

_____
Employee

2-20 CHANGE OF STATUS

Date:_____

Employee name: _____ Employee number: _____

Department: _____ Social Security number: _____

Effective date of change(s): _____

    Please make the following changes to the above employee's personnel records.

Job classification from _____ To _____

Job title from _____ To _____

Pay change from _____ To _____

Shift change from _____ To _____

Full-time/part-time change from _____ To _____

Temporary/permanent change from _____ To _____

Other changes (describe) _____

_____

_____

Submitted by _____ Date _____

Approved by _____ Date _____

2-21　ORIENTATION CHECKLIST

Date: _____

Employee name: _____ Employee number: _____

Department: _____ Social Security number: _____

Date of employment: _____

Subjects/Items reviewed:

_____ Company goals		_____ Company policies
_____ Work schedule		_____ Job training
_____ Salary		_____ Record-keeping requirements

_____ Overtime policies and procedures for approval

Supplies and storage:

_____ Use of company property, telephones, letterhead

_____ Equipment and tools

_____ Employee benefits

_____ Employee assistance groups

_____ Parking

_____ Credit union

_____ Vacation and holidays

_____ Safety and first aid

_____ Probationary period

_____ Other _____

　　I acknowledge that I have received an orientation on the above initialed subjects. I understand the information and have no additional questions regarding it.

Date: _____　　　　　　Date: _____

_____　　　_____
Employee　　　　　　　　　　　Supervisor

2-22   NEW EMPLOYEE CHECKLIST

Date: _____

Employee name: _____   Employee number: _____

Department: _____   Social Security number: _____

Date of employment: _____

Chart or Document	When Needed	Completed
Employment application	_____	_____
Personal data sheet	_____	_____
W–4 (FICA) form	_____	_____
Physical exam report	_____	_____
Employment agreement	_____	_____
Noncompetition agreement	_____	_____
Trade secret agreement	_____	_____
Indemnity agreement	_____	_____
Conflict of interest statement	_____	_____
Fidelity bond	_____	_____
Emergency data sheet	_____	_____
Other	_____	_____
Other	_____	_____

_____
Supervisor

PAY RATE HISTORY

Employee name: _____   Employee number: _____

Department: _____   Social Security number: _____

Date of employment: _____

Effective Date	Change	Job Title		Pay Rate		Performance Rating
		From	To	From	To	

Change Codes:

P—promotion   C—cost of living increase   D—demotion

M—merit increase   L—longevity increase   R—reclassification

N—negotiated increase

2-24 EMPLOYEE TIME SHEET

Employee name: _____   Employee number: _____

Department: _____   Social Security number: _____

Date of employment: _____

Date	Time Started	Time Finished	Lunch Time	Overtime	Total Hours Worked

2-25 WEEKLY TIME SHEET

For Week Ending _____

Employee	Mon.	Tues.	Wed.	Thurs.	Fri.	Sat.	Sun.	Total

2-26 DAILY TIME SHEET

Date: _____

Employee	Time Work Began	Time Work Ended	Lunch Break	Overtime Hours	Total

2–27 WEEKLY WORK SCHEDULE

For week ending: _____

Employee	Hours						
	Sun.	Mon.	Tues.	Wed.	Thur.	Fri.	Sat.

2–28 FLEXTIME SCHEDULE

Employee:		Week Ending:		
Day	A.M.	Lunch	P.M.	Hours for Day

2-29 OVERTIME AUTHORIZATION

Employee name: _____   Employee number: _____

Department: _____   Social Security number: _____

    The above-named employee is approved to work overtime for a maximum of _____ hours between the dates of _____ to _____. The employee's overtime is approved for the purposes of:

_____

_____

The overtime pay rate shall be paid as per company policy.

Requested by: _____   Date: _____

Approved by: _____   Date: _____

2-30 REQUEST FOR COMPENSATORY TIME OFF

Employee name: _____   Employee number: _____

Department: _____   Social Security number: _____

Compensatory time off is requested for the below periods of time:

Date(s) from _____ To _____

Time(s) from _____ To _____

Total hours request off: _____

To compensate for time worked on:

Date(s)_____

_____
Employee Signature

Date submitted: _____

Supervisory Action Taken on Request

_____ Approved   _____ Disapproved

Comment:

Date employee notified: _____

_____
Supervisor Signature

2-31　PHYSICIAN'S REPORT

Date: _____

Doctor: _____

Re: [employee's name]

Dear Doctor:

The above-referenced employee has been absent from work on the days noted below. We have been advised that the employee has been receiving treatment from you. It is our company policy to verify prolonged medical absences. Accordingly, we would appreciate your completing the form below and returning it to our personnel office.

Dates of absences: _____

Sincerely,

_____

Date: _____

    I consent to the release of the above information.

_____

Employee Signature

- -

    I certify that _____ has been under my medical care during the above absences and that the absences listed were medically necessary or reasonable based on the employee's medical condition.

Date: _____   _____

Doctor Signature

2-32 INJURY REPORT

Employee name: _____ Employee number: _____

Department: _____ Social Security number: _____

Age: _____ Sex: _____

Was the injury or illness related to employment? _____

Date of injury or illness: _____ Time: _____

Describe in detail how the injury occurred, and parts of the body affected:

_____

_____

_____

_____

Date employee returned to work after incident: _____

Type and location of medical treatment, including name of physician, if any:

_____

_____

_____

Names of witnesses:

_____

_____

_____

Comments:

_____

_____

_____

Signature of employee: _____ Date signed: _____

Signature of supervisor or first aid person: _____

2-33 SUPERVISOR'S REPORT OF INJURY

Employee name: _____ Employee number: _____

Department: _____ Social Security number: _____

Date of injury or illness: _____ Time: _____

Describe the nature of the injury or illness:

_____

_____

How did injury or illness occur?

_____

What was first aid treatment given:

_____

_____

Name and address of treating physician, if any:

_____

_____

If employee was hospitalized, name and address of hospital:

_____

_____

Names of witnesses:

_____

_____

Steps taken to prevent future incidents:

_____

Was injury reported to insurance carrier, if applicable? _____

Report prepared by: _____

Date report prepared: _____

Report reviewed by: _____

2-34 RECORD OF INJURY REPORTS

Starting date of log: _____ Ending date: _____

Employee Name	Date of Injury	Date Report Submitted

2-35 REPORT OF ABSENCE FOR MILITARY DUTY

Employee name: _____   Employee number: _____

Department: _____   Social Security number: _____

I hereby request absence or leave from my employment for the purposes of temporary active duty training with the military.

My military unit is: _____

The exclusive dates of my absence from work are as follows:

From: _____   To: _____

I agree to furnish the company with a copy of my orders for service or such other documentation of active duty as the company may require.

_____
Employee Signature

2-36 REQUEST FOR TRANSFER

Employee name: _____   Employee number: _____

Department: _____   Social Security number: _____

I hereby request transfer to the following position:

[Describe position and identify department in which position is located.]

My reason(s) for transfer:

_____

Employee signature

Supervisor's Action

Supervisor's comments and recommendation:

_____

Supervisor signature

Action Taken

Date received: _____

Action taken: _____

Reasons for action: _____

Employee notified on: _____
                        [date]

_____

Action Officer signature

2-37 GRIEVANCE REPORT

Date: _____

Employee name: _____   Employee number: _____

Department: _____   Social Security number: _____

1. Nature of incident/grievance: _____
   _____
   _____

2. Date of incident/grievance:_____
   _____
   _____

3. Witnesses: _____
   _____
   _____

4. Requested resolution of incident/grievance: _____
   _____
   _____

5. Reported to: _____   Date reported: _____

6. Action taken:_____
   _____
   _____

7. Action reviewed by: _____   Date reviewed: _____

2–38 SALARY REVIEW REQUEST

Employee name: _____   Employee number: _____

Department: _____   Social Security number: _____

I request that my salary be reviewed.

Present salary: _____

Date of last salary increase: _____

Nature of change in salary or benefits requested: _____

_____

Justification for an increase or change in salary or benefits:_____

_____

I (have) (have not) discussed this request with my immediate supervisor.

- -

Action Taken

_____ Increase approved. From $_____ to $_____

Effective date: _____

_____ Request disapproved.

    _____ not in budget

    _____ based on performance analysis

    _____ other: _____

    _____

_____ Employee notified on [date]: _____

2-39 RECEIPT FOR COMPANY PROPERTY

Employee name: _____   Employee number: _____

Department: _____   Social Security number: _____

    I acknowledge receipt of the below listed company property. I agree to maintain the property in good condition and to return it when I terminate employment with the company or when requested by my supervisor. In addition, if I no longer need any of the items, I will report this information to my supervisor. I agree to notify the company if any of the items are damaged, destroyed, or lost.

Receipt Date Issued	Item	Serial No.	Returned to	Return Date

_____
Employee Signature

_____
Date

2-40   EMPLOYEE PERFORMANCE RATING (SUMMARY)

Employee name: _____   Employee number: _____

Department: _____   Social Security number: _____

Date of review: _____   Reviewer: _____

Factors	Excellent	Satisfactory	Fair	Poor
Honesty				
Attendance				
Work quality				
Technical skills				
Consistency				
Dependability				
Enthusiasm				
Cooperation				
Working relations				
Appearance				
Punctuality				

2-41 EMPLOYEE PERFORMANCE RATING (NARRATIVE)

Employee name: _____   Employee number: _____

Department: _____   Social Security number: _____

Date of Review: _____   Reviewer: _____

Factors	Rating	Comments
Overall performance		
Dependability		
Honesty		
Job knowledge		
Attendance		
Judgment		
Attitude		
Reliability		
Productivity		

_____ Report discussed with employee

_____

Supervisor

Review by: _____   Date: _____

2-42   GENERAL PERFORMANCE SUMMARY

Employee name: _____   Employee number:_____

Department: _____   Social Security number: _____

Date summary completed: _____   Period covered by report: _____

Report reviewed by: _____   Date: _____

Report discussed with employee: _____   Date: _____

Comments

1. Overall performance of work: _____

_____

2. Dependability:_____

_____

3. Quality of work:_____

_____

4. Quantity of work:_____

_____

5. Working relationships with fellow employees:_____

_____

6. Knowledge of job:_____

_____

7. Technical skill:_____

_____

Overall rating:_____

_____

_____   Date:_____
Supervisor

2-43 PERFORMANCE ANALYSIS WORKSHEET

Employee name: _____   Employee number: _____

Department: _____   Social Security number: _____

In preparation for your upcoming performance review, please answer the following questions.

1. How successful do you feel you have been in meeting your overall job qualifications during this appraisal period?

2. What areas do you feel that you have excelled in?

3. What areas do you feel that you need to work on?

4. What are your immediate employment goals?

5. What are your long-term employment goals?

6. What additional training do you need to improve your overall performance of duty?

7. Is there anything about your job that you would like to change?

8. In what ways may the company help you become more proficient in the performance of your job duties?

2-44   EMPLOYEE RESPONSE TO PERFORMANCE REVIEW

Employee name: _____   Employee number: _____

Department: _____   Social Security number: _____

Date of review: _____

I have reviewed the performance evaluation of my past work performance.

I agree with the following conclusions:

I disagree with the following conclusions:

My performance review is not fair and impartial because of the following reasons:

I believe that the following changes should be made in my evaluation:

The following changes or improvements should be made in company policies or procedures:

_____   Date: _____
Employee

_____   Date: _____
Supervisor

_____   Date: _____
Evaluator's Supervisor

2-45   **LETTER OF COMMENDATION**

Date: _____

To: [name of employee being commended]

From: [CEO of company]

    We are please to commend you for the excellent performance of duty during the period from _____ to _____. Your efforts are greatly appreciated. Devoted and tireless contributions of valued employees like yourself are needed to help our company grow and be more responsive to our customers and employees.

    On behalf of the company and your associates, we salute you for a job well done.

Sincerely,

2-46 FIRST WARNING NOTICE

Employee name: _____   Employee number: _____

Department: _____   Social Security number: _____

Date of warning: _____

Date and time violation or incident occurred: _____

Witnesses to incident: _____

Nature of violation:

_____ Substandard work   _____ Absenteeism
_____ Carelessness   _____ Tardiness
_____ Disruptive conduct   _____ Intoxication
_____ Other: _____

Additional remarks

_____

_____

_____

_____

Employee comments

_____

_____

_____

_____

Signatures:

_____   _____
Employee   Supervisor

_____
Human Resources Dept.

2-47 SUBSEQUENT WARNING NOTICE

Employee name: _____   Employee number: _____

Department: _____   Social Security number: _____

Date of warning: _____

Date and time violation or incident occurred: _____

Witnesses to incident: _____

Nature of violation:

_____ Substandard work   _____ Absenteeism
_____ Carelessness   _____ Tardiness
_____ Disruptive conduct   _____ Intoxication
_____ Other: _____

Additional remarks

_____

_____

_____

_____

Employee comments

_____

_____

_____

_____

This is not the first warning that you have received concerning your employment with the company. Future violations may lead to immediate dismissal without further notice or warning.

Signatures:

_____   _____
Employee   Supervisor

_____
Human Resources Dept.

2–48   REPORT OF MISCONDUCT

Employee name: _____   Employee number: _____

Department: _____   Social Security number: _____

Date of incident or misconduct: _____

Date and time incident or misconduct occurred: _____

Witnesses to incident: _____

Nature of violation:

_____	Substandard work	_____	Absenteeism
_____	Carelessness	_____	Tardiness
_____	Disruptive conduct	_____	Intoxication
_____	Other: _____		

Additional remarks

_____

_____

_____

_____

Action taken

_____

_____

_____

_____

The above misconduct has (has not) been noted and recorded as part of the employee's personnel file.

_____   Date: _____
Human Resources Dept.

2-49   ACKNOWLEDGMENT OF WORK RULES

Employee name: _____   Employee number: _____

Department: _____   Social Security number: _____

    I have read and understand the company work rules. I acknowledge that I am expected to conform to those rules and that I am subject to termination for failure to conform to the said rules. It is understood that any modification to the work rules must be in writing and signed by [individual with the authority to modify work rules]. In addition, I acknowledge that I have a duty to report to [supervisor] any violations of the work rules by other employees.

Acknowledged by: _____   Date: _____

2–50 NOTICE OF PROBATION

Employee name: _____ Employee number: _____

Department: _____ Social Security number: _____

Date of Notice: _____

To: [employee]

On [date] you were warned regarding your [poor performance of duty; absenteeism, tardiness, etc.].

The above mentioned misconduct constitutes adequate grounds to terminate your employment with the company. We, however, want to give you another opportunity to prove your value to our company, and are therefore placing you on probation for a period of six months commencing on the above date. In the event there is a repeat incident or other problem, we shall have no choice but to terminate your employment without further notice.

Hopefully, this probationary period will provide you with an opportunity to prove to us that our confidence in you is justified.

On receipt of this letter, please report to the personnel department to clarify the conditions of your probation and to assist you in any way possible toward improved performance.

Sincerely,

copies to:

2–51   NOTICE OF EXTENDED PROBATION

Employee name: _____   Employee number: _____

Department: _____   Social Security number: _____

Date of notice: _____

To: [employee]

On [date] you were placed on probation regarding your [poor performance of duty; absenteeism, tardiness, etc.].

Although we have noticed improvement in your job performance during this probationary period, we feel that it would be in the best interest of the company and yourself to continue your probationary period for an additional six months. This will allow us to monitor your performance and make appropriate recommendations regarding your employment status.

It is hoped that this additional probationary period will provide you with an opportunity to prove to us that our confidence in you is justified.

On receipt of this letter, please report to the personnel department so that they can clarify the conditions of your extended probation and assist you in any way possible toward improved performance.

Sincerely,

copies to:

2-52 TRAINING EVALUATION FORM

In an effort to better serve you by presenting training that provides topics applicable to your position and that provides you with the most effective information, I would appreciate your completing this form. Also, it will assist me in your evaluation of my presentation. Thank you.

1. Did this program meet your expectations?

    If not, what would you recommend be covered in more detail?

2. Quality of handouts/material.

    _____Excellent   _____Satisfactory   _____ Other

3. Suggestions to improve presentation/or recommended future topics:

4. Would you be interested in a follow-up program, possibly annually?

5. Were the training location and facilities satisfactory?

6. Additional comments and overall review of the program.

_____   _____
Name (optional)   Department (optional)

2-53 NOTICE OF DISMISSAL

Date:_____

To: [employee]

The purpose of this letter is to notify you that your employment with this company is hereby terminated. The termination is effective on [date]. The reasons for your termination are set forth below:

[unsatisfactory work performance, absenteeism, tardiness, etc.]

Severance pay shall be paid as per company policy if you meet the qualifying criteria. Within 30 days of termination we will issue you a statement of benefits. Insurance benefits will continue for the time required by statutes or regulations. For a briefing on your termination benefits, please contact [name] in the personnel office.

Your final pay check may be obtained from the personnel office on your final day of employment.

We sincerely regret this action and wish you the best of luck in finding a new employment situation.

Sincerely,

copies to:

2–54 NOTICE OF DISMISSAL FOR VIOLATION OF WORK RULES

Date: _____

To: [employee]

The purpose of this letter is to notify you that your employment with this company is hereby terminated. The termination is effective on [date]. This termination of employment is necessary due to your violation of company work rules on [date]. Your violations were as follows:

[list the specific work rules violated]

Severance pay shall not be paid because your termination was for cause. Within 30 days of termination we will issue you a statement of benefits. Insurance benefits will continue for the time required by statutes or regulations. For a briefing on your termination benefits please contact [name] in the personnel office.

Your final paycheck shall be for the period ending [date] and may be obtained from the personnel office on your final day of employment.

We sincerely regret this action and wish you the best of luck in finding a new employment situation.

Sincerely,

copies to:

2-55 NOTICE OF DISMISSAL FOR EXCESSIVE ABSENCES

Date: _____

To: [employee]

The purpose of this letter is to notify you that your employment with this company is hereby terminated. The termination is effective on [date]. The reason for your termination is an excessive number of unauthorized absences.

You were previously warned regarding the unauthorized absences on [date of warning]. Should you have any questions regarding the dates of your absences, a copy of your attendance record is available in the personnel office for your review.

Severance pay will be paid as per company policy if you meet the qualifying criteria. Within 30 days of termination we will issue you a statement of benefits. Insurance benefits will continue for the time required by statutes or regulations. For a briefing on your termination benefits, please contact [name] in the personnel office.

Your final paycheck may be obtained from the personnel office on your final day of employment.

We sincerely regret this action and wish you the best of luck in finding a new employment situation.

Sincerely,

copies to:

2-56 NOTICE OF DISMISSAL FOR EXTENDED ABSENCE

Date:_____

To: [employee]

The purpose of this letter is to notify you that your employment with this company is hereby terminated. The termination is effective on [date employee last worked]. The reason for your termination is your continued unauthorized absence. It is noted that you failed to report to work on [date] and have continued to be absent from work since that date. You also failed to notify the company of the reasons for your continued absence.

In accordance with company policy, there will be no severance pay because your termination was for cause. Within 30 days of termination, we will issue you a statement of benefits. Insurance benefits will continue for the time required by statutes or regulations. For a briefing on your termination benefits, please contact [name] in the personnel office.

Your final paycheck may be obtained from the personnel office on your final day of employment.

We sincerely regret this action and wish you the best of luck in finding a new employment situation.

Sincerely,

copies to:

2-57 RESIGNATION

Date: _____

To: [employer]

Re: Letter of resignation

    Please accept this letter as my resignation from the company, effective on [date]. It is my intention to terminate my employment in all capacities with the company.

    I will return all company property prior to the above termination date. I am also aware that I am under an obligation to protect and keep confidential all company trade secrets.

    Please send all monies due me to the address below.

    This is a voluntary resignation.

Sincerely,

_____

[signature of employee]

_____

[print name]

_____

[street]

_____

[city] [state] [zip code]

2-58   EXIT INTERVIEW

Employee name: _____   Employee number: _____

Department: _____   Social Security number: _____

Date of interview: _____   Interviewer: _____

Last date of employment: _____

Employee informed of the following restrictions:

_____ trade secrets and other confidential data

_____ noncompetition agreement (if applicable)

_____ insurance benefits [COBRA requirements]

_____ other: _____

Employee has returned the following items:

_____ company documents and data (including any computer records)

_____ tools

_____ equipment

_____ company credit cards

_____ keys

_____ identification badges, and the like

_____ uniforms

_____ company automobile

Exit Questions

1. What is your reason for leaving the company?
2. What recommendations do you have for improving the company?
3. Do you feel that you received adequate training for your position?
4. Was management supportive of your efforts?
5. Do you feel that you were fairly treated by the company?
6. Would you consider reemployment with the company at a later date?
7. Was your work rewarding?
8. Do you feel that you were paid an adequate salary?
9. How can the company improve working conditions?

10. What are the strengths of the company?

11. What are the weaknesses of the company?

12. Have you observed any frequent violations of company policies or thefts of company property? If so, please list below.

13. Other comments:

NOTE: YOUR COMMENTS ARE HELD STRICTLY CONFIDENTIAL.

2–59   SAMPLE CONTRACT PROVISIONS TO PROTECT YOUR BUSINESS

Employee agrees not to compete with employer for a period of two years after termination of subject employment.

The employee shall not acquire or hold any interest as a stockholder, partner, owner, director, agent or otherwise in any business in competition with employer without the written consent of the employer, and shall not engage in any business competing with that of the employer.

Employee agrees to have no contact for business purposes with customers of the employer for a period of one year after termination of subject employment. This includes, but is not limited to, contacting clients by telephone, mail, or in person for any purposes that directly or indirectly affect the business of the employer.

Employee agrees that the names and addresses of employer's customers constitute trade secrets of the employer and that the sale or unauthorized use or disclosure of any of the employer's trade secrets obtained by employee during employment constitutes unfair competition. Employee agrees not to participate in any form of unfair competition against employer.

For a period of two years after termination of subject employment, employee agrees not to directly or indirectly make known to any person, business, or corporation, the names and addresses of the customers of the employer or any other information pertaining to the customers.

In the event of breach of this agreement, the employee will be liable for damages as determined by a court of law.

2-60 CHECKOUT RECORD

Item Returned	Date Returned	Initials of Receiver
Company documents		
Company credit cards		
Company auto		
Keys		
Customer lists		
ID cards and badges		
Petty cash advances		
Company tools		
Company equipment		
Other		
Completed Items and Briefings		
Exit interview		
Confidentiality briefing and form completed		
Expense reports		
COBRA briefing		
Other		

Date checkout record reviewed: _____

_____
Signature of Reviewer

_____
[title]

2-61 TERMINATION REPORT

Employee name: _____   Employee number: _____

Department: _____   Social Security number: _____

1. Termination date: _____

2. Last date paid: _____

3. Reasons for termination: _____

_____

4. Eligible for unemployment compensation: _____

   If no, explain: _____

_____

5. Assessment of employee: _____

_____

_____

6. Employee eligible for rehire: _____

7. Eligible for continued benefits: _____

8. Other: _____

_____

_____

Date: _____   _____
                      Supervisor

2–62   ACCRUED BENEFITS STATEMENT

Employee name: _____   Employee number: _____

Department: _____   Social Security number: _____

Interim report: _____   Final report: _____

The below benefits are accrued as of the date of _____.

Vacation (days): _____

Vacation (pay): _____

Sick (hours): _____

Sick (pay): _____

Profit sharing (vested) _____

Profit sharing (nonvested) _____

Stock dividend (value) _____

Pension (vested) (nonvested) _____

Life insurance _____

Surrender value of insurance _____

Severance pay _____

Others: _____

_____

_____

Date: _____   _____

                                                Supervisor

2-63　REPLY TO REFERENCE REQUEST

Date: _____

To: _____

Re: Your request for a reference on [name]

We are in receipt of your request for a reference on [name]. Please be advised that it is our policy not to provide references on present or past employees.

We do confirm that the above person was employed by our company from _____ to _____ as a [position].

Sincerely,

2-64   TELEPHONE REFERENCE LOG

Date: _____   Time: _____

Reference requested on: _____

Name of individual requesting reference: _____

Company: _____

Reasons for reference: _____

Summary of the information provided: _____

_____

_____

_____

_____

Specific questions and answers: _____

_____

_____

_____

_____

_____

_____

Name of individual supplying above information: _____

_____
Signature

2-65 SKELETON INTERVIEW

Questions that may be asked in most states:

1. Would you tell us about your last job?
2. What were your major duties and responsibilities?
3. Describe a typical day on your last employment.
4. What are some of the problems involved in your last job?
5. Which problems frustrated you the most?
6. How did you overcome the problems encountered?
7. How did your previous job prepare you for this position?
8. What were your goals at your last job? Did you reach them?
9. What position did your immediate supervisor hold?
10. Why do you want this position?
11. What can you contribute to this company?
12. What qualifications do you have for this position?
13. Do you know of any reasons or problems that would prevent you from working normal hours? Overtime?
14. Do you know of any reasons that would prevent you from traveling? [only if traveling is a part of the job]
15. What do you consider your strong points?
16. What do you consider your weak points?
17. What is your strongest personal quality and weakest?
18. What do you want to do in your next job that you cannot do in your present one?
19. Do you have any special skills or knowledge? Are your skills recent?
20. When did you last use a [machine or skill]?
21. What is your career objective?
22. What do you intend to do to reach your career objective?
23. In what subjects did you make good grades in school?
24. What was your major? Why?
25. Are you interested in continuing your education?
26. How did your education prepare you for this job?
27. What professional organizations that are relevant to your job do you belong to?
28. Have you ever worked for this company under a different name?

29. In checking your references and work record, are there any other names or nicknames you have used that we should check under?

30. If hired, can you provide proof of citizenship or right to work in this country?

We are committed to providing a comfortable and productive work environment for both women and men. The work environment should be free from sexual harassment. Sexual harassment will not be tolerated.

This policy applies to all phrases of employment.

Prohibited sexual harassment includes the following:

Unsolicited and unwelcome contact that has sexual overtones; verbal contact, such as sexually suggestive or obscene comments, threats, slurs, epithets, jokes about gender-specific traits, sexual propositions.

Physical contact, such as intentional touching, pinching, brushing against another's body, impeding or blocking movement, assault, coercing sexual intercourse.

Visual contact, such as leering or staring at another's body, gesturing, displaying sexually suggestive objects or pictures, cartoons, posters, or magazines.

Written contact such as sexually suggestive or obscene letters, notes, and invitations.

Sexual harassment also includes continuing to express sexual or social interest after being informed directly that the interest is unwelcome and using sexual behavior to control, influence, or affect the career, salary, or work environment of another employee.

It is impermissible to suggest, threaten, or imply that failure to accept a request for a date or sexual intimacy will affect an employee's job prospects. For example, it is forbidden either to imply or actually withhold support for an appointment, promotion, or change of assignment, or suggest that a poor performance report will be given because an employee has declined a personal proposition.

Also, offering benefits, such as promotions, favorable performance evaluations, favorable assigned duties or shifts, recommendations or reclassification in exchange for sexual favors is forbidden.

Supervisors shall take all reasonable steps to see that this policy prohibiting sexual harassment is followed by all employees, supervisors, and others who have contact with our employees. This prevention plan will include training sessions, ongoing monitoring of the worksite, and a confidential employee survey to be conducted and evaluated every six months.

Any employee found to have violated this policy shall be subject to appropriate disciplinary action, including warnings, reprimand, suspension, or discharge, according to the findings of the complaint investigation.

Any employee bringing a sexual harassment complaint or assisting in investigating such a complaint will not be adversely affected in terms and conditions of employment, or discriminated against or discharged because of the complaint. Complaints of such retaliation will be promptly investigated and punished.

[Name of counselor] is designated as the Sexual Harassment Counselor. All complaints of sexual harassment and retaliation for reporting or participating in an investigation shall be directed to the Sexual Harassment Counselor or to a supervisor of your choice, either in writing, by filling out a complaint form, or by requesting an individual interview. All complaints shall be handled as confidentially as possible. The Sexual Harassment Counselor will promptly investigate and resolve complaints involving violations of this policy and recommend to management the appropriate sanctions to be imposed against violators.

A yearly training session for all employees concerning their rights to be free from sexual harassment and the legal options available if they are harassed will be established. In addition, training sessions will be held for supervisors and managers, educating them in how to keep the workplace as free from harassment as possible and in how to handle sexual harassment complaints.

A copy of the policy will be distributed to all employees and posted in areas where all employees will have the opportunity to freely review it. We welcome your suggestions for improvements to the policy.

2-67 SAMPLE SEXUAL HARASSMENT COMPLAINT

Name: _____

Department: _____ Job Title: _____

Immediate Supervisor: _____

1. Who was responsible for the harassment? _____

2. Describe the sexual harassment. _____

_____

First incident: _____

_____

Approximate date, time, and place: _____

What was your reaction? _____

Second incident: _____

_____

Approximate date, time, and, place: _____

What was your reaction? _____

Subsequent incidents: _____

_____

Approximate date, time, and place: _____

What was your reaction? _____

3. List any witnesses to the harassment:

_____

_____

I UNDERSTAND THAT THESE INCIDENTS WILL BE INVESTI-GATED, BUT THIS FORM WILL BE KEPT CONFIDENTIAL TO THE HIGHEST DEGREE POSSIBLE.

Employee signature: _____

Date:_____

FOR ADMINISTRATIVE USE

Dates of investigation of complaint: _____

Date of final report: _____

Copy sent to employee: _____

Action taken: _____

_____

_____

_____

Date of follow-up conference with employee: _____

Results: _____

_____

_____

_____

Date of follow-up conference with employee: _____

Results: _____

_____

_____

_____

Date of follow-up conference with employee: _____

Results: _____

_____

_____

_____

2–68   APPLICANT CHECKLIST

Employment Position: _____

Name of Applicant: _____

Address: _____

Telephone: _____

_____ Completed application for employment received.

_____ Copies of supporting documents received.

_____ Written references received.

_____ Education credentials checked.

References

1. Former employers:

    Name   Recommendations

    a. _____

    b. _____

    c. _____

2. Character references:

    Name   Recommendations

    a. _____

    b. _____

    c. _____

Interview Process

    Interviewer   Comments

1. _____

2. _____

3. _____

Personnel recommendations: _____

_____

Employment decision: _____

2-69 MEDICAL CONSENT

To: [doctor]

I, the undersigned individual, hereby give my consent for the limited purpose of employment consideration to the below listed medical examination procedures:

[list procedures here]

I am over the age of eighteen years. I authorize this consent without limitation or uncertainty. I also understand that the results of the examination will be forwarded to:

[company]

Date: _____   _____
                                               Employee

2-70 EXPENSE REIMBURSEMENT CONTRACT

The undersigned employee hereby agrees to reimburse the [name of company] for any employee business expenses or advances that are determined to be covered by any of the below situations:

1. Advances in excess of actual expenses
2. Expenses that are determined to be unjustified by management
3. Expenses that are determined by the Internal Revenue Service not to constitute a deductible business expense pursuant to the Internal Revenue Code of 1986.
4. Any expenses that are not properly documented

The amount to be repaid under the above situations is only that amount in excess of that determined to be appropriate.

Date: _____   _____
                                               Employee

2-71 EMPLOYEE EXPENSE REPORT

Employee name: _____   Employee number: _____

Department: _____   Social Security number: _____

Expenses authorized by: _____

Purpose of travel or expense: _____

Destination and dates of travel: _____

Company or personnel visited: _____

_____

Specific Expenses:

Hotel/Motel $ _____

Meals   _____

Tips   _____

Auto Expense:

    Mileage at ____ cents per mile   _____

    Tolls   _____

    Parking   _____

Telephone   _____

Other expenses:

_____   _____

_____   _____

_____   _____

    Total Expenses $ _____

2-72 REQUEST UNDER FREEDOM OF INFORMATION ACT

Date: _____

To: [Governmental agency with records]

Pursuant to the Freedom of Information Act, I request disclosure of any information on me that may be maintained in your files, and to the extent the disclosure is required by law.

Please forward the information to the address below:

[complete mailing address at this point]

Sincerely,

_____
[signature]

_____
[printed name]

_____
[date of birth]

_____
[Social Security number]

Signature witnessed by: _____
[signature]

_____
[printed name]

Chapter 3

Real Estate Forms and Agreements

This chapter contains the forms and agreements that are generally used when dealing with an ownership interest in real estate. Chapter 4 contains forms used in the rental or lease of real property.

Deeds

In all states, any interest in real estate must be conveyed (i.e., transferred) by written documents. In the vast majority of cases, the documents involving interest in real estate are deeds. The most popular are the *grant deed* and the *warranty deed*. In a grant deed, you grant an interest in the real property to someone. In a warranty deed, not only do you grant an interest, but you also make certain warranties of title. A *quit claim deed* transfers only the interest that you have in a property without any warranties of ownership or right to transfer. Statutes and customs dictate which types of deeds should be used in various situations. Always have your deed reviewed by an attorney.

Recording

Any interest in real estate should normally be recorded in the county in which the land is located. An unrecorded document that evidences an interest in real estate is normally not valid for value against an innocent purchaser who did not know of the document. The purpose of recording is to provide constructive notice to everyone that you have an interest in the property.

Most states require that documents be notarized by a notary public before the documents may be recorded. Accordingly, it is advisable to have documents that transfer any interest in real estate executed (i.e., signed) before a notary public.

Zoning Laws and Other Restrictions

Zoning ordinances regulate the character and use of property. They are imposed under the local policy power to regulate for the health and welfare of the community. Building codes regulate the construction or remodeling of building.

In most cases, it is the responsibility of the businessowner, not the landlord, to ascertain whether a prospective business complies with the local zoning laws. There should be a clause in the lease that will allow the business tenant to cancel the lease if the appropriate permits cannot be obtained to operate the business in that location or if a change in ordinances or laws makes it illegal to continue operation in that location. *Note:* It is the landlord's responsibility to ensure that at the time the premises are turned over to the tenant the premises comply with the appropriate building codes. If the tenant does any remodeling after taking possession, the tenant is responsible for ensuring that the remodeling conforms to the building codes.

Easements

Any easements or restrictions that limit the right of the tenant to use the property should be disclosed by the landlord prior to the signing of the final lease. An easement is any right, privilege or benefit that one enjoys in the land of another. For example, if the utility company has an easement to place utility lines across the property, the landlord has a duty to inform the tenant of this easement if it will interfere with the right of the tenant to use the property. Any deed restrictions or easements should be disclosed to the tenant. Any undisclosed easements or restrictions that interfere with the tenant's use of the premises may be grounds for reducing the rent or canceling the lease.

Forms

- FORM 3–1: PURCHASE OPTION AGREEMENT. Obtains an option to purchase real estate.

- FORM 3–2: OFFER TO PURCHASE REAL ESTATE. Submits a written offer to purchase real estate.

- FORM 3–3: ESCROW AGREEMENT. Establishes an escrow during the purchase of real estate.

- FORM 3–4: QUITCLAIM DEED. Transfers interest in real property without having to give a warranty as to the title of the property. A quitclaim deed transfers only what you own and does not guarantee that you own any interest in the property.

- FORM 3–5: WARRANTY DEED. Transfers interest in real property with a warranty as to the title of the property. A warranty deed warrants that you are transferring a good and marketable title in the property.

- FORM 3–6: GRANT DEED. Grants an interest in real property.

- FORM 3–7: GRANT DEED WITH RESERVATION OF MINERAL RIGHTS. A grant deed whereby the seller retains the mineral interest in the property.

- FORM 3–8: GRANT DEED WITH THE ASSUMPTION OF ENCUMBRANCES (NOTE). The buyer assumes and promises to pay the promissory note on the land.

- FORM 3–9: GRANT DEED WITH THE ASSUMPTION OF ENCUMBRANCES (LEASE). The buyer assumes the lease of the premises.

- FORM 3–10: GRANT DEED CREATING A JOINT TENANCY. Creates a joint tenancy for the buyers.

- FORM 3–11: GRANT DEED (BY JOINT TENANTS TO THIRD PERSON). Joint tenants transfer property to a third person.

- FORM 3–12: GRANT DEED OF LIFE ESTATE. Grants a person a life estate whose duration is limited to the life of a person holding it. On that person's death, the property then goes to the other named person.

- FORM 3–13: GRANT DEED RESERVING LIFE ESTATE. The grantor retains a life estate in the property for himself or herself.

- FORM 3–14: DISCHARGE AND SATISFACTION OF MORTGAGE. Records the discharge and satisfaction of a mortgage on real property.

- FORM 3–15: EXTENSION OF DEED OF TRUST. Extends payment time on a loan secured by a deed of trust.

- FORM 3–16: APPOINTMENT OF SUBSTITUTE TRUSTEE. Names a new trustee to a deed of trust.

- FORM 3–17: NOTICE OF EXERCISE OPTION TO PURCHASE. When used by a lessee (tenant), provides landlord with notice of the exercise of an option to purchase the leased property.

- FORM 3–18: DEED: GRANT OF EASEMENT. Formalizes and records the grant of an easement.

- FORM 3–19: DEED: GRANT OF EASEMENT (LIMITED). Grants a limited easement.

- FORM 3–20: DEED: GRANT OF EASEMENT (RESTRICTED). Grants an easement that is restricted to certain uses (e.g., noncommercial).

- FORM 3–21: NOTICE OF DEFAULT ON LAND CONTRACT. Notifies the individuals involved that they are in dispute of a contract to buy real estate.

- FORM 3–22: NOTICE OF DISCHARGE AND SATISFACTION OF MORTGAGE. Notifies third persons of the discharge and satisfaction of a mortgage.

- FORM 3–23: NOTICE OF CANCELLATION OF OPTION TO PURCHASE REAL ESTATE. Notifies a third party that an option pertaining to real estate has been canceled.

- FORM 3–24: DECLARATION OF COVENANTS AND RESTRICTIONS. Records covenants and restrictions on property. Normally used only when the land is being subdivided.

- FORM 3–25: NOTICE OF AGREEMENT REGARDING (DISPUTED) BOUNDARY LINES. Settles a dispute regarding boundary lines.

- FORM 3–26: NOTICE OF AGREEMENT REGARDING (CHANGING) BOUNDARY LINE. Changes boundary lines between two pieces of land.

- FORM 3–27: DECLARATION OF HOMESTEAD (BY UNMARRIED PERSON). Declares a homestead by an unmarried head of a family.

- FORM 3–28: DECLARATION OF HOMESTEAD (BY MARRIED COUPLE). Declares a homestead by a married couple.

- FORM 3–29: DECLARATION OF HOMESTEAD (BY PERSON NOT HEAD OF HOUSEHOLD). Used by a single person, not a head of a household, to declare a homestead.

- FORM 3–30: ABANDONMENT OF HOMESTEAD (BY SINGLE HEAD OF HOUSEHOLD). Declares abandonment of a previously declared homestead by a single person who is head of a household.

- FORM 3–31: ABANDONMENT OF HOMESTEAD (BY SINGLE PERSON NOT HEAD OF HOUSEHOLD). Declares abandonment of a previously declared homestead by a single person who is not a head of household.

- FORM 3–32: ABANDONMENT OF HOMESTEAD (BY MARRIED COUPLE). Declares abandonment of a previously declared homestead by a married couple.

3-1   PURCHASE OPTION AGREEMENT

This Purchase Option Agreement is hereby entered into between _____ [owner] and _____ [buyer]. Buyer hereby pays to Owner the sum of $_____ in consideration for the option set forth in this agreement. The terms of the option are as follows:

1. Buyer has the option and right to buy: [describe property according to both its legal description and its street address].

2. The purchase price of the property is $_____. The following payment terms are acceptable to Owner:

3. This option will remain in effect until [date and time], unless sooner exercised.

4. To exercise this option, the Buyer must notify the Owner by certified mail of its exercise within the option period.

5. If Buyer exercises this option, Owner will complete and sign the enclosed contract of sale within 10 days.

6. This option agreement shall be binding upon and inure to the benefit of the parties, their assigns, and personal representatives.

Signed under seal this date:

_____
Owner

Signed under seal this date:

_____
Buyer

WITNESSED the hands of said Grantor(s) this _____ day of _____, 19_____.

_____

_____

State of   )
County of   ) SS

On this date, [list names of person(s) who signed above] personally appeared before me and acknowledged that the above signature(s) are valid and binding.

Notary Public

_____

My Commission expires:

3-2   OFFER TO PURCHASE REAL ESTATE

The undersigned Buyer hereby offers to purchase from _____ , Owner, the parcel of real estate known as: [legal description of land and street address], [city or town] located in the County of _____ State of _____ .

The terms of the offer are as follows:

Total purchase price: _____
          paid as follows
Deposit here in paid: _____
On signing of contract: _____
Balance due at closing: _____

This offer is subject to Buyer's obtaining a real estate mortgage of at least $ _____ payable over _____ years at an interest rate not to exceed _____% within 60 days of the acceptance of this offer.

This offer is also subject to a satisfactory home inspection and termite–pest report within 30 days of the acceptance of this offer.

This offer is also subject to a good and marketable title being provided by Owner, and the property is to be sold free and clear of all encumbrances.

The closing shall be within 60 days of the acceptance of this offer.

The parties are to execute a standard purchase and sales agreement in accordance with the above terms within 10 days of the acceptance of this offer.

Signed under seal on this _____ day of _____, 19_____.

_____
Buyer

Accepted on this _____ day of _____, 19_____.

_____
Owner

3-3 ESCROW AGREEMENT

This Escrow Agreement between _____ (Seller); _____ (Buyer); and _____ (Escrow Agent) is entered into at the same time that the Seller and Buyer have entered into a Contract for the Sale and Purchase of Real Estate. This agreement is to be construed together with the Contract for the Sale and Purchase of Real Estate (Contract).

The closing of the real estate will take place on [date] at [time A.M./P.M.] at the offices of _____ located at [address of offices] or at such other time and place as may be agreed on by Seller and Buyer.

As per the Contract, Buyer has deposited with the Escrow Agent a down payment of $ _____.

At closing, the Escrow Agent will pay the amount deposited to the Seller or in accordance with Seller's instructions. At which time, the Escrow Agent will make the necessary transfer of title to the said property to the Buyer.

If there is no closing according to the Contract, the Escrow Agent shall withhold all monies received until he or she receives written instructions signed by both parties regarding the disposition of the monies. If Escrow Agent does not receive proper instructions signed by both parties, the Agent may either bring action or proceedings to determine the correct disposition of the monies or the Agent may continue to hold the monies. The Agent is under no obligation to bring an action or proceeding to determine the disposition of the monies.

Escrow Agent assumes only the liability of a stakeholder. The Agent shall incur no liability to anyone except for acts in bad faith willful misconduct, or gross negligence. All parties excuse and release the Agent for acts done or omitted in good faith.

Signed this date:

_____
Buyer

Signed this date:

_____
Seller

Signed this date:

_____
Escrow Agent

3-4   QUITCLAIM DEED

BE IT KNOWN, That [name of person making deed] Grantor, County of _____, State of _____, hereby QUITCLAIM and transfers to [person receiving the interest in the property], of the County of_____, State of _____; the following described real property located in _____ County of _____, State of _____, more particularly described as: [enter legal description at this point].

The consideration for this transfer is the payment of $_____ and for other good and valuable consideration. The transfer is made with QUIT-CLAIM COVENANTS ONLY.

WITNESSED the hands of said Grantor(s) this _____ day of _____, 19_____.

_____

_____

State of   )

County of   ) SS

On this date, [list names of person(s) who signed above] personally appeared before me and acknowledged that the above signature(s) are valid and binding.

_____
Notary Public

My Commission expires:

3-5   WARRANTY DEED

BE IT KNOWN, That [name of person making deed] Grantor, County of _____, State of _____, hereby conveys and transfers to [person receiving the interest in the property], of the County of_____, State of _____; the following described real property located in _____, County of _____ , State of _____, more particularly described as: [enter legal description at this point].

The consideration for this transfer is the payment of $_____ and for other good and valuable consideration. The transfer is made with WARRANTY COVENANTS. The warranty includes that the Grantor(s) for himself/herself, heirs, and assigns, that Grantor(s) is the owner of the above described title to the property and is hereby giving a good and marketable title to the said property. The Grantor and his or her heirs will forever warrant and defend the property so granted to the Grantee, his or her heirs, and assigns, against every person lawfully claiming the same or any part of the property.

This property being the same property conveyed to the Grantors by deed of _____, dated _____, 19_____.

WITNESSED the hands of said Grantor(s) this _____ day of _____, 19___.

_____

_____

_____

State of   )

County of   ) SS

On this date, [list names of person(s) who signed above] personally appeared before me and acknowledged that the above signature(s) are valid and binding.

_____
Notary Public

My Commission expires:

3-6   GRANT DEED

BE IT KNOWN, That [name of person making deed] Grantor, County of _____, State of _____, hereby conveys, grants and trans fers to [person receiving the interest in the property], of the County of _____, State of _____; the following described real property located in _____, County of _____, State of _____, more particularity described as: [enter legal description at this point]. together with all the tenements, hereditament, and appurtenances thereto belonging and the reversions, remainders, rents, and profits, if any, thereof.

The consideration for this transfer is the payment of $_____ and for other good and valuable consideration.

WITNESSED the hands of said Grantor(s) this _____ day of _____, 19_____.

_____

_____

State of   )

County of   ) SS

On this date, [list names of person(s) who signed above] personally appeared before me and acknowledged that the above signature(s) are valid and binding.

_____
Notary Public

My Commission expires:

3–7 GRANT DEED WITH RESERVATION OF MINERAL RIGHTS

BE IT KNOWN, That [name of person making deed] Grantor, County of _____, State of _____, hereby conveys, grants, and transfers, subject to the reservation stated below, to [person receiving the interest in the property], of the County of _____, State of _____; the following described real property located in _____, County of _____, State of _____, more particularity described as: [enter legal description at this point]

together with all the tenements, hereditament, and appurtenances thereto belonging and the reversions, remainders, rents, and profits, if any, thereof.

Reserving and excepting therefrom, however, _____ percent of the mineral rights in the property for the Grantor and Grantor's heirs, executors, and assigns. This reservation includes by its terms, oil, gas, and any other minerals on, in, and under the property conveyed.

The consideration for this transfer is the payment of $_____ and for other good and valuable consideration.

WITNESSED the hands of said Grantor(s) this _____ day of _____, 19_____.

_____

_____

State of   )

County of   ) SS

On this date, [list names of person(s) who signed above] personally appeared before me and acknowledged that the above signature(s) are valid and binding.

_____
Notary Public

My Commission expires:

3-8 GRANT DEED WITH THE ASSUMPTION OF ENCUMBRANCES (NOTE)

BE IT KNOWN, That [name of person making deed] Grantor, County of _____, State of _____, hereby conveys and transfers to [person receiving the interest in the property], of the County of_____, State of _____; the following described real property located in _____, County of _____, State of _____, more particularity described as: [enter legal description at this point]

together with all the tenements, hereditament, and appurtenances thereto belonging and the reversions, remainders, rents, and profits, if any, thereof.

The Grantee expressly assumes by the acceptance of this deed all the agreements, rights, duties, and obligations of the Grantor, including the payments of all sums due or becoming due on the debt evidenced by a promissory note in the principle sum of $_____, dated_____19XX and recorded in Book_____, Page_____, of the Records of_____County.

The consideration for this transfer is the payment of $_____ and for other good and valuable consideration.

WITNESSED the hands of said Grantor(s) and Grantee(s) this _____ day of _____, 19_____.

_____

_____

State of   )

County of   ) SS

On this date, [list names of person(s) who signed above] personally appeared before me and acknowledged that the above signature(s) are valid and binding.

_____
Notary Public

My Commission expires:

3-9 GRANT DEED WITH THE ASSUMPTION OF ENCUMBRANCES (LEASE)

BE IT KNOWN, That [name of person making deed] Grantor, County of _____, State of _____, hereby conveys and transfers to [person receiving the interest in the property], of the County of_____, State of _____; the following described real property located in _____, County of _____, State of _____, more particularity described as: [enter legal description at this point]

together with all the tenements, hereditament, and appurtenances thereto belonging and the reversions, remainders, rents, and profits, if any, thereof.

The Grantee expressly assumes by the acceptance of this deed all the agreements, rights, duties, and obligations of the Grantor in the below described lease:

[describe lease]

The consideration for this transfer is the payment of $_____ and for other good and valuable consideration.

WITNESSED the hands of said Grantor(s) and Grantee(s) this _____ day of _____, 19_____.

_____

_____

State of   )

County of   ) SS

On this date, [list names of person(s) who signed above] personally appeared before me and acknowledged that the above signature(s) are valid and binding.

_____
Notary Public

My Commission expires:

3–10 GRANT DEED CREATING A JOINT TENANCY

BE IT KNOWN, That [name of person making deed] Grantor, County of _____, State of _____, hereby conveys, grants, and transfers to [persons receiving the interest in the property], of the County of_____, State of _____; as joint tenants, the following described real property located in _____, County of _____, State of _____, more particularity described as: [enter legal description at this point]

together with all the tenements, hereditament, and appurtenances thereto belonging and the reversions, remainders, rents, and profits, if any, thereof.

The consideration for this transfer is the payment of $_____ and for other good and valuable consideration.

WITNESSED the hands of said Grantor(s) this _____ day of _____, 19___.

_____

_____

State of _____)

County of _____) SS

On this date, [list names of person(s) who signed above] personally appeared before me and acknowledged that the above signature(s) are valid and binding.

_____
Notary Public

My Commission expires:

3-11   GRANT DEED (BY JOINT TENANTS TO THIRD PERSON)

BE IT KNOWN, That we, [names of persons making deed] Joint Tenants, County of _____, State of _____, hereby convey and transfer to [person receiving the interest in the property], of the County of_____, State of _____; the following described real property located in _____, County of _____, State of _____, more particularity described as: [enter legal description at this point].

together with all the tenements, hereditament, and appurtenances thereto belonging and the reversions, remainders, rents, and profits, if any, thereof.

The consideration for this transfer is the payment of $_____ and for other good and valuable consideration.

WITNESSED the hands of said Grantor(s) this _____ day of _____, 19_____.

_____

_____

State of _____   )

County of _____   ) SS

On this date, [list names of person(s) who signed above] personally appeared before me and acknowledged that the above signature(s) are valid and binding.

_____
Notary Public

My Commission expires:

3-12   GRANT DEED OF LIFE ESTATE

BE IT KNOWN, That [name of person making deed] Grantor, County of _____, State of _____, hereby conveys, grants, and transfers a life estate to [person receiving the interest in the property], of the County of_____, State of _____; in the following described real property located in _____, County of _____, State of _____, more particularity described as: [enter legal description at this point]

together with all the tenements, hereditament, and appurtenances thereto belonging.

On the death of the Grantee, the property will go in fee simple to [person receiving the property on the death of the grantee].

The consideration for this transfer is the payment of $_____ and for other good and valuable consideration.

WITNESSED the hands of said Grantor(s) this _____ day of _____, 19_____.

_____

_____

State of   )

County of   ) SS

On this date, [list names of person(s) who signed above] personally appeared before me and acknowledged that the above signature(s) are valid and binding.

_____
Notary Public

My Commission expires:

3-13 GRANT DEED RESERVING LIFE ESTATE

BE IT KNOWN, That [name of person making deed] Grantor, County of _____, State of _____, hereby conveys, grants, and transfers to [person receiving the interest in the property], of the County of_____, State of _____; in the following described real property located in _____, County of _____, State of _____, more particularity described as:

[enter legal description at this point]

subject to the reservation herein made below.

The Grantor reserves to himself/herself the exclusive possession, use, and enjoyment of the rents, issues, and profits in the above described property for and during the natural lifetime of Grantor.

The consideration for this transfer is the payment of $_____ and for other good and valuable consideration.

WITNESSED the hands of said Grantor(s) this _____ day of _____, 19____.

_____

_____

State of   )

County of   ) SS

On this date, [list names of person(s) who signed above] personally appeared before me and acknowledged that the above signature(s) are valid and binding.

_____
Notary Public

My Commission expires:

3-14 DISCHARGE AND SATISFACTION OF MORTGAGE

BE IT KNOWN, We, the holders of a real estate mortgage from [name of persons holders of mortgage], for value received, hereby acknowledge full satisfaction and discharge of the below listed mortgage: [enter a complete mortgage description at this point],

the said mortgage was recorded in Book or Volume _____, Page _____, of the _____ County Registry of Deeds.

Signed under seal this _____ day of _____, 19_____.

_____

_____

State of   )

County of   ) SS

On this date, [list names of person(s) who signed above] personally appeared before me and acknowledged that the above signature(s) are valid and binding.

_____
Notary Public

My Commission expires:

3-15 EXTENSION OF DEED OF TRUST

This note is given for and represents the sum [amount paid to extend note] ($_____), advanced and paid to the grantor on this date by [person paying sum]. The consideration is for the extension of the deed of trust between [enter parties to deed of trust] and more fully described and duly recorded in [cite the page and volume where trust deed is recorded, official name of records, and location of records].

Grantor acknowledges that the deed of trust referenced above is a valid and subsisting lien against the property. The lien is renewed, extended, and continued in force to secure the payment of the note that is secured here.

_____   _____
(signed by Grantor)   (signed by Grantee)

_____

_____

State of   )
County of   ) SS

On this date, [list names of person(s) who signed above] personally appeared before me and acknowledged that the above signature(s) are valid and binding.

_____
Notary Public

My Commission expires:

3-16   APPOINTMENT OF SUBSTITUTE TRUSTEE

State of _____

County of _____

In a deed of trust dated _____, recorded in the [state where recorded, including page and volume of records] of _____ County, _____[name of substitute trustee—also include address of new trustee] is hereby appointed as substitute trustee because the originally appointed trustee is [unable, unwilling to act or has died] to act in this matter. The substitute trustee is granted the same rights, powers, and duties as the original trustee.

Dated: _____

[signature of parties]

_____

_____

State of   )

County of   ) SS

On this date, [list names of person(s) who signed above] personally appeared before me and acknowledged that the above signature(s) are valid and binding.

_____
Notary Public

My Commission expires:

3-17 NOTICE OF EXERCISE OPTION TO PURCHASE

Certified Mail, Return Receipt Requested

[date]

[company name
 and address]

Re: Notice to exercise option to purchase property

To: [lessor]

This is to officially notify you that we are exercising our option to purchase the leased property located at [address of property].

Under the terms of the present lease, we have the option to purchase the said property. Pursuant to lease, we hereby exercise the option to purchase the property at the option price of $_____. Enclosed is our required down payment in the amount of $_____.

Sincerely,

_____
Lessee

3-18   DEED: GRANT OF EASEMENT

Recording Requested by:
[name and address of person recording grant]

DEED: GRANT OF EASEMENT

County of   )
State of   )

For Valuable Consideration, receipt of which is acknowledged; I,
_____ ,
grantor, to the owners of the adjoining property, to wit:

_____

In consideration for construction of a boundary fence between the parties to this deed, grantor grants to grantee, its successors, and assigns, the right to erect, construct, or replace a boundary fence between the properties of the grantor and the grantee at the present location of boundary fence which is located on the below described land. This Deed shall act as a grant of easement against the property located in the State of _____, County of _____, and described as follows:

Executed on _____, 19_____ at [city and state].

_____
[signature of person granting
easement]

State of   )
County of   ) SS.
   On this_____day of_____,19____, before me, the undersigned, a Notary Public in and for the State of_____, personally appeared _____ personally known to me or proved to me on the basis of satisfactory evidence to be the person whose name is subscribed to the within instrument, and acknowledged to me that he executed it.

WITNESS my hand and official Seal.

_____
Notary Public in and for
Said State

DEED: GRANT OF EASEMENT (LIMITED)

Recording Requested by:
[name and address of person recording grant]

DEED: GRANT OF EASEMENT (LIMITED)

County of)
State of)
    For Valuable Consideration, receipt of which is acknowledged; I,

_____,

grantor, to the owners of the adjoining property, to wit:

_____

    In consideration for construction of a boundary fence between the parties to this deed, grantor grants to grantee, its successors, and assigns, the right to erect, construct, or replace a boundary fence between the properties of the grantor and the grantee at the present location of boundary fence which is located on the below described land. This Deed shall act as a grant of easement against the property located in the State of_____, County of_____, and described as follows:

    This grant of easement shall terminate without further action on the part of the grantor _____ years from the date of the execution of this document.

    Executed on _____, 19___ at [city and state].

                                    _____

                                    [Signature of person granting easement]

State of)
County of) SS
    On this_____ day of_____, 19___, before me, the undersigned, a Notary Public in and for the State of_____, personally appeared _____
personally known to me or proved to me on the basis of satisfactory evidence to be the person whose name is subscribed to the within instrument, and acknowledged to me that he executed it.

WITNESS my hand and official Seal.

                                    _____

                                    Notary Public in and for
                                    Said State

3-20 DEED: GRANT OF EASEMENT (RESTRICTED)

Recording Requested by:
[name address of person recording grant]

DEED: GRANT OF EASEMENT (RESTRICTED)

County of   )
State of   )
For Valuable Consideration, receipt of which is acknowledged; I,

_____

grantor, to the owners of the adjoining property, to wit:

_____

The Grantor grants to grantee, its successors, and assigns, the right to pass through the properties of the grantor on the private road presently located on the below described land.

This Deed shall act as a grant of easement against the property located in the State of_____, County of_____, and described as follows:

This grant of easement shall terminate without further action on the part of the grantor _____ years from the date of the execution of this document.

This grant of easement is limited only to personal and noncommercial travel on the subject road. Vehicles exceeding the following weights (_____) or with more than two axles may not use the subject road.

Executed on _____, 19_____ at [city and state].

_____
[Signature of person granting easement]

State of   )
County of   ) SS
On this_____day of_____,19___, before me, the undersigned, a Notary Public in and for the State of_____
personally appeared _____
personally known to me or proved to me on the basis of satisfactory evidence to be the person whose name is subscribed to the within instrument, and acknowledged to me that he executed it.

WITNESS my hand and official Seal.

_____
Notary Public in and for
Said State

3-21

NOTICE OF DEFAULT ON LAND CONTRACT

Date:

To: [debtor]

Dear [name of debtor]:

We entered into a contract to sell a parcel of land to you during _____, 19____. The only contingency was that the "buyer obtain a construction loan." It now appears that you refused to complete the escrow based on the fact that you could not "presell" your proposed construction. Since this was not a stated contingency, you are in violation of the contract with us.

Please advise me within 10 days of your intentions regarding the subject contract. If your proposals are not satisfactory, I intend to file civil action against you.

As I am sure you are aware, if this matter goes to suit, all court costs, process server's fees, sheriff's fees, attorney fees where permitted, and other postjudgment costs will be added to the damages in this case.

Sincerely,

3-22   NOTICE OF DISCHARGE AND SATISFACTION OF MORTGAGE

BE IT KNOWN, that the below described mortgage has been paid and the mortgage holder has acknowledged full satisfaction and discharge of the below listed mortgage: [enter a complete mortgage description at this point],

the said mortgage was recorded in Book or Volume _____ Page _____, of the _____ County Registry of Deeds.

Signed under seal this _____ day of _____, 19_____.

_____

_____

State of   )
County of   ) SS

On this date, [list names of person(s) who signed above] personally appeared before me and acknowledged that the above signature(s) are valid and binding.

_____
Notary Public

My Commission expires:

3-23 NOTICE OF CANCELLATION OF OPTION TO PURCHASE REAL ESTATE

Certified Mail, Return Receipt Requested

BE IT KNOWN, that the below described option to purchase real estate located at [description of real estate in question] has been canceled in that the holder of the option has failed to comply with the terms of the option agreement.

Description of option: [enter a complete option description at this point]

Description of terms of option that were not complied with: [describe the acts on which the cancellation is based, e.g., failed to pay a prescribed amount by a certain date]

the said mortgage was recorded in Book or Volume _____, Page _____, of the _____ County Registry of Deeds.

Signed under seal this _____ day of _____, 19___.

_____

_____

State of   )

County of   ) SS

On this date, [list names of person(s) who signed above] personally appeared before me and acknowledged that the above signature(s) are valid and binding.

_____
Notary Public

My Commission expires:

3-24 DECLARATION OF COVENANTS AND RESTRICTIONS

BE IT KNOWN, That [name of person declarations] Declarant, County of _____, State of _____, hereby declares that the property located in the County of_____ State of _____; the following described real property located in _____, County of _____, State of _____, more particularly described as:

[enter legal description at this point]

is subject to the following restrictions:

[list the restrictions]

The declarant imposes on such property beneficial restrictions under a general plan of improvement for the benefit of all future owners thereof. The parcels of property conveyed from the original parcel described above shall be subject to the above restrictions.

WITNESSES the hands of said Declarant(s) this _____ day of_____, 19_____.

_____

_____

State of   )

County of   ) SS

On this date, [list names of person(s) who signed above] personally appeared before me and acknowledged that the above signature(s) are valid and binding.

_____
Notary Public

My Commission expires:

3-25

NOTICE OF AGREEMENT REGARDING (DISPUTED) BOUNDARY LINE

BE IT KNOWN, that the below signed property holders to once and forever settle the dispute regarding the boundary lines of their property have agreed that the [describe boundary line, e.g. north/south] boundary line between their respective properties is located at:

[describe in detail the location of the boundary line]

This agreement affects and is binding on the following parcels of property:

[legal description of the two parcels of land affected by the boundary line agreement]

Signed under seal this _____ day of _____, 19_____.

_____

_____

State of   )

County of   ) SS

On this date, [list names of person(s) who signed above] personally appeared before me and acknowledged that the above signature(s) are valid and binding.

_____

Notary Public

My Commission expires:

3-26 NOTICE OF AGREEMENT REGARDING (CHANGING) BOUNDARY LINES

BE IT KNOWN, that the below signed property holders for good and valuable consideration, receipt of which is hereby acknowledged, the boundary lines of their property have agreed to change the [describe boundary line, e.g. north/south] boundary line between their respective properties. The new boundary line is located at:

[describe in detail the location of the boundary line]

This agreement affects and is binding on the following parcels of property:

[legal description of the two parcels of land affected by the boundary line agreement]

Signed under seal this _____ day of _____, 19_____.

_____

_____

State of   )

County of   ) SS

On this date, [list names of person(s) who signed above] personally appeared before me and acknowledged that the above signature(s) are valid and binding.

_____
Notary Public

My Commission expires:

3-27 DECLARATION OF HOMESTEAD (BY UNMARRIED PERSON)

BE IT KNOWN, That [name of person making the declaration] Declarant, County of _____, State of _____, hereby declares that the property located in the County of_____, State of _____; the following described real property located in _____, County of _____, State of _____, more particularity described as: [enter legal description at this point]

is our homestead.

I further declare that:

1. I am unmarried and the head of a family. My family consists of the following members:

2. The above described property is currently occupied and resided in by my family and me as our home and is therefore our homestead.

3. I have made no former declarations of homestead [or the previous declaration of homestead made by me on [date] has been abandoned.

WITNESSED the hands of said Declarant(s) this _____ day of _____, 19_____.

_____

_____

State of   )

County of   ) SS

On this date, [list names of person(s) who signed above] personally appeared before me and acknowledged that the above signature(s) are valid and binding.

_____
Notary Public

My Commission expires:

3-28

DECLARATION OF HOMESTEAD (BY MARRIED COUPLE)

BE IT KNOWN, That we, [names of married couple making the declaration] Declarants, County of _____, State of _____, hereby declare that the property located in the County of_____, State of _____; the following described real property located in _____, County of _____, State of _____, more particularity described as: [enter legal description at this point]

is our homestead.

We further declare that:

1. We are husband and wife and the heads of a family. Our family consists of the following members:

2. The above described property is currently occupied and resided in by our family and us as our home and is therefore our homestead.

3. We have made no former declarations of homestead [or the previous declaration of homestead made by us on [date] has been abandoned.

WITNESSED the hands of said Declarant(s) this _____ day of _____, 19_____.

_____

_____

State of   )

County of   ) SS

On this date, [list names of person(s) who signed above] personally appeared before me and acknowledged that the above signature(s) are valid and binding.

_____
Notary Public

My Commission expires:

3-29 DECLARATION OF HOMESTEAD (BY PERSON NOT HEAD OF HOUSEHOLD)

BE IT KNOWN, That I, [name of person making the declaration] Declarant, County of _____, State of _____, hereby declare that the property located in the County of_____, State of_____; the following described real property located in _____, County of _____, State of _____, more particularly described as: [enter legal description at this point]

is my homestead.

I further declare that:

1. I am an unmarried person.
2. The above described property is currently occupied and resided in by me as my home and is therefore my homestead.
3. I have made no former declarations of homestead [or the previous declaration of homestead made by me on [date] has been abandoned.

WITNESSED the hands of said Declarant(s) this _____ day of _____, 19_____.

_____

_____

State of   )

County of   ) SS

On this date, [list names of person(s) who signed above] personally appeared before me and acknowledged that the above signature(s) are valid and binding.

_____
Notary Public

My Commission expires:

3-30   ABANDONMENT OF HOMESTEAD (BY SINGLE HEAD OF HOUSEHOLD)

BE IT KNOWN, That I, [name], Declarant, County of _____, State of _____, hereby abandoned the homestead declared by me on [date] and recorded on [date recorded] in Book_____, Page_____of the official records of_____County, [state] on that the property located in the County of_____, State of _____; the following described real property located in _____, County of _____, State of _____, more particularity described as:

[enter legal description at this point]

At the time that the homestead was declared, I was an unmarried head of household. My present status is unmarried, head of household.

WITNESSED the hands of said Declarant(s) this _____ day of _____, 19_____.

_____

_____

State of   )

County of   ) SS

On this date, [list names of person(s) who signed above] personally appeared before me and acknowledged that the above signature(s) are valid and binding.

_____

Notary Public

My Commission expires:

3-31

ABANDONMENT OF HOMESTEAD (BY SINGLE PERSON NOT HEAD OF HOUSEHOLD)

BE IT KNOWN, That I, [name] Declarant, County of _____, State of _____, hereby abandoned the homestead declared by me on [date] and recorded on [date recorded] in Book_____, page_____ of the official records of _____ County, [state] on that the property located in the County of _____, State of _____; the following described real property located in _____, County of _____, State of _____, more particularity described as:

[enter legal description at this point]

WITNESSED the hands of said Declarant(s) this _____ day of _____, 19_____.

_____

_____

State of   )

County of   ) SS

On this date, [list names of person(s) who signed above] personally appeared before me and acknowledged that the above signature(s) are valid and binding.

_____
Notary Public

My Commission expires:

3-32 ABANDONMENT OF HOMESTEAD (BY MARRIED COUPLE)

BE IT KNOWN, That we, [names of married couple making the declaration] Declarants, County of _____, State of _____, hereby abandoned the homestead declared by us on [date] and recorded on [date recorded] in Book____, page____of the official records of____County, [state] on that the property located in the County of_____, State of _____; the following described real property located in _____, County of _____, State of _____, more particularity described as:

[enter legal description at this point]

WITNESSED the hands of said Declarant(s) this _____ day of _____, 19____.

_____

_____

State of   )

County of   ) SS

On this date, [list names of person(s) who signed above] personally appeared before me and acknowledged that the above signature(s) are valid and binding.

_____
Notary Public

My Commission expires:

Chapter 4

Leases and Rental Forms and Agreements

This chapter discusses the legal aspects of leasing and the forms and agreements that are used in the leasing and rental of business equipment, and buildings.

Leasing Business Property

Before agreeing to lease any property, you should be familiar with the state laws that establish the rights and liabilities of both tenant and landlord. The laws vary from state to state; therefore only the general principles subject are discussed here.

A formal written lease is not necessary to establish a landlord–tenant relationship. The relationship may be created by an oral agreement, it may arise out of the conduct of the parties, or it may result from the operation of law. *Note*: Most states require that a lease for a period longer than one year be in writing. In those states, failure to have a written document when the lease is for longer than a year automatically makes the lease a month-to-month lease. In any case, however, a written lease is strongly recommended. *Note*: Traditionally, preprinted form leases are printed to favor the landlord.

The two basic types of leases are the *fixed-term lease* and the *periodic lease*. Under a fixed-term lease, the length of the lease is set, as is the rent schedule and amount. Except for specific reasons, neither the tenant nor the landlord may cancel the lease or vary the amount of rent without mutual consent. A periodic lease is an open-ended agreement for an indefinite period. This type of lease is also called a *month-to-month lease*.

The fixed-term lease protects the tenant against being forced out of the premises until the lease expires and against having the rent raised. It has the disadvantage of binding the tenant, businessperson, to paying the stated rent for the duration of the lease, even if the businessperson discontinues the business or moves to a different location. A periodic lease binds neither the tenant nor the landlord beyond the periodic rent period. The periodic lease, however, provides little stability for the business owner and thus should be used with caution.

Before signing any lease, read it carefully and make sure you understand all its provisions, conditions, and terms. If you are in doubt, check with a local attorney. Any verbal assurances by the landlord should be written and included in the written lease before you sign it. In most cases, when verbal understandings are followed by a written lease, the courts look to the written agreement to determine the rights of the parties. This is especially true in those cases where the written document is in conflict with the earlier verbal agreements or understandings. For example, if there is verbal agreement between the building owner and the tenant that the rent could be paid on the fifteenth of each month and the written lease provides that the monthly rental is to be paid not later than the fifth, the courts would probably enforce the written provision rather than the verbal agreement.

Lease Provisions

A written lease is a contract between the tenant and the landlord. Its provisions, if not illegal, establish the terms and the conditions of the lease. If the lease is silent as to the duration of it, it is considered as a tenancy-at-will lease. If the lease fails to indicate the starting date, it will normally begin when the tenant takes possession of the premises.

Examine the lease document for the following provisions and conditions. Because it is unlikely that all the provisions listed below may be included in the lease in a manner that is favorable to you, consider each one as at least a bargaining point with the landlord.

1. Is there a clear provision regarding the return of the security deposit, the cleaning deposit, or both at the termination of the lease?

2. What are the requirements on the landlord to maintain the property according to certain standards?

3. Under what circumstances or conditions may either you or the landlord cancel the lease before its expiration?

4. Does the lease provide you with an option to renew the lease in order to protect your rights to stay in the same location?

5. Does the lease allow the landlord to enter the property at any time without any prior notice to you?

6. Does the landlord retain a set of keys to your business?

7. Does the lease obligate you to follow any rules formulated by the landlord any time after the lease is signed?

8. Does the lease release the landlord from responsibility for any damages to your property, even if it is the landlord's fault?

9. Are you, under the terms of lease, required to maintain any fixtures, appliances, or portions of the property?

10. Does the security or any other deposit that you are required to post pay interest?

11. Do you have the right to put up signs for your business without the landlord's permission?

12. Do you have the right to sublease the premises for the duration of the lease if your business closes or if you can no longer use the property?

13. Can you use the property for any lawful purpose?

14. Is the landlord prohibited from renting other space in the same building or nearby to tenants who will compete with your business?

15. What rights do you have in the use of the common property such as hallways, driveways, elevators, and parking lots?

16. If the amount of your rent is based on gross receipts of your business, are provisions made for deductions for returned merchandise, delivery or installation charges, refundable deposits, and sales tax?

Landlord's Liability

Unless required to do so by the rental agreement, the landlord is under no obligation to repair the leased premises. The tenant takes the premises as they are and promises to return them to the landlord at the end of the lease in the same condition, less normal wear and tear. Generally, a landlord is not liable for injuries caused by defects in the premises unless such liability is provided for in the lease or unless the landlord was aware of the defects and the defects could not be reasonably discovered by the tenant on inspection of the premises. For example, if the landlord leases the entire building to one tenant and at the time the tenant takes possession the stairs are in need of repair and the condition is apparent, the landlord is normally not liable for anyone injured. There would be a different result if the building were rented to several tenants and the stairs were in common use by more than one tenant.

Rents

Rents are due and payable at periods established in the agreement between the landlord and the tenant. As a matter of practice, landlords require advance payment of rent. If nothing is agreed on between the parties as to rent, the courts assume that the parties agreed to a reasonable rent and payable at the end of the lease, not in advance. *Caution* for your protection, make an agreement and get it in writing.

When the rents are based on gross receipts or a percentage of the income, care should be exercised that all parties understand the exact method to be used in computing the rent and what deductions are taken before the rent is computed. In addition, the rights of the landlord to look at the books or accounts of the tenant to determine or ascertain the amount of rent due must be understood.

Forfeiture of Lease

Leases may be terminated by the landlord when the tenant fails to comply with any major provision of the lease agreement. For example, all states have statutes providing for the termination of a tenancy for the nonpayment of rent. Other actions that may result in a forfeiture of the lease include using the premises for unlawful activities, violation of local zoning ordinances, willful destruction of the property, and violations of lease provisions.

When the landlord declares a forfeiture of the lease, he must, in most cases notify the tenant in writing of the election. In some cases, the landlord is required to give the tenant an opportunity to correct the problem. For example, for nonpayment of rent in Massachusetts, a tenant is given a 14-day notice to quit the premises unless the tenant has received a similar notice within the past 12 months. If the tenant has received a similar notice within the past year, then the period in which he must quite the premises is only five days. In California, the landlord may serve the tenant a three-day notice to pay rent, or quit. In either case, if the tenant tenders full payment of the rent within the granted period, the lease is not forfeited.

Right of Landlord to Enter Premises

Unless permitted by the lease in most states, a landlord has no right to enter premises that have been leased to others without their permission. An exception to this rule is when it is necessary to enter the premises to preserve the property. Most standard leases have provisions regarding the right of the landlord to enter the premises. The right to enter in those cases must, therefore, be in accordance with the terms of the lease.

Before Taking Possession

Before you accept possession of the premises, there are certain steps you should take to protect yourself in the event any disputes occur during the term of the lease or when you vacate the premises.

1. Keep a record of all transactions between you and the landlord during the lease negotiations. *Note*: Also keep copies of the lease, notices, letters between you and the landlord, receipts for rent, and so on.

2. Before you move in, complete a detailed checkoff list or inventory as to the condition of the premises and of any property included with the building. Keep one copy and forward one to the landlord. For example, if the walls need painting, make that notation on your list even if the landlord promises to paint it later.

3. If necessary to accurately reflect the condition of the premises, take pictures.

Security and Cleaning Deposits

Most state statutes include specific rules relating to the holding and return of security and cleaning deposits. These statutes usually provide that the landlord may keep only that part of the deposit necessary to clean the premises, repair any damages (except for normal wear and tear), and for unpaid rent. Unless the lease provides otherwise, a landlord cannot charge you for normal wear and tear on a building. At the end of the lease, the landlord is required to notify you in writing within a certain period (normally 15 days) of any deductions from your deposit. The burden is on the landlord to establish any right to withhold any portion of the deposit. In most states, the landlord cannot make the deposit nonrefundable. Accordingly, the landlord is normally required to return the entire deposit if you leave the premises in good, clean condition and there are no damages or unpaid rent chargeable to you.

State statutes usually require the landlord to pay interest on security deposits. The landlord is also required to refund the deposit or give a detailed written explanation for withholding any part of the deposit within a certain time, usually not more than 15 days. *Note*: To withhold any part of the deposit for damages caused by the tenant, the landlord must establish that the damages are in excess of those caused by normal wear and tear.

In most states, failure to provide a detailed accounting to the tenant within the required time results in the landlord's being unable to make any deductions and may also subject him or her to a penalty. If the security deposit is not returned as required, you should seek assistance from any tenant associations in your area or consider using the small claims court. If these options are not available, consult an attorney. *Note*: Most leases provide for attorney fees and court costs to the landlord if the tenant violates the lease. If there is a provision whereby one party may obtain attorney fees and court costs, this provision is also available to the other side (the tenant).

Equipment Leasing

Another way to partially finance a business is to use a security lease. The businessperson signs a long-term lease rather than buying the needed business equipment. At the end of the lease, the equipment belongs to the businessowner. This arrangement permits you to structure your financing over a much longer useful life of the equipment than that which you would usually be allowed on a loan or chattel mortgage on the equipment.

In many cases, the lease is structured so that the cash flow the equipment generates is tied into the number of lease payments due. Another possible advantage in using the lease method of equipment financing is the fact that the lessor may allow you to finance a greater percentage of the equipment's cost than that which would be available in the usual loan situation.

Forms in This Chapter

- FORM 4–1: RESIDENTIAL RENTAL APPLICATION. For a landlord's use in taking a rental application. Contains sufficient data to enable landlord to check applicant's creditworthiness.

- FORM 4–2: RESIDENTIAL LEASE. Leases residential property to tenants.

- FORM 4–3: AMENDMENT TO RESIDENTIAL LEASE. Amends a lease for residential property.

- FORM 4–4: RENT GUARANTY. Used when a third person guarantees rent for a tenant. Attached to the residential lease.

- FORM 4–5: RESIDENTIAL SUBLEASE. Subleases residential property to tenants.

- FORM 4–6: COMMERCIAL LEASE. Leases commercial property to tenants.

- FORM 4–7: AMENDMENT TO COMMERCIAL LEASE. Amends a lease for commercial property.

- FORM 4–8: COMMERCIAL SUBLEASE. Subleases commercial property to tenants.

- FORM 4–9: EXTENSION OF LEASE. Extends a lease for real property.

- FORM 4–10: NOTICE OF ADDITIONAL CHARGES. Notifies tenants of additional charges under a lease.

- FORM 4–11: NOTICE OF CHANGE IN RENT. Notifies tenants of an increase in rent.

- FORM 4–12: NOTICE OF TRANSFER OF SECURITY DEPOSIT. Notifies tenants that the security deposit under a lease has been transferred to the new owners of the property.

- FORM 4–13: LESSEE'S NOTICE OF TERMINATION OF LEASE. A tenant's notification to lessor of termination of a month-to-month lease.

- FORM 4–14: NOTICE TO EXERCISE OPTION TO EXTEND LEASE. A tenant's notification to lessor of the exercise of an option to extend a lease.

- FORM 4–15: LESSOR'S NOTICE OF TERMINATION OF LEASE. A lessor's notice of termination of a month-to-month lease.

- FORM 4–16: NOTICE OF DEFAULT IN RENT. A lessor's notice to tenants that they are in default of rental payments. (*Note*: Check local requirements for any special clauses that need to be included.)

- FORM 4–17: NOTICE OF CURABLE DEFAULT. Notifies tenants that they are in default of the lease for other than rental payments. (*Note*: Check local requirements for any special clauses that need to be included.)

- FORM 4–18: NOTICE OF NONCURABLE DEFAULT. Notifies tenants that they are in default of lease for other than rental payments and default is noncurable. (*Note*: Check local requirements for any special clauses that need to be included.)

- FORM 4–19: MUTUAL RELEASE BETWEEN LANDLORD AND TENANT. Mutually releases both landlord and tenant from the provisions of a lease.

- FORM 4–20: NOTICE OF BELIEF OF ABANDONMENT OF LEASED PROPERTY (POSSESSIONS REMOVED). Notifies tenants of lessor's belief that they have abandoned the property and that lessor intends to reclaim it. In most states, the rent of the property must be past due and the tenants have apparently removed *all* their possessions when the notice is mailed.

- FORM 4–21: NOTICE OF BELIEF OF ABANDONMENT OF LEASED PROPERTY (SOME POSSESSIONS REMAINING). Notifies tenants of lessor's belief that they have abandoned the property and that lessor intends to reclaim it. In most states, the rent of the property must be past due and the tenants have left some of their possessions on the premises when the notice is mailed.

- FORM 4–22: DEMAND ON COTENANT FOR PAYMENT. Places a demand on a cotenant for payment of past due rent or damages.

- FORM 4–23: DEMAND ON GUARANTOR FOR PAYMENT. Places a demand on a guarantor for payment of past due rent or damages.

- FORM 4–24: EQUIPMENT LEASE. A straightforward equipment lease.

- FORM 4–25: EQUIPMENT LEASE (WITH OPTION TO PURCHASE). A lease with an option to purchase.

- FORM 4–26: EQUIPMENT LEASE (WITH TITLE TRANSFERRING TO LESSEE AT END OF LEASE). A lease that transfers the title to the lessee at the end of the lease.

- FORM 4–27: AMENDED EQUIPMENT LEASE (SUBSTITUTION OF EQUIPMENT). Substitutes equipment on an equipment lease.

- FORM 4–28: EXTENSION OF EQUIPMENT LEASE. Extends an equipment lease.

- FORM 4–29: MUTUAL CANCELLATION OF EQUIPMENT LEASE. Mutually cancels an equipment lease.

- FORM 4–30: LEASE PROVISIONS CHECKLIST. Used to ensure that any lease agreement contains the necessary provisions.

- FORM 4–31: WAIVER OF CLAIM TO FIXTURES. Consent of the landlord to remove fixtures attached by tenant.

- FORM 4–32: NOTICE ENDING AT-WILL TENANCY. Notifies a tenant that tenancy will be terminated.

4–1   RESIDENTIAL RENTAL APPLICATION

Name: _____   Social Sec. No._____

Spouse: _____   Social Sec. No._____

Present Address:

_____

Previous Address:

_____

Driver's Lic. No. _____   Birthdate: _____

Spouse's Driver's Lic. _____   Birthdate: _____

How long have you lived at your present address?   _____

Name of landlord: _____   Telephone: _____

Employer: _____   Position: _____

Salary: _____   How long? _____

Spouse's Employer: _____   Telephone: _____

Salary: _____   How long? _____

Name of Bank:_____

Address: _____

Checking acc't no. :_____   Savings acc't no.:_____

Personal References:

Name	Relationship	Telephone
_____	_____	_____
_____	_____	_____

Credit References:

_____	_____	_____
_____	_____	_____

The above information is correct to the best of my knowledge and belief. I authorize you to check my credit and employment references in connection with processing of this application.

Date: _____   _____

                                                Applicant

4-2 RESIDENTIAL LEASE

This residential lease is entered into between _____ (Landlord) and _____ and _____, (Tenant(s)). The Landlord hereby leases the below described residential property to the Tenant(s). The Tenant(s) hereby accepts the lease. The terms of the lease are as follows:

1. The lease pertains to the property located at:

   _____

2. The lease shall be for a period of _____, commencing on _____ day of _____, 19____ and ending on _____ day of _____ 19____.

3. The Tenant shall pay Landlord the monthly rent of $_____, payable on the first day of every month. There will be a late fee of $_____ if the rent is not paid by the 5th of the month. The Tenant agrees to pay to Landlord the sum of $ _____ as a security deposit, to be promptly returned upon the termination of the lease and compliance with all provisions of this lease.

4. The Tenant shall be responsible for providing all utilities.

5. The Tenant agrees to return possession of the premises at the conclusion of the lease in its present condition, except for normal wear and tear.

6. Only the following persons will reside on the premises:

   _____.

7. The Tenant shall not assign or sublease the premises without written permission of the landlord.

8. No material or structural alterations of the premises will be made without the prior written permission of the landlord.

9. The Tenant will comply with all zoning, health, and use ordinances.

10. Pets are not allowed on the premises without prior written permission of the Landlord.

11. This lease shall be subordinate to all present and future mortgages against the premises.

12. In the event that legal action is necessary to enforce any provisions of this contract, attorney fees may be recovered by the prevailing party.

13. Additional lease terms: _____

_____
_____
_____
_____

Signed under seal this _____ day of_____, 19_____.

_____   _____
Landlord   Tenant

                                     _____
                                     Cotenant

4-3 AMENDMENT TO RESIDENTIAL LEASE

This amendment modifies the residential lease between the below parties which was entered into on [date of original lease] between _____ (Landlord) and _____ and _____, (Tenant(s)).

The Landlord and Tenant(s) for good and valuable consideration hereby modify and amend the said lease only as to the following terms:

[list new terms here]

All other terms of the original lease shall remain in force.

Signed under seal this _____ day of _____, 19_____.

_____
Landlord

_____
Tenant

_____
Cotenant

RENT GUARANTY

As an inducement for the Landlord to enter into a residential lease of the premises located at [location of rental property] to [name of renters] and for other good and valuable consideration, the undersigned hereby jointly and severally guaranty to the Landlord, his or her assigns, and or successors the prompt and full payment of all rents and other charges that may become due and owing to the Landlord under the terms of the attached lease or any renewal or extension thereof.

Signed under seal this _____ day of _____ 19_____.

_____   _____
Landlord   Tenant

                                                                   _____
                                                                   Cotenant

RESIDENTIAL SUBLEASE

This residential sublease is entered into between _____ (Tenant), _____ (Subtenant), and _____, (Tenant(s)). The Tenant hereby subleases the below described residential property to the Subtenant(s). The Subtenant(s) hereby accepts the lease, and the Landlord by signing this sublease agrees to the sublease. The terms of the sublease are as follows:

1. The sublease pertains to the property located at:

   _____

2. The sublease shall be for a period of _____, commencing on _____ day of _____, 19_____ and ending on _____ day of _____, 19_____.

3. The Subtenant shall pay Tenant the monthly rent of $_____ payable on the first day of every month. There will be a late fee of $_____ if the rent is not paid by the 5th of the month. The Subtenant agrees to pay to Tenant the sum of $_____ as a security deposit, to be promptly returned upon the termination of the sublease and compliance with all provisions of this sublease.

4. The Subtenant shall be responsible for providing all utilities.

5. The Subtenant agrees to return possession of the premises at the conclusion of the lease in its present condition, except for normal wear and tear.

6. Only the following persons will reside on the premises:

   _____
   _____ .

7. The subtenant shall not further assign or sublease the premises without written permission of the Landlord and the Tenant.

8. No material or structural alterations of the premises will be made without the prior written permission of the Landlord and Tenant.

9. The Subtenant will comply with all zoning, health, and use ordinances.

10. Pets are not allowed on the premises without prior written permission of the Landlord and Tenant.

11. This sublease shall be subordinate to all present and future mortgages against the premises.

12. In the event that legal action is necessary to enforce any provisions of this contract, attorney fees may be recovered by the prevailing party.

13. Additional sublease terms:

_____

_____

_____

_____

Signed under seal this _____ day of _____, 19___.

_____
Landlord

_____
Tenant

_____
Subtenant

4–6   COMMERCIAL LEASE

This commercial lease is entered into between _____ (Landlord) and _____ and _____, (Tenant(s)). The Landlord hereby leases the below described commercial property to the Tenant(s). The Tenant(s) hereby accepts the lease. The terms of the lease are as follows:

1. The lease pertains to the property located at:

    _____

2. The lease shall be for a period of _____, commencing on_____ day of_____, 19_____ and ending on _____ day of_____, 19_____ .

3. The Tenant shall pay Landlord, the monthly rent of $_____ payable on the first day of every month. There will be a late fee of $_____, if the rent is not paid by the 5th of the month. The Tenant agrees to pay to Landlord the sum of $_____ as a security deposit, to be promptly returned upon the termination of the lease and compliance with all provisions of this lease.

4. The Tenant shall be responsible for providing all utilities.

5. The Tenant agrees to return possession of the premises at the conclusion of the lease in its present condition, except for normal wear and tear.

6. The premises shall be used for the purpose of conducting the following business activities:

    _____

    _____ .

7. The Tenant shall not assign or sublease the premises without written permission of the Landlord.

8. No material or structural alterations of the premises will be made without the prior written permission of the landlord.

9. The Tenant will comply with all zoning, health, and use ordinances.

10. This lease shall be subordinate to all present and future mortgages against the premises.

11. In the event that legal action is necessary to enforce any provisions of this contract, attorney fees may be recovered by the prevailing party.

12. Additional lease terms: _____

    _____

    _____

    _____

Signed under seal this _____ day of _____19_____.

_____   _____
Landlord   Tenant

                                         _____
                                         Cotenant

4-7   AMENDMENT TO COMMERCIAL LEASE

This amendment modifies the commercial lease between the below parties which was entered into on [date of original lease] between _____ (Landlord) and _____ and_____, (Tenant(s)).

The Landlord and Tenant for good and valuable consideration hereby modify and amend the said lease only as to the following terms:

[list new terms here]

All other terms of the original lease shall remain in force.

Signed under seal this _____ day of _____,19_____.

_____
Landlord

_____
Tenant

_____
Cotenant

4-8   COMMERCIAL SUBLEASE

This sublease of commercial property is entered into between _____ (Tenant), _____ (Subtenant) and_____, (Tenant(s)). The Tenant hereby subleases the below described residential property to the Subtenant(s). The Subtenant(s) hereby accepts the lease and the Landlord by signing this sublease agrees to the sublease. The terms of the sublease are as follows:

1. The sublease pertains to the property located at:

    _____

2. The sublease shall be for a period of_____ , commencing on____ day of_____, 19____ and ending on _____ day of_____, 19____.

3. The Subtenant shall pay Tenant, the monthly rent of $_____ payable on the first day of every month. There will be a late fee of $_____, if the rent is not paid by the 5th of the month. The Subtenant agrees to pay to Tenant the sum of $_____ as a security deposit, to be promptly returned upon the termination of the sublease and compliance with all provisions of this sublease.

4. The Subtenant shall be responsible for providing all utilities.

5. The Subtenant agrees to return possession of the premises at the conclusion of the lease in its present condition, except for normal wear and tear.

6. Only the following types of businesses will be conducted on the premises:

    _____
    _____

7. Subtenant shall not further assign or sublease the premises without written permission of the Landlord and the Tenant.

8. No material or structural alterations of the premises will be made without the prior written permission of the Landlord and Tenant.

9. The Subtenant will comply with all zoning, health, and use ordinances.

10. This sublease shall be subordinate to all present and future mortgages against the premises.

11. In the event that legal action is necessary to enforce any provisions of this contract, attorney fees may be recovered by the prevailing party.

12. Additional sublease terms:

    _____
    _____

Signed under seal this _____ day of _____,
19____ .

_____   _____
Landlord   Tenant

                                        _____
                                        Subtenant

4-9

EXTENSION OF LEASE

This amendment extends the lease between the below parties which was entered into on [date of original lease] between_____, (Landlord), and_____ and_____, (Tenant(s)).

The Landlord and Tenant for good and valuable consideration hereby extend the said lease for a period of _____ years commencing on _____ and terminating on _____, 19_____.

All other terms of the original lease as hereby extended shall remain in force.

Signed under seal this _____ day of _____, 19_____.

_____   _____

Landlord   Tenant

                                                        _____

                                                        Cotenant

4-10 NOTICE OF ADDITIONAL CHARGES

Date:

To: [tenant]

Pursuant to the terms of your lease, you are hereby notified that an additional sum of $_____ is due on or before [date].

The additional sum is due to the below factors:

[list reasons for additional charges]

Payment of the additional sum should be made directly to the undersigned.

_____
Landlord

4-11 NOTICE OF CHANGE IN RENT

Date:

To: [tenant]

Pursuant to the terms of your lease, you are hereby notified that starting on the 1st day of_____ , 19_____, the monthly rent on your leased property will be increased to the monthly total of $_____.

This is a change from your present rate of $_____.

_____
Landlord

4-12 NOTICE OF TRANSFER OF SECURITY DEPOSIT

Date:

To: [tenant]

As you are aware, the leased property that you occupy has been sold to new owners. Pursuant to the terms of your lease, you are hereby notified that the security deposit in the amount of $_____ has also been transferred to the new owners.

The new owners and present holders of your security deposit are listed below:

[list name and address of new owners]

_____
Previous Landlord

I acknowledge that the above listed security deposit has been received by the undersigned.

_____
New Owner/New Landlord

4-13   LESSEE'S NOTICE OF TERMINATION OF LEASE

Date:

[Company name
and address]

Re: Notice of Termination of Lease

To: [lessor]

    This is to officially notify you that we are exercising our option to cancel our lease and to deliver up possession of the property located at [address of property], which we presently occupy, on [date the possession of property will be surrendered].

Sincerely,

_____

Tenant

4–14 NOTICE TO EXERCISE OPTION TO EXTEND LEASE

Certified Mail, Return Receipt Requested

Date:

[Company name
 and address]

Re: Notice to exercise option to extend lease

To: [lessee]

   This is to officially notify you that we are exercising our option to extend the lease on the property located at [address of property].

   Under the terms of the present lease, we have the option to extend or renew the said lease for a _____ term. Pursuant to lease options, we advise you that it is our election to so exercise the option to renew or extend the lease on the terms of the present lease.

Sincerely,

_____

Lessee

4-15   LESSOR'S NOTICE OF TERMINATION OF LEASE

Certified Mail, Return Receipt Requested

Date:

[Company name
 and address]

Re: Notice of Termination of Lease

To: [lessee]

    This is to officially notify you that we are exercising our option to cancel your lease and to direct you to deliver up possession of the property located at [address of property], which you presently occupy, on [date the possession of property will be surrendered].

Sincerely,

_____

Lessor

4-16 NOTICE OF DEFAULT IN RENT

Certified Mail, Return Receipt Requested

To: [name(s) of tenant(s)]

Regarding the property located at [address of property], this is to notify you that you are presently in default of the terms of the rental agreement on the subject property. Presently you owe rent from [date] to [date] for a total past due rent of $_____ .

You are hereby directed to pay the past due rent within _____ days or surrender possession of the property (quit).

If payment is not received within the above period or possession of the property is not surrendered, legal proceeding may be commenced against you without any further notice.

Sincerely,

_____

Lessor

4-17 NOTICE OF CURABLE DEFAULT

Certified Mail, Return Receipt Requested

To: [name(s) of tenant(s)]

Regarding the property located at [address of property], this is to notify you that you are presently in default of the terms of the rental agreement on the subject property. The default is as follows:

[describe the conduct that constitutes a violation of the lease]

If you do not remedy the above default within _____ days, legal proceeding may be commenced against you without any further notice.

Sincerely,

_____
Lessor

4–18   NOTICE OF NONCURABLE DEFAULT

Certified Mail, Return Receipt Requested

To: [name(s) of tenant(s)]

Regarding the property located at [address of property], this is to notify you that you are presently in default of the terms of the rental agreement on the subject property. The default is as follows:

[describe the conduct that constitutes a violation of the lease]

The default constitutes a forfeiture of your rights under the lease. Accordingly, unless you surrender possession of the subject property within _____ days, legal proceeding may be commenced against you without any further notice.

Sincerely,

_____

Lessor

4-19 MUTUAL RELEASE BETWEEN LANDLORD AND TENANT

Both _____ (Landlord) and _____ (Tenant) release and discharge one and the other from any and all claims arising out of the lease of the premises located at:

Landlord also acknowledges that possession of the premises have been returned to him/her and that any claims for damages to the property or past due rent are hereby waived.

Tenant acknowledges that he/she has received all monies due from the security deposit.

Signed under seal this _____ day of _____, 19____.

_____   _____
Landlord   Tenant

                                                    _____
                                                    Cotenant

4-20

NOTICE OF BELIEF OF ABANDONMENT OF LEASED PROPERTY (POSSESSIONS REMOVED)

Certified Mail, Return Receipt Requested

[date]

[tenant name(s)
and address(es)]

Re: Notice of belief of abandonment of leased property
    located at:

To: [tenant(s)]

The rent on the above property is past due and owing since [date rent was due]. It also appears that you have abandoned the said property since there are no possessions of yours located on the property.

Please be advised that unless I receive a written notice from you within the next 15 days stating both (1) that it is your intent not to abandon the property and (2) providing me with an address whereby legal process may be served on you by certified mail, I will consider the property has been abandoned and will reclaim possession of the property.

Sincerely,

_____

Landlord

4-21

NOTICE OF BELIEF OF ABANDONMENT OF LEASED PROPERTY (SOME POSSESSIONS REMAINING)

Certified Mail, Return Receipt Requested

[date]

[tenant name(s)
and address(es)]

Re: Notice of belief of abandonment of leased property
located at:

To: [tenants]

The rent on the above property is past due and owing since [date rent was due]. It also appears that you have abandoned the said property.

Please be advised that unless I receive a written notice from you within the next 15 days stating both (1) that it is your intent not to abandon the property and (2) providing me with an address whereby legal process may be served on you by certified mail, I will consider the property has been abandoned and will reclaim possession of the property.

Be advised also that unless I receive instructions from you regarding the disposition of the property you left on the premises, action will be taken to dispose of the property in accordance with state law.

If the abandoned property has a market value of less than $300, the undersigned may dispose of the property after 15 days in any manner deemed reasonable. If the property value exceeds $300, the property will be sold at a public auction. After expenses of sale, past due rent, and other allowable damages have been deducted, any excess sums will be forwarded to your last known address.

[Note: check state statutes to see if there are any different requirements]

Sincerely,

_____

Landlord

4–22   DEMAND ON COTENANT FOR PAYMENT

Certified Mail, Return Receipt Requested

Date:

To: [name and address of
cotenant]

In the lease of property between you, [the Landlord], and [Tenant] entered into on [date lease was signed], you agreed to the terms of the lease.

Please be advised that the sum of $_____ is owed to the undersigned for the following:

Since this debt was incurred in respect to the leased property in which you were a Cotenant, demand is hereby made upon you for the payment of $_____.

If payment or satisfactory arrangements for payment are not made within 15 days, I will take the necessary legal action to collect the sum due me, including if applicable, court costs and attorney fees.

Sincerely,

_____
Landlord

4-23   DEMAND ON GUARANTOR FOR PAYMENT

Certified Mail, Return Receipt Requested

Date:

To: [name and address of
    guarantor]

By attachment to the lease of property between [Landlord] and [Tenant] entered into on [date lease was signed], you guaranteed the payment of rent and related charges for [name of Tenant].

Please be advised that the sum of $ _____ is owed to the undersigned for the following:

Since this debt was incurred in respect to the property in which you agreed to act as the guarantor, demand is hereby made upon you for the payment of $ _____.

If payment or satisfactory arrangements for payment are not made within 15 days, I will take the necessary legal action to collect the sum due me, including if applicable, court costs and attorney fees.

Sincerely,

_____
Landlord

4–24   EQUIPMENT LEASE

This equipment lease is entered into between_____ (Lessor) and_____ and_____, (Lessee(s)). The Lessor hereby leases the below described equipment to the Lessee(s). All of the undersigned parties hereby accept the lease and all of its terms. The terms of the lease are as follows:

1. The lease pertains to the equipment described as follows:

2. The lease shall be for a period of_____ , commencing on_____ day of_____, 19_____ and ending on _____ day of_____, 19_____.

3. The Lessee shall pay to the Lessor, the monthly rent of $_____ payable on the first day of every month. There will be a late fee of $_____ if the rent is not paid by the 5th of the month. The Lessee also agrees to pay to Lessor the sum of $_____ as a security deposit, to be promptly returned upon the termination of the lease and compliance with all provisions of this lease.

4. Title to the equipment shall be and remain in Lessor at all times during the term of the lease.

5. The Lessee agrees to return equipment at the conclusion of the lease in its present condition, except for normal wear and tear resulting from proper use thereof.

6. The Lessee shall at all times during the term of the lease at its expense shall insure the equipment to the amount of $_____ for such risks as Lessor shall require. In the event of damage or loss, the proceeds of the insurance policy shall be used to replace or repair the property. If it is not practicable to replace or repair the property, the Lessor shall be entitled to all proceeds collected under the policy.

7. Lessor [Lessee] agrees at its own expense to keep the equipment in good working condition during the term of the lease.

8. Lessor shall have the right to inspect the equipment at any time during the lease.

9. No delay or omission to exercise any right, power, or remedy accruing to Lessor on any breach or default by Lessee under this lease shall impair any such right, power, or remedy of Lessor, nor shall it be construed to be a waiver of any such breach or default or acquiescence therein.

10. Lessee shall indemnify Lessor against, and hold Lessor harmless from all claims, actions, proceedings, costs, damages, and liabilities including

attorney fees, arising out of or connected with, or resulting from the lease or the leased equipment.

11. The lease shall be governed by the laws of the State of_____ .

12. In the event that legal action is necessary to enforce any provisions of this contract, attorney fees may be recovered by the prevailing party.

13. Additional lease terms:_____
    _____
    _____
    _____

LESSOR MAKES NO WARRANTIES, EXPRESS OR IMPLIED, AS TO THE EQUIPMENT LEASED, AND ASSUMES NO RESPONSIBILITY FOR ITS CONDITION.

Signed under seal this_____ day of_____, 19_____.

_____   _____
Lessor   Lessee

4-25

EQUIPMENT LEASE (WITH OPTION TO PURCHASE)

This equipment lease is entered into between_____ (Lessor) and_____ and _____ , (Lessee(s)). The Lessor hereby leases the below described equipment to the Lessee(s). All of the undersigned parties hereby accept the lease and all of its terms. The terms of the lease are as follows:

1. The lease pertains to the equipment described as follows:

   _____

2. The lease shall be for a period of _____, commencing on _____ day of_____, 19____ and ending on _____ day of_____, 19____.

3. The Lessee shall pay to the Lessor the monthly rent of $_____ payable on the first day of every month. There will be a late fee of $_____ if the rent is not paid by the 5th of the month. The Lessee also agrees to pay to Lessor the sum of $_____ as a security deposit, to be promptly returned upon the termination of the lease and compliance with all provisions of this lease.

4. Title to the equipment shall be and remain in Lessor at all times during the term of the lease. Except that Lessor hereby grants to Lessee the option to purchase the equipment at the expiration of this lease for a price of $_____ provided that the Lessee shall give Lessor written notice of his/her intention to so purchase the equipment not later than one month prior to end of the lease. This option to purchase is conditioned on complete performance by the lessee of terms of this lease, including full payment of the rents.

5. Except as provided for in paragraph 4, the Lessee agrees to return equipment at the conclusion of the lease in its present condition, except for normal wear and tear resulting from proper use thereof.

6. The Lessee at all times during the term of the lease at its expense shall insure the equipment to the amount of $_____ for such risks as Lessor shall require. In the event of damage or loss, the proceeds of the insurance policy shall be used to replace or repair the property. If it is not practicable to replace or repair the property, the Lessor shall be entitled to all proceeds collected under the policy.

7. Lessor [Lessee] agrees at its own expense to keep the equipment in good working condition during the term of the lease.

8. Lessor shall have the right to inspect the equipment at any time during the lease.

9. No delay or omission to exercise any right, power, or remedy accruing to Lessor on any breach or default by Lessee under this lease shall

impair any such right, power, or remedy of Lessor, nor shall it be construed to be a waiver of any such breach or default or acquiescence therein.

10. Lessee shall indemnify Lessor against, and hold Lessor harmless from all claims, actions, proceedings, costs, damages, and liabilities including attorney fees, arising out of or connected with, or resulting from the lease or the leased equipment.

11. The lease shall be governed by the laws of the State of _____ .

12. In the event that legal action is necessary to enforce any provisions of this contract, attorney fees may be recovered by the prevailing party.

13. Additional lease terms: _____
    _____
    _____
    _____

LESSOR MAKES NO WARRANTIES, EXPRESS OR IMPLIED, AS TO THE EQUIPMENT LEASED, AND ASSUMES NO RESPONSIBILITY FOR ITS CONDITION.

Signed under seal this _____ day of _____, 19_____.

_____   _____
Lessor   Lessee

4-26   EQUIPMENT LEASE (WITH TITLE TRANSFERRING TO LESSEE AT END OF LEASE)

This equipment lease is entered into between_____ (Lessor) and_____ and_____ , (Lessee(s)). The Lessor hereby leases the below described equipment to the Lessee(s). All of the undersigned parties hereby accept the lease and all of its terms. The terms of the lease are as follows:

1. The lease pertains to the equipment described as follows:

2. The lease shall be for a period of_____, commencing on _____ day of_____, 19_____ and ending on _____ day of _____, 19_____.

3. The Lessee shall pay to the Lessor the monthly rent of $_____ payable on the first day of every month. There will be a late fee of $_____ if the rent is not paid by the 5th of the month. The Lessee also agrees to pay to Lessor the sum of $_____ as a security deposit, to be promptly returned upon the termination of the lease and compliance with all provisions of this lease.

4. Title to the equipment shall be and remain in lessor at all times during the term of the lease. Except that Lessor hereby grants to Lessee the option to assume ownership and title of the equipment at the expiration of this lease without the payment of any additional sums of money. This option to assume ownership is conditioned on complete performance by the Lessee of terms of this lease, including full payment of the rents.

5. Except as provided for under paragraph 4, the Lessee agrees to return equipment at the conclusion of the lease in its present condition, except for normal wear and tear resulting from proper use thereof.

6. The Lessee at all times during the term of the lease at its expense shall insure the equipment to the amount of $_____ for such risks as Lessor shall require. In the event of damage or loss, the proceeds of the insurance policy shall be used to replace or repair the property. If it is not practicable to replace or repair the property, the Lessor shall be entitled to all proceeds collected under the policy.

7. Lessor [Lessee] agrees at its own expense to keep the equipment in good working condition during the term of the lease.

8. Lessor shall have the right to inspect the equipment at any time during the lease.

9. No delay or omission to exercise any right, power, or remedy accruing to Lessor on any breach or default by Lessee under this lease shall impair any such right, power, or remedy of Lessor, nor shall it be construed to be a waiver of any such breach or default or acquiescence therein.

10. Lessee shall indemnify Lessor against, and hold Lessor harmless from all claims, actions, proceedings, costs, damages, and liabilities including attorney fees, arising out of or connected with, or resulting from the lease or the leased equipment.

11. The lease shall be governed by the laws of the State of_____ .

12. In the event that legal action is necessary to enforce any provisions of this contract, attorney fees may be recovered by the prevailing party.

13. Additional lease terms: _____

_____

_____

_____

LESSOR MAKES NO WARRANTIES, EXPRESS OR IMPLIED, AS TO THE EQUIPMENT LEASED, AND ASSUMES NO RESPONSIBILITY FOR ITS CONDITION.

Signed under seal this _____ day of _____ , 19_____ .

_____   _____
Lessor   Lessee

4-27 AMENDED EQUIPMENT LEASE (SUBSTITUTION OF EQUIPMENT)

The Lessor and Lessee entered into an equipment lease on [date] for the lease of the following equipment:

By the execution of this amended equipment lease, the parties desire to substitute the equipment described below in place of the original leased equipment. Substituted equipment:

[describe replacement equipment]

The Lessee agrees to return the original equipment no later than [date]. The Lessor agrees to provide the substituted equipment no later than [date]. The Lessee shall be responsible for transporting the equipment from the Lessor's place of business.

Except as indicated below, all other terms of the original lease entered into on [date] shall remain effective and enforceable.

Modifications of terms are as follows:

LESSOR MAKES NO WARRANTIES, EXPRESS OR IMPLIED, AS TO THE EQUIPMENT LEASED, AND ASSUMES NO RESPONSIBILITY FOR ITS CONDITION.

Signed under seal this _____ day of _____,19_____.

_____   _____
Lessor   Lessee

4-28   EXTENSION OF EQUIPMENT LEASE

The Lessor and Lessee entered into an equipment lease on [date] for the lease of the following equipment:

By the execution of this amended equipment lease, the parties desire to extend the length of the lease until [date].

Except as indicated below, all other terms of the original lease entered into on [date] shall remain effective and enforceable.

Modifications of terms other than the expriation date are as follows:

[if no modifications indicate none]

LESSOR MAKES NO WARRANTIES, EXPRESS OR IMPLIED, AS TO THE EQUIPMENT LEASED, AND ASSUMES NO RESPONSIBILITY FOR ITS CONDITION.

Signed under seal this_____ day of _____,19_____.

_____   _____
Lessor   Lessee

4-29

MUTUAL CANCELLATION OF EQUIPMENT LEASE

The Lessor and Lessee entered into an equipment lease on [date] for the lease of the following equipment:

By the execution of this agreement, the parties hereby mutually cancel the subject lease effective on [date].

The Lessee will return the leased equipment no later than [time and date].

On the return of the leased equipment, the Lessee shall be liable for lease payments in the amount of $_____ covering the period of [months]. The parties mutually agree that in addition to the payment of the above listed sum by the Lessee to the Lessor, the parties will take the following actions:

LESSOR MAKES NO WARRANTIES, EXPRESS OR IMPLIED, AS TO THE EQUIPMENT LEASED, AND ASSUMES NO RESPONSIBILITY FOR ITS CONDITION.

Signed under seal this _____ day of _____,19_____.

_____   _____
Lessor   Lessee

4-30 LEASE PROVISIONS CHECKLIST

1. Is there a clear provision regarding the return of the security and cleaning deposits at the termination of the lease?

2. What are the requirements on the landlord to maintain the property according to certain standards?

3. Under what circumstances or conditions may either you or the landlord cancel the lease prior to its expiration?

4. Does the lease provide you with an option to renew the lease in order to protect your rights to stay in the same location?

5. Does the lease allow the landlord to enter the property at any time without any prior notice to you?

6. Does the landlord retain a set of keys to your business?

7. Does the lease obligate you to follow any rules formulated by the landlord any time after the lease is signed?

8. Does the lease release the landlord from responsibility for any damages to your property, even if it is his or her fault?

9. Under the terms of lease, are you required to maintain any fixtures, appliances, or portions of the property?

10. Does the security or any other deposit that the tenant is required to post pay interest?

11. Do you have the right to put up signs for your business without the landlord's permission?

12. Do you have the right to sublease the premises for the duration of the lease if your business closes or if you can no longer use the property?

13. Can you use the property for any lawful purpose?

14. Is the landlord prohibited from renting other space in the same building or nearby to tenants who will compete with your business?

15. What rights do you have in the use of the common property such as hallways, driveways, elevators, and parking lots.

16. If the amount of your rent is based on gross receipts of your business, are provisions made for deductions for returned merchandise, delivery or installation charges, refundable deposits, and sales tax?

4-31 WAIVER OF CLAIM TO FIXTURES

For good and valuable consideration, receipt of which is acknowledged, [name], Landlord hereby surrenders any claim to fixtures that have been attached to the real property by the Tenant under the lease dated [date of lease].

The Landlord hereby waives any claim to any personal property installed on the property leased by the Tenant, even if that property is considered as a fixture.

The Landlord acknowledges and admits that said fixtures retain their status as personal property and may be removed by the Tenant.

WITNESSED the hands of said Landlord, this _____ day of _____ , 19_____.

_____

_____

State of   )

County of   ) SS

On this date, [list names of person(s) who signed above] personally appeared before me and acknowledged that the above signature(s) are valid and binding.

_____
Notary Public

My Commission expires:

4-32 NOTICE ENDING AT-WILL TENANCY

Certified Mail, Return Receipt Requested

Date:

To: [tenant]

You are presently occupying the property located at:

under the terms of a lease dated [date]. Under that lease, your tenancy is a tenancy at will. Your tenancy shall end on [date]. You must vacate the premises no later than that date.

Under the terms of the lease, you are required to leave the premises in a clean condition.

Sincerely,

_____

Landlord

Chapter 5

Credit and Collection Forms and Agreements

This chapter discusses establishing credit terms, debt collection restrictions, the advantages and disadvantages of using a collection agency, using small claims court to collect debts, enforcing debt judgments, and dealing with credit reporting agencies. The chapter also includes forms involved in credit and collection transactions.

Establishing Credit Terms

Most businesses deal in credit; therefore, credit can be the key to your business' success or failure. In a recent government study, three out of five retail shoppers used credit to make retail purchases. Accordingly, the retailer who sells only for cash only limits the availability of customers. In addition, people are more apt to be repeat customers if they have an account with a store. Using credit also increases the ability of small, and medium-sized businesses to compete with the larger stores that routinely offer their own credit systems.

There are some distinct disadvantages in extending credit to your customers. First, there is the added cost associated with operating a collection system. Foremost is the added expense of financing a credit program. Bad debt losses will occur, and historically a larger percentage of credit sales results in sales returns than those made with cash. Consider all the advantages and disadvantages before deciding to establish a credit system. In many cases, the best system for your business is to use the major charge card systems, such as Visa and MasterCard. The clear advantages of using these major

---

Taking Credit Cards

When using the major credit cards, a business is required to observe the following practices:

- Honor any valid card (*Note*: You may refuse cards for small sales. For example, a statement that, "Credit cards accepted only for sales in excess of $10.00" is permissible.)
- You must use the proper forms provided by the credit card issuer.
- You must refuse any suspicious cards and report your suspicions to the credit card issuer.
- You must forward all credit slips to the card issuer within a certain period, normally seven days.
- You are required to indemnify the credit card issuer from any claims resulting from defects in products or services obtained on the card.
- You are required to pay a percentage of your monthly credit card sales to the credit card issuer, normally 3 to 5 percent.

---

cards are that more people are likely to possess them and they eliminate the need to have your own credit system. The obvious disadvantage is the approximately 5-percent service fee charged for their use. Your sales are automatically discounted by that amount.

Legal restrictions involved in the granting of credit usually fall into four general categories:

1. The credit application and investigative process.
2. The amount of carrying charges or late fees that you can legally charge.
3. The type of information that you must provide to all of your customers who purchase on credit.
4. The restrictions on the practices you can engage in when collecting debts.

A related problem involves employee misconduct in using a credit card system. Either willful misconduct or negligence by your employees could open your business to liability from cardholders. It is not unusual for employees to engage in credit card fraud.

In getting the information you need to make a decision to extend credit to a specific individual, there are certain legal restrictions on the questions that you may ask. For example, on the credit application you may not ask for the race, color, sex, national origin, or religious beliefs of the applicant, and you may not ask for a statement of the applicant's philosophical or political beliefs. You may ask the applicant's sex for identification purposes only, not to help you decide whether to grant or deny credit. You may not deny credit because an applicant lives in a certain part of the community (commonly known as "red-lining"). A businessperson must avoid making any decisions based on discrimination.

To avoid discrimination, most credit agencies have developed a numbering system to help determine an individual's creditworthiness. For example, a certain number of points are awarded for the length of time an applicant has lived in the neighborhood and held the same job. Other points are based on the ratio of the applicant's debts to salary. This objective formula helps to avoid any charges of discrimination, either open or unconscious.

The finance, or carrying, charges you may impose on an account depend on state law. In every state, there are laws regarding the maximum amount of interest—that is, the finance charges—that a merchant can charge. State laws also determine whether or not you can consider late charges to be finance charges. Check with your Better Business Bureau or your local retail credit agency to find out what the regulations and laws are in your state.

The Federal Truth in Lending Act requires that anyone who offers consumer credit provide sufficient information regarding the credit terms to enable the customer to make a knowledgeable decision. In addition to the Federal Truth in Lending Act, discussed in detail later in this chapter, similar state statutes may apply to the granting of retail credit in your state.

Certain restrictions apply to individuals who collect debts. Most of the restrictions are stated in the Federal Fair Debt Collection Practices Act of 1978, discussed later in this chapter. There are also state restrictions on debt collection.

Equal Credit Opportunity Act of 1974

The federal government passed the Equal Credit Opportunity Act (ECOA) in 1974 to prevent and eliminate many of the abuses in granting credit that were occurring up to that time. This law forbids discrimination in any aspect of a credit decision because of a person's sex, marital status, race, national origin, age, religion, or receipt of welfare income, or because the person has sued a previous creditor in good faith. The ECOA also prohibits a creditor from discounting the income that a credit applicant receives from part-time employment. The act gives both the Federal Trade Commission and the courts authority to impose certain restrictions on debt collections and to eliminate certain unethical practices. Before the passage of the Equal Credit Opportunity Act, lenders routinely refused to grant credit to married women or to allow them to get credit in their own name. Before one major creditor would grant credit to a working wife, she was required to promise in writing that she would practice birth control or get an abortion if she became pregnant. These practices are now illegal under the ECOA.

Since the enactment of the ECOA, one major credit card company was successfully sued because they canceled a woman's credit when she got married. A major oil company was required to pay a $200,000 judgment for discriminating against women because it failed to consider any income they had from alimony, child support, or separate maintenance payments. Miscellaneous provisions under the ECOA require that if you apply for a credit card or a loan, the creditor must either issue credit within 30 days or notify you that your application is denied.

The credit card company must provide you with written notification if your application is denied. The notification must include the reason, or advise you of your right to request the reasons, for the denial of credit. One major problem in this regard is that the notice may use vague language, such as insufficient income or poor credit history, and not give specific reasons.

Other restrictions on credit decisions in the ECOA include the fact that you cannot deny people credit because they are over a certain age. A creditor may ask your age, but if you are over the age of 18 or 21, depending upon your state law, the creditor cannot turn you down or decrease your credit. The creditor cannot ignore your retirement income in rating your application or close your credit account or require you to reapply when you reach a certain age limit. The creditor also cannot refuse to grant you credit if credit life insurance is not available to persons in your age group. In regard to age, however, the law does permit a creditor to consider such information as length of time until an applicant's retirement and length of time applicant's current income is expected to continue.

Creditors may not ask about your birth control practices, or whether you plan to have children, or assume anything about your plans regarding children. They may not consider whether you have a telephone listed in your name, because this has been determined to discriminate against most married women. However, they may consider whether or not there is a telephone in your home.

Federal Truth-in-Lending Law

The Federal Truth-in-Lending Act requires businesses to give certain basic information to credit applicants regarding the cost of buying on credit or taking out a loan. The basic theory behind the act is that credit transactions should be an open and knowing transaction between the creditor and the debtor.

The Finance Charge and the Annual Percentage Rate

Under the Truth-in-Lending Act, the creditor must explain the finance charge and the annual percentage rate (APR) to the debtor in writing and before the debtor signs any agreement. The finance charge is the difference between a cash price and the total dollar amount paid when a person uses credit. It includes interest cost, service charges, credit-related insurance, appraisals, cash discounts, and so on.

The APR is the percentage cost or relative cost of credit on a yearly basis. It is the most important figure to use in comparing credit costs and should apply regardless of the credit amount or the amount of time a person takes to repay the credit. The Federal Truth-in-Lending Act does not regulate interest rates or credit charges. It merely requires their disclosure so that the debtor can compare credit costs.

The Truth-in-Lending Act also requires a certain degree of accuracy in the advertising of any credit terms. If a business advertises important features of a credit, sale, or lease, such as a down payment or the length of time to pay, it must also state the annual percentage rate. For example, an ad saying that you can buy a new car for $99 down must also state the annual percentage rate.

Fair Credit Billing Act

The Fair Credit Billing Act is another federal statute designed to protect consumers. It basically requires businesses offering credit to set up procedures for promptly correcting any billing mistakes. It also allows debtors to refuse to make credit card payments on defective goods, and it requires creditors to promptly credit any payments to a debtor's account.

Under the Fair Credit Billing Act, a creditor is required to correct errors promptly and without damaging a person's credit rating. Under the law, errors are defined as charges for items you have not purchased, purchases made by someone who was not authorized to use your account, charges not properly identified on your bill, amounts that differed from the actual purchase price, amounts entered on a date different from the purchase date, and something you did not accept on delivery or that was not delivered according to your agreement. Billing errors also include errors in arithmetic, the failure to promptly reflect payment or other credit to your account, and the failure to mail your statement to you at least 15 days before the due date, provided you have notified the creditor of your appropriate address at least 20 days before the billing period.

If you as the debtor feel that an error has been made in your billing and if you notify the creditor within 60 days after the bill was mailed, you are not required to pay that part of the bill until the credit company conducts an inquiry into the circumstances. The creditor must acknowledge your letter within 30 days unless the bill can be corrected sooner. The bill must be corrected, or the creditor must explain to you why the bill is believed to be correct within two billing periods or within 90 days.

The Fair Credit Billing Act also allows you to withhold payment for any damaged or shoddy goods as long as you are making an attempt to solve the problem with the merchant. Your right to withhold payment for defective goods or services is limited if your card was not issued by the store where you made the purchase. If the card was a bank, travel, or entertainment card, the sale must have been for more than $50 and must have taken place in your home state or within 100 miles of your home address.

Federal Fair Credit Reporting Act

The Federal Fair Credit Reporting Act allows debtors to examine information in their credit files, and it has set up procedures to correct any errors they discover. If a lender refuses credit because your report contains unfavorable information, you have a right to know the name and address of the credit reporting agency keeping the report, and you have the right to request the information from the credit agency, either by mail or in person. Although you do not have the right to get a copy of your file, you will at least be provided with a summary of it. In addition, the credit agency must help you interpret the data. If you have been refused credit within the past 30 days, the credit agency cannot charge you a fee for giving you that information. However, you can be charged a fee if you have not been denied credit but you still want a summary of your credit report.

The act also requires that bankruptcies be removed from a debtor's credit history after 10 years and that suits, judgments, tax liens, arrest records, and other kinds of unfavorable information be removed after seven years.

The Fair Credit Reporting Act also guarantees the right of privacy in regard to the credit information that your business may wish to obtain on a person. Only individuals with a legitimate business may get such credit information. In most cases the information may be given out only upon the written consent of the person involved.

Regulation Z

Regulation Z, issued by the Federal Reserve Board, also substantially restricts certain types of credit transactions. The regulation applies to any businessperson who sells consumer goods by using installment sales. If your business arranges for or provides credit for a finance charge on which debt is payable in four or more payments, Regulation Z applies.

Note: If the debt is due in one sum, but the customer takes four or more payments to pay the debt, the debt is not considered as payable in four or more installments for the purposes of Regulation Z. For example, if you sell a customer $1,000 of merchandise, net within 30 days, and the customer makes four payments of $250 each, this would not be an installment sale unless you charged a finance charge.

Regulation Z applies only to consumer credit. The following transactions are not subject to Regulation Z:

Commercial and business credit

Transactions involving securities and commodities with brokers registered with the Security Exchange Commission

Credit over $25,000 that is not on real estate

Student loans

Credit to public agencies

Agricultural transactions

Requirements of Regulation Z are as follows:

Specific language and disclosure forms are required to be used.

Certain disclosures are required to be given.

Credit records must be maintained by the business for at least two years.

The annual percentage rate of the finance charge must be stated to the nearest 1/8 of 1 percent.

The customers must be advised of the total finance charge that they will be required to pay.

Credit is divided into two categories: open-ended credit and closed-ended credit.

Buyers must be informed of all credit fees, which includes interest, loan fees, finder's fees, any time–price differential, points, any credit insurance fees, or prepaid interest.

Residential mortgage must include the right to rescind within three days.

All payments must be credited promptly.

Debtors must be advised of billing error rights.

In open-ended credit, debtors must be advised of the method used to determine the balance against which a finance charge will be imposed and how the actual finance charge is calculated.

Debtors must be informed of the conditions under which additional finance or any additional charges may be made.

Note: The Federal Reserve Board is required to publish model forms and clauses. A copy of the Federal Reserve Board's Regulation Z with appendixes (which contain the model forms and clauses) may be obtained from the nearest major library or from the U.S. Government Printing Office, Washington, DC 20402.

Penalties under Federal Statutes

Each of the federal statutes mentioned has criminal penalties in the form of fines, and in several cases there is imprisonment for up to one year. In addition, persons whose rights have been violated under these statutes may bring a civil suit. If they are successful in court, they can recover damages, court costs, and an additional penalty fee in the form of punitive damages. Check with the Federal Trade Commission for more information regarding violations of these statutes.

Uniform Consumer Credit Code

Many states have adopted the Uniform Consumer Credit Code (UCCC). In most cases, the protection provided by the state UCCCs are more extensive than those provided by federal regulations.

Debt Collection

Because debt collection has a history of abuse, there are both state and federal statutes setting forth debt collectors' responsibilities and prohibiting certain acts. For example, a debt collector may not collect or attempt to collect a consumer debt by force, threat of force, or criminal means to cause harm to the debtor or the debtor's reputation or property.

In most states debt collectors are prohibited from trying to collect a debt by using profane or obscene language, by placing telephone calls without disclosing the collectors' identity, by calling collect, or by causing the telephone to ring repeatedly to annoy the person being called. Nor can collectors telephone or see the debtors with a frequency that would constitute harassment.

Contacting debtors' employers is also restricted. In most states, creditors are not allowed to inform debtors' employers about the debtors' payment of a consumer debt. An exception to this is a communication necessary to the collection of the debt if it is made only to verify the debtors' employment, locate debtors, or garnish the wages of debtors.

Debt collectors may not communicate with debtors in the name of an attorney or counselor-at-law or upon stationery bearing the name of an attorney or counselor-at-law, unless such communications are previously authorized by an attorney.

Collectors may not threaten to increase the consumer debt by the addition of attorney fees, investigative fees, service or finance charges if such fees or charges may not be legally added to an existing obligation. Collectors may not falsely represent themselves as being representatives of a credit reporting agency.

The Federal Fair Debt Collection Practices Act of 1978 supplements state restrictions. Basically, the act prohibits telephone calls from being made to debtors at unusual or inconvenient times, which is usually interpreted to mean calls before 8:00 A.M. or after 9:00 P.M. Repeated calls are prohibited even if they are made during convenient hours. If debtors are represented by an attorney and request that the creditors communicate only with the attorney, then all future communications must be with the attorney. Creditors may contact debtors' places of employment only to obtain the debtors' current addresses. Creditors may not call neighbors, relatives, or third parties of the debtors, except in a bonafide effort to locate them.

If debtors write stating that they do not intend to pay the debt, then collectors must stop all communications with debtors except to inform them of any legal action being taken.

The penalties for violations of this act are $10,000 plus attorney fees. In addition, the act provides for civil suits against the collector, in which the collecting agency may be held liable for $500,000 or up to 1 percent of the creditor's net worth, whichever is less.

A Systematic Approach to Reducing Delinquent Debts

According to the experts, the key to reducing delinquent debts is to use a systemic strategy with a timetable for action. Asking customers for payment is not pleasant. Most collection experts agree that the biggest problem that small business owners have is waiting too long before asking for payment. Research indicates, also, that a systematic collection program conducted in a professional manner does not alienate good customers. The longer you wait, however, the less likely you will get paid. According to many experts, if you wait until you are aggravated, you have waited too long. For example, if terms are net within 30 days, you should call on the thirty-first day about payment. During the call, indicate that you expect payment arrangements be kept.

Collecting a Debt

According to a recent study by the Commercial Law League of America, the percentages that follow show the percentage of debt that you can expect to collect in the intervals given:

Less than 1 month delinquent	90 percent
More than 1 month delinquent	85 percent
More than 2 months delinquent	70 percent
More than 3 months delinquent	50 percent
More than 12 months delinquent	25 percent

If the bills remain unpaid after 60 days, it is recommended that you restrict credit and institute a cash-on-delivery (C.O.D.) system until all past due accounts are paid. In cases involving service contracts, stop work on the contract when past due payments extend beyond 60 days. After 90 days, taking your case to a small claims court or to a collection agency may be appropriate.

Letters of Credit

A letter of credit is by a bank or other financial institution to a supplier or other individual creditor you are dealing with that states that the bank will advance credit on presentation of an invoice from the supplier. Therefore instead of your making C.O.D. purchases, the supplier delivers supplies to you and invoices the bank. The bank pays the supplier direct. When the bank makes the payment, it is in effect a loan fromthe bank to you. Letters of credit were once used almost exclusively in trade between foreign countries. They are becoming more common in domestic commercial arrangements.

Revolving Credit Accounts

If you have a revolving credit account with a bank, the bank approves a certain credit limit and then allows you to draw to that limit, repay, and redraw funds again throughout the term of the loan, according to your specific needs. You pay interest on the outstanding balance but not on any of the unused credit. The advantage of a revolving credit account is that you are not required to borrow money until you need it. This is a critical advantage because one of the most common mistakes new businessowners make is failing to have an adequate cash reserve. Another big advantage of revolving credit is that as you repay your loan, you automatically rebuild the amount of credit you may use in the future.

Forms in This Chapter

- FORM 5–1: CREDIT APPLICATION (CONSUMER). Obtains the necessary information to evaluate an individual's request for consumer credit.

- FORM 5–2: CREDIT APPLICATION (COMMERCIAL). Obtains the necessary information to evaluate an individual's request for commercial credit.

- FORM 5–3: ACTION ON CREDIT REQUEST. Notifies applicants that their applications for credit have been denied.

- FORM 5–4: CREDIT REFERENCE REQUEST. Requests a reference on an applicant for credit.

- FORM 5–5: DISCLOSURE OF CREDIT INFORMATION. Requests disclosure of credit information that a credit reporting agency has on the requester.

- FORM 5–6: AUTHORIZATION TO RELEASE CREDIT INFORMATION. Obtains authorization to release credit information.

- FORM 5–7: ADVERSE CREDIT INFORMATION REQUEST. Requests information about adverse credit report.

- FORM 5–8: REQUEST TO CORRECT CREDIT INFORMATION. Requests correction of credit information contained on an adverse credit report.

- FORM 5–9: COLLECTION LETTER. Notifies a debtor that legal action is being considered in order to collect a past due account.

- FORM 5–10: COLLECTION LETTER (AUTOMOBILE). Notifies a debtor that legal action is being considered in order to collect a past due account for the purchase of an automobile.

- FORM 5–11: FINAL NOTICE BEFORE LEGAL ACTION. Notifies a debtor that unless payment is forthcoming, legal action will be taken.

- FORM 5–12: NOTICE OF DEFAULT ON SETTLEMENT AGREEMENT. Notifies debtor of default in a case when a settlement agreement exists between the two parties.

- FORM 5–13: NOTICE OF DEFAULT ON PROMISSORY NOTE. Notifies a debtor of being in default on a promissory note. In most cases, a formal notice is necessary before the entire balance of the note may be collected.

- FORM 5–14: NOTICE OF DEFAULT ON OPEN BOOK ACCOUNT. Notifies a debtor of being in default on an open book account.

- FORM 5–15: DEMAND ON GUARANTORS. Places a formal notice of default and a demand on guarantors of a debt for payment.

- FORM 5–16: DEMAND ON ENDORSER. Places a formal notice of default and a demand on endorser for payment.

- FORM 5–17: PAYMENT ON SPECIFIC ACCOUNTS. Notifies a creditor as to which accounts an enclosed payment should be credited to when there is more than one account.

- FORM 5–18: RECEIPT FOR PAYMENT IN FULL. Acknowledges payment in full on an account.

- FORM 5–19: NOTICE OF DISPUTED ACCOUNT BALANCE. Notifies a creditor that borrower does agree with the last statement of account submitted by creditor.

- FORM 5–20: REQUEST FOR INFORMATION ON ACCOUNT BALANCE. Notifies a creditor that borrower may not agree with the last statement of account submitted by creditor but that additional information is needed to verify the amount owed.

- FORM 5–21: SETTLEMENT OF DISPUTED ACCOUNT BALANCE. Settles a disputed account balance.

- FORM 5–22: COMPROMISE. Compromises an account or claim.

- FORM 5–23: RELEASE OF ALL CLAIMS (INSTALLMENT PAYMENTS). Settles claims when an individual has a claim against a business for an incident such as an automobile accident.

- FORM 5–24: RELEASE OF ALL CLAIMS (LUMP SUM PAYMENT). Releases all claims against a business, but settlement is made by one lump-sum payment.

- FORM 5–25: COLLECTION TRANSMITTAL. Forwards an account to a collection agent.

- FORM 5–26: PROPOSAL TO COLLECT PAST DUE ACCOUNTS. Establishes an agreement between a business and a collection agency.

- FORM 5–27: NOTICE OF DISHONORED CHECK. Attempts to collect on a dishonored check.

- FORM 5–28: NOTICE OF DISHONORED CHECK (STOP PAYMENT). Used when a customer wrongly stops payment on a check.
- FORM 5–29: CHECK STOP-PAYMENT ORDER. Stops payment on a check; used only when there is a valid reason for stopping the check.
- FORM 5-30: BANK COLLECTION—DISHONORED CHECK. Forwards a dishonored check to the bank for collection.
- FORM 5–31: NOTICE OF LOST OR STOLEN CREDIT CARD. Reports a lost or stolen credit card.
- FORM 5–32: REQUEST FOR CREDIT CHARGEBACK. Requests a credit card company to decline a credit charge or to charge back a charge.
- FORM 5–33: NOTICE OF RESCISSION. Cancels a contract that has a three-day cooling-off period.
- FORM 5–34: NOTICE OF BILLING ERROR RIGHTS (MODEL UNDER THE FAIR CREDIT BILLING ACT). Notifies debtors of their rights under the Fair Credit Billing Act.
- FORM 5–35: NOTICE OF DEBTOR'S RIGHTS AND CREDITOR'S RESPONSI-BILITIES WHEN BILL IS DISPUTED. Used when a debtor challenges the correctness of a bill.

5-1 CREDIT APPLICATION (CONSUMER)

Date: _____

Name: _____ Birthdate: _____

Known by any other names? _____

Address: _____ City: _____

State: _____ Zip _____

Telephone: _____ Soc. Sec. no.: _____

How long at that address? _____ Own or rent? _____

Previous Address: _____

Employed by: _____ Position: _____

Address: _____ Telephone: _____

No. of dependents: _____ Type of car owned: _____

Outstanding obligations: _____ _____

_____

Other income (sources and monthly amount): _____

_____

_____

Personal references with telephone numbers: _____

_____

Credit references (include account numbers & telephone numbers):

_____

_____

Notice

I understand that in making this application for credit an investigation of my credit history may be made. The investigation may include the examination of my credit record and interviews of personal and credit references provided on this form. In addition, the individual making the investigation has the right to ask for additional information from me. I certify that the above information is true.

_____

Applicant

5-2 CREDIT APPLICATION (COMMERCIAL)

Date: _____

Business name: _____ Type of business: _____

Trade name (if different): _____

Address: _____ City: _____

State: _____ Zip: _____

Telephone: _____ Owner/President: _____

How long in business: _____ Credit rating: _____

Trade references (names and addresses):

_____

_____

_____

_____

Bank references (include account numbers & addresses):

_____

_____

_____

_____

Location of financial statements:

Notice

The undersigned authorizes an inquiry as to the credit information of the business. In addition, credit if granted may be withdrawn at any time. I certify the above information to be true.

_____
Owner/President

5-3　ACTION ON CREDIT REQUEST

Date:

To: [applicant]

We regret to inform you that your application for credit has been refused for the reason(s) checked below:

_____ Incomplete information [you may resubmit with additional information]

_____ Unable to verify credit data

_____ Insufficient credit references

_____ Insufficient income

_____ Unacceptable credit references

_____ Irregular employment history

_____ Temporary employment

_____ Bankruptcy

_____ Limited credit experience

_____ Inadequate term of residence

_____ Excessive obligations

_____ Collection actions against you

_____ Outstanding judgments or liens

_____ Poor credit performance with us

_____ Other:

_____ Adverse credit reports (You may contact the credit reporting agencies directly for a copy of the credit report. Their addresses are [list addresses of each credit reporting agency used.])

CREDIT REFERENCE REQUEST

Date:

To: [name & address of
    credit reference]

Re: [name of person seeking a credit reference]

Dear Madam/Sir:

The above referenced person has applied for credit with our company and has listed you as a credit reference. To assist us in making our credit decision, please provide us with the below requested information:

High credit limit:
Present balance:
Payment history:
Number of payments more than 30 days late:
Length of time account open:
Other information that we should consider:

Any information received from you will be held confidential. Enclosed for your convenience is a stamped return envelope.

Sincerely,

DISCLOSURE OF CREDIT INFORMATION

Date:

To: [creditor reporting agency]
    [address]

Dear Madam/Sir:

    I hereby request a complete disclosure of my credit file to include the sources of any information in my file and the name and addresses of any party who has received any credit information on me or my credit report. This request is made pursuant to the Federal Fair Credit Reporting Act.

_____
Signature

_____
Printed name

_____
Address

_____
Telephone number

5-6

AUTHORIZATION TO RELEASE CREDIT INFORMATION

Date:

To: [creditor]
   [address]

Dear Madam/Sir:

I have a credit account with your company. I hereby authorize the release of my credit information and request that a report of my credit history with your company be forwarded to the below listed credit reporting agencies.

[name and addresses of credit reporting agencies]

Sincerely,

_____
Signature

_____
Address

5-7 ADVERSE CREDIT INFORMATION REQUEST

Date

To: [business denying credit application]
    [address]

Dear Madam/Sir:

I applied for credit with your company. My credit application was denied. Accordingly, under the provisions of the Federal Fair Credit Reporting Act, I hereby request a full and complete disclosure of the reasons for the denial including the sources of any adverse credit information received from any person, company, business, and so on.

_____
Signature

_____
Printed name

_____
Address

_____
Telephone number

5-8 REQUEST TO CORRECT CREDIT INFORMATION

Date:

To: [creditor reporting agency]
  [address]

Re: Credit report of _____

In reviewing a copy of my credit report received from your agency I discovered the below error:

[list erroneous information here]

Please be advised that the above information is incorrect, and pursuant to the provisions of the Federal Fair Credit Reporting Act demand is hereby made on you to correct the said information. I also request that this letter be made a part of my credit report and transmitted with any credit reports disseminated on me.

Sincerely,

_____
Signature

_____
Printed name

_____
Address

_____
Telephone number

Date:

To: [name and
    address of debtor]

Re: Your account with [name of company]

Dear [name of debtor]:

Your delinquent account with [company name] has been referred to my office for collection action. You are currently several payments behind on the above referenced account.

I have been instructed to bring legal action against you as may be necessary, which may result in levies against your property or other assets after judgment.

The file indicates that you have failed or refused to pay the above claim even though it appears just, owing, and correct.

You are hereby further advised that if payment is not received within 15 days of the date of this letter, suit in small claims court may be commenced against you forthwith and without further notice for the amount indicated above, together with prejudgment interest. Instead of small claims court, this matter may be referred to our attorney for suit in municipal court.

As I am sure you are aware, if this matter goes to suit, all court costs, process server's fees, sheriff's fees, attorney fees where permitted, and other postjudgment costs will be added to the amount that you already owe.

You can avoid the unnecessary inconvenience and added expenses of a lawsuit by making immediate payment to us within 15 days.

Sincerely,

_____

Collections Manager

5-10 COLLECTION LETTER (AUTOMOBILE)

Date:

To: [name and
    address of debtor]

Re: Your [describe automobile]

Dear [name of debtor]:

Your delinquent account for the purchase of the above-referenced automobile with our company has been referred to my office for collection action. Currently, you are several payments behind on the above referenced account.

I have been instructed to bring legal action against you, as may be necessary, which may result in levies against your property or other assets after judgment. In addition, the automobile may be repossessed.

The file indicates that you have failed or refused to pay the above claim even though it appears just, owing, and correct.

You are hereby further advised that if payment is not received within 15 days of the date of this letter, suit in small claims court may be commenced against you forthwith and without further notice for the amount indicated above, together with prejudgment interest. Instead of small claims court, this matter may be referred to our attorney for suit in municipal court.

As I am sure you are aware, if this matter goes to suit, all court costs, process server's fees, sheriff's fees, attorney fees where permitted, and other postjudgment costs will be added to the amount that you already owe.

You can avoid the unnecessary inconvenience and added expenses of a lawsuit by making immediate payment to us within 15 days.

Sincerely,

_____

Collections Manager

5-11 FINAL NOTICE BEFORE LEGAL ACTION

Date:

To: [name and
address of debtor]

Re: Your past due account

Dear [name of debtor]:

We have made numerous requests for payment on your long overdue account. The balance is currently $_____.

Since you have failed to pay this account, we are by copy of this letter forwarding the account to our attorney. You may, however, still avoid legal action if you contact us within the next 10 days and make satisfactory arrangements for payment.

This is your final opportunity to avoid legal action.

Sincerely,

5-12

NOTICE OF DEFAULT ON SETTLEMENT AGREEMENT

Date:

To: [name and
address of debtor]

Dear [name of debtor]:

This is to advise you that you are in default of the monthly payments for _____. Accordingly, unless the account is current within 20 days after you receive this letter, my client has instructed me to file a notice of default with the court and to take action necessary to collect the balance due under the agreement.

Sincerely,

5-13   NOTICE OF DEFAULT ON PROMISSORY NOTE

Date:

To: [name and
    address of debtor]

Notice is hereby given that you are in default under your promissory note of [date note was entered into]. The below payments are due and owing:

Payment due date : _____   Amount due: $_____

Your total arrears: $

Accordingly, demand is hereby made for full payment of the balance due of $_____ unless the above noted past due payments are received within the next _____ days. If payment is not forthcoming, we will forward this note to our attorneys for legal action.

Sincerely,

5–14 NOTICE OF DEFAULT ON OPEN BOOK ACCOUNT

Date:

To: [name and
address of debtor]

Notice is hereby given that you are in default under your open book account with our company. The below payments are due and owing:

Invoice / Payment due date: _____   Amount due: $_____

Your total arrears: $_____

Accordingly, demand is hereby made for full payment of the balance due of $_____. Unless the above noted past due payments are received within the next _____ days, your open book credit account will be closed. If payment is not forthcoming, we will forward this note to our attorneys for legal action.

Sincerely,

5-15   DEMAND ON GUARANTORS

Date:

To: [name and
     address of guarantors]

You are hereby notified that the debt between [creditor] and [debtor] is in default. Since you are the guarantor of that debt and the undersigned is the holder of that guaranty, demand is hereby made on you for payment of the debt.

You guaranteed the debt by a written document entered into between the Creditor, Debtor, and you on [date document was entered into]. Accordingly, you are now responsible for paying the amount due, which as of this date is $_____.

If payment is not made within _____ days, we shall proceed to enforce against you our rights to collect this debt. Please note that if legal action is necessary, under the terms of the guaranty, you are responsible for attorney's fees and costs of collection.

Sincerely,

5-16 DEMAND ON ENDORSER

Date:

To: [name and
    address of endorser]

You are hereby notified that the check/note made between [creditor] and [debtor] and which you endorsed has been dishonored. As an endorser, you are the guarantor of that check/note and the undersigned is the holder of that guaranty. Demand is hereby made on you for payment of the check/note.

Date of check/note: _____
Face amount: _____
Maker of check/note: _____

The amount due as of this date is $_____. The amount due includes the face amount of the check/note of $_____ and bank/check return charges of $_____.

If payment is not made within _____ days, we shall proceed to enforce against you our rights to collect on your warranties of endorsement of this check/note.

Sincerely,

5–17   PAYMENT ON SPECIFIC ACCOUNTS

Date:

To: [creditor,
     address]

Enclosed is a check in the amount of $_____. This payment is to be applied to the below listed accounts only:

Invoice no.   Payment due date   Amount to credit

Please ensure that the above amounts are credited to the correct accounts.

Sincerely,

5-18 RECEIPT FOR PAYMENT IN FULL

Date:

To: [name and
address of debtor]

The undersigned Creditor hereby acknowledges the receipt of $_____ from [debtor]. This sum is accepted as payment in full for the below described account.

[describe account here]

_____
Creditor

5–19

NOTICE OF DISPUTED ACCOUNT BALANCE

Date:

To: [creditor,
    address]

Notice is hereby given that your invoice or statement of [date] is incorrect for the following reasons:

_____ Payment of [date] not reflected on statement.
_____ The goods have been returned.
_____ The price listed for the goods is incorrect.
_____ The goods listed on the statement have not been received.
_____ Goods were not ordered and are being held for your instructions regarding return.

_____ Other: _____

The correct balance on the statement should be: $ _____

Sincerely,

5-20 REQUEST FOR INFORMATION ON ACCOUNT BALANCE

Date:

To: [creditor,
    address]

Notice is hereby given that regarding your invoice or statement of [date], we feel that it may be incorrect. In order that we may verify the correctness of the account, please provide us with the below requested items or information:

_____ Copies of the purchase orders received from us
_____ List of goods claimed to have shipped to us
_____ Any debt memoranda that is outstanding

_____ Other: _____

When we have received the above information, we will audit the account and provide you with our conclusions.

Sincerely,

5-21   SETTLEMENT OF DISPUTED ACCOUNT BALANCE

Date:

By this agreement between, [name of Creditor], Creditor and [name of Debtor] Debtor resolve and forever settle and adjust the below listed claim. Both parties agree that there is a bona fide dispute regarding the amount due the Creditor on this account. Accordingly, the parties agree that the Debtor shall pay to the Creditor the sum of $_____ no later than [date] as payment in full on the below described account or claim.

Should Debtor fail to pay the agreed sum by the above listed date, then Creditor has the right to pursue the full amount claimed and is no longer under obligation to take the agreed sum as payment in full. If Debtor pays the agreed amount on or prior to the above listed date, Creditor will accept the payment as payment in full.

This agreement covers the below described account:

[describe the account or claim in this space]

This agreement shall be binding on all parties involved, their assigns, successors, and personal representatives.

Sincerely,

5-22 COMPROMISE

For good and valuable consideration, [name of Creditor], Creditor and [name of Debtor] Debtor hereby agree to compromise and discharge the indebtness owed to the Creditor by the Debtor according to the following terms:

1. The Debtor acknowledges that the sum of the present debt due the Creditor is $ _____.

2. The Creditor agrees to accept the sum of $ _____ as payment in full and agrees to discharge, release, and accept as satisfaction of all monies presently due.

3. Agreement of the Creditor to accept a lesser sum is binding only if payment by the Debtor is made within _____ days of the signing of this agreement.

4. If Debtor fails to pay the agreed sum within _____ days of the signing of this agreement, the Creditor shall have the right to pursue his/her claim for the full amount.

5. In the event of default, the defaulting parties agree to pay reasonable attorney fees and costs.

6. The agreement shall be binding on parties, their heirs, assigns, successors, and personal representatives.

Signed this_____ day of _____ 19_____.

_____
Creditor

_____
Debtor

RELEASE OF ALL CLAIMS (INSTALLMENT PAYMENTS)

FOR AND IN CONSIDERATION of the sum of _____ Dollars and No Cents ($ _____) which will be paid as follows: $_____ on the execution of this document and the balance paid in _____ monthly installments of $ _____ and the final monthly installment of $_____ with the monthly installments commencing on _____, 19____; and with each succeeding monthly installment due of the _____ of each succeeding month until paid with the final installment of $_____ due on_____, 19___; the undersigned, _____, his/her assigns, successors, and any other in privity with the undersigned, do

HEREBY RELEASE AND FOREVER DISCHARGE [name of person being released] and their agents, employees, employers, principals, partners, and all others in privity with said Releases (agreeing parties) of and from any and all claims, demands, rights, liens, damages, injuries, losses, contracts, convenants, suits, causes of action, expenses, judgments, orders and liabilities of any kind and nature, whether now known or unknown, suspected or unsuspected, foreseen or unforeseen, and whether or not concealed and hidden, which may have existed or may not have existed, or which can, may or shall hereafter exist or which have accrued or may hereafter accrue, on account of, or in any way relating to the _____ which occurred on or about _____, 19_____ in the City of _____, between _____ and an employee of _____ which accident allegedly gave rise to the claims of _____ against the agreeing parties.

It is understood and agreed by all parties and the undersigned does hereby state that this is a full and final Release in accord with its terms, applying to all unknown, unanticipated and unsuspected injuries, damages, claims, and expenses as set forth above, arising out of said accident, as well as to those now known or disclosed.

It is understood and agreed, and the undersigned does hereby state that reliance is placed wholly upon his judgment, belief, and knowledge as to the nature, cause, extent, and duration of any injuries and damages; and that no statement with regard thereto made by the Releases has in any way influenced the making of this compromise settlement and the execution of this Release.

It is understood and agreed that this offer and/or compromise shall not be deemed or construed as an admission of liability as to any of the agreeing parties.

The undersigned does hereby expressly represent to the releases that no medical liens are involved and there is no claim for reimbursement being made by any governmental agency or other third party and no third party has asserted any right to claim any proceeds of this settlement. Such representations have been relied upon by the releases herein and are deemed to be a material element of this settlement.

Having read and understood the terms of this Release of All Claims, and in witness whereof, the undersigned have hereunto set his/her hand this _____ day of _____, 19_____.

_____
Signature(s) of person being released

5-24 RELEASE OF ALL CLAIMS (LUMP SUM PAYMENT)

FOR AND IN CONSIDERATION of the sum of _____ Dollars ($_____) which will be paid as follows: $_____ by certified check or money order within 15 days after this signed document is received by _____ the undersigned.

_____, his assigns, successors, and any other in privity with the undersigned, do

HEREBY RELEASE AND FOREVER DISCHARGE [person being released from claim] and their agents, employees, employers, principals, partners, and all others in privity with said Releases (agreeing parties) of and from any and all claims, demands, rights, liens, damages, injuries, losses, contracts, convenants, suits, causes of action, expenses, judgments, orders and liabilities of any kind and nature, whether now known or unknown, suspected or unsuspected, foreseen or unforeseen, and whether or not concealed and hidden, which may have existed or may not have existed, or which can, may or shall hereafter exist or which have accrued or may hereafter accrue, on account of, on in any way relating to the

[describe incident, e.g. car accident]

The undersigned does hereby state that this is a full and final Release in accord with its terms, applying to all unknown, unanticipated and unsuspected injuries, damages claims and expenses as set forth above, arising out of the above incident, as well as to those now known or disclosed.

It is understood and agreed, and the undersigned does hereby state that reliance is placed wholly upon his and his attorney's judgment, belief and knowledge as to the nature, cause, extent, and duration of any injuries and damages; and that no statement with regard thereto made by the Releases has in any way influenced the making of this compromise settlement and the execution of this Release.

It is understood and agreed that this offer and/or compromise shall not be deemed or construed as an admission of liability as to any of the agreeing parties.

Having read and understood the terms of this Release of All Claims, and in witness whereof, the undersigned has hereunto set their hands this _____ day of _____, 19____ .

_____
Signature of person releasing claim

5-25   COLLECTION TRANSMITTAL

Date:

To: [attorney or
     collection agent]

Dear Madam/Sir:

The below listed accounts are being turned over to your office for collection in accordance with your standard fee schedule. Also enclosed are the supporting documents for each account.

If additional information is required, please contact [name of contact person and telephone number].

We would appreciate your expedited efforts in collecting these accounts.

List of accounts being forwarded:

[list accounts here and attach supporting documents to this letter]

Sincerely,

5-26 PROPOSAL TO COLLECT PAST DUE ACCOUNTS

[Agency] will collect past due accounts for _____ subject to the below terms and conditions:

1. [name of client] (hereinafter referred to as Client) is under no obligation to forward any cases for collection to Agency. The agency has a right to refuse any individual cases where there is a possible conflict of interest, etc.

2. The agreement may be canceled by either party with a 30-day notice.

3. If payment is collected without court action, the division of payment will be 35 percent to agent and 65 percent to client.

4. If court action is required, first payments received will be applied toward costs associated with the court action. Thereafter, the division of payment will be 40 percent to agent and 60 percent to client.

5. If no payments are received on a case, the agent will *not* seek reimbursement of court costs or associated fees from client.

6. Client will cooperate with agent by providing witnesses to court trials when the debts are disputed.

7. Client when forwarding a case for collection will include a ledger or balance sheet indicated balance due, copy of lease, copy of credit application and any other information regarding the Debtor that is reasonably available.

Dated:

_____
Agency

Dated:

Above terms are accepted.

_____
Client

5-27 NOTICE OF DISHONORED CHECK

NOTICE

Date:

To:

    The undersigned is the payee of a check you wrote for $_____ . The check was refused by your bank because of insufficient funds, and the payee demands payment.

    If you fail to pay the payer the full amount of the check in cash within 30 days after this notice is mailed, you could be sued and held responsible to pay at least all of the following:

1. The amount of the check.
2. Damages
3. The cost of mailing this notice.

    Upon receipt of good replacement funds, the check will be returned to you.

    You may wish to contact a lawyer to discuss your legal rights and responsibilities.

    Amount due: Check amount $_____ ; check return fee $_____

Total due: $_____

Sincerely,

5-28

NOTICE OF DISHONORED CHECK (STOP PAYMENT)

NOTICE

Date:

To:

The undersigned is the payee of a check you wrote for_____. The check was not paid because you stopped payment, and the payee demands payment. You may have a good faith dispute as to whether you owe the full amount. If you do not have a good faith dispute with the payee and fail to pay the payer the full amount of the check in cash within 30 days after this notice is mailed, you could be sued and held responsible to pay at least all of the following:

1. The amount of the check.
2. Damages
3. The cost of mailing this notice.

If the court determines that you do have a good faith dispute with the payee, you will not have to pay the damages and mailing cost mentioned above. If you stopped the payment because you have a good faith dispute with the payee, you should try to work out your dispute with the payee. You can contact the payee's attorney at the below listed address.

You may wish to contact a lawyer to discuss your legal rights and responsibilities.

Amount due: Check amount $_____; check return fee $_____
       Total due: $_____

Sincerely,

5-29 CHECK STOP-PAYMENT ORDER

Date:

To: [bank,
    address]

Please stop payment on the below check. This stop payment order remains in effect until you receive other written instructions. If the below check has already been paid, please advise me immediately.

Date of check:
Name of payee:
    Amount of check:
Check number:

Sincerely,

5-30   BANK COLLECTION–DISHONORED CHECK

Date:

To: [bank
address]

Dear Sir/Madam:

    The enclosed dishonored check is placed with you for collection. Any funds collected should, after deducting your standard charges, be credited to our account.

    Date of check:
    Name of maker:
       Amount of check:
    Check number:
      Drawee bank:
      Account number:

Sincerely,

_____
Signature

_____
Account name

_____
Account number

5-31   NOTICE OF LOST OR STOLEN CREDIT CARD

Date:

To: [credit card company,
    address]

Re: Lost or stolen credit card: [card number and name as listed on the card]

  The above referenced credit card has been lost or stolen. Accordingly, please cancel it and provide me with a replacement.

Sincerely,

_____
Card Holder Signature

_____
Address

5-32 REQUEST FOR CREDIT CHARGEBACK

Date:

To: [credit card company,
      address]

Re: Credit chargeback; [card number and name as listed on the card]

Dear Sir/Madam:

On [date] a charge was placed on the above referenced account on a transaction with [name of business]. Please do not honor that charge, or if it has been honored, please reverse the charge. This request is based on the following reason:

[state reasons such as; the merchandise was defective or the merchandise was not as ordered, etc.]

Thank you for your assistance in this matter.

Sincerely,

_____
Card Holder Signature

_____
Address

5-33 NOTICE OF RESCISSION

Date:

To: [company,
    address]

Re: Rescission of contract with your company dated [date]

Dear Sir/Madam:

You are hereby notified that I am exercising my rights to rescind the contract entered into with your company on [date]. Accordingly, please cancel said contract and return my deposit of $_____. Please note that under the provisions of the Federal Truth-in-Lending Act, I have three days to cancel the said contract and this rescission is pursuant to that right.

In addition, you are requested to cancel any lien against our property within ten days as required by law.

Sincerely,

_____
Card Holder Signature

_____
Address

5-34   NOTICE OF BILLING ERROR RIGHTS (MODEL UNDER THE FAIR CREDIT BILLING ACT)

Your Billing Rights
Keep This Notice for Future Use

If you think your bill is wrong, or if you need more information about a transaction on your bill, write us at this address (address inserted here). You must notify us within 60 days after we send you the first bill on which the error or problem appears. You may contact us by telephone, but doing so will not preserve your rights. You should include the following information in your letter:

Your name and account number
The dollar amount of the suspected error or questionable transaction
A description of the error and an explanation of why you believe that the item or transaction is an error
A request for any additional information needed to verify the correctness of your bill

If we are authorized to pay your credit card bill automatically from your banking institution or credit union, you may stop the payment of any amount that you think is wrong. To stop the payment your letter must reach us at least three business days before the automatic payment is scheduled to occur.

5-35　NOTICE OF DEBTOR'S RIGHTS AND CREDITOR'S RESPONSIBILITIES WHEN BILL IS DISPUTED

Your Rights and Our Responsibilities
After Written Notice Is Received by Us

Your letter will be acknowledged within 30 days unless we have corrected the error by then. We must either correct the error or explain why we believe the bill is correct.

After we receive your written notice, we cannot try to collect any amount you question or report you as delinquent. We can continue to bill you for the amount that you question including finance charges, and we can apply any unpaid amount against your credit limit. You are not required to pay any questioned amount while we are investigating, but you are still obligated to pay the parts of your bill that are not in question.

If we find that we made a mistake on your bill, you will not have to pay any finance charges related to any questioned amount. If we find that the amount billed is correct, you may be required to pay finance charges, and you will have to make up any missed payments on the questioned amount. In either case, you will be sent a statement of the amount you owe and the date it is due.

If you fail to pay the amount that we think you owe, we may report you as delinquent. However, if our explanation does not satisfy you and you write to us within ten days telling us that you still refuse to pay, we must tell anyone we report you to that you have a question about your bill. We must, also, tell you the name of anyone we reported you to. If the matter is settled between us, we must tell anyone we reported you to that the matter has been settled.

If we do not follow the above rules, we can not collect the first $50 of the questioned amount, even if the bill was correct.

Chapter 6

Assignments

This chapter contains those forms and agreements commonly used in assigning rights and properties.

Assignment in the legal sense has a comprehensive meaning. It means the transfer or setting over of property or some right or interest. It is also an act by which one person causes his or her property rights to vest in another. The person making the assignment is referred to as the *assignor*, and the person receiving the assignment is referred to as the *assignee*. For a right or interest to be assignable, it must have either an actual or potential existence. The assignment of certain rights is prohibited by either federal or state statutes. For example in most states, a person may not assign right to receive welfare payments.

Except for those assignments involving the transfer of real estate, there are no particular forms required. The form used, however, should afford a clear identification of the parties, the rights assigned, and the rights reserved. In most states, assignments are required to be in writing. In those assignments that affect an interest in real estate, most states require that the assignments be recorded in the county in which the real estate is located. The tax aspects should be considered when an assignment is being contemplated. In most cases, the assignment of income does not shift the burden of paying income tax on the income from the assignor to the assignee. If the property produces income, the assignment of the property will normally result in the assignee's being responsible for paying taxes on all future income from the property.

Assignment of Wages

In some states, wages that have not yet been earned cannot be assigned. Other states restrict the percentage of gross wages that can be assigned, the requirement being that a spouse consent to the assignment. Assignment of wages is a closely regulated area by the statutes of many states.

Assignment of Contracts

An assignment of a contract occurs when one party to the contract transfers his or her interest and rights under the contract to another person. Most contracts can be assigned. The following questions must be examined to determine if a contract can be assigned by one party to a third person:

Is the contract of a personal nature or of the type that limits its performance to the named individuals in the contract?

Do the contract terms permit assignment of the rights and benefits under the contract?

Does the assignment violate law or public policy?

Does the assignment impose additional duties, rights, or obligations on the other parties to the contract?

Does the assignment jeopardize the rights of the other parties to the contract to receive their benefits under the contract?

In regard to the first question, an assignment of personal service contracts is usually prohibited when the nature of the services to be performed under the contract is unique. The theory behind this prohibition is that the nature of the contract is changed when the services contracted from one individual are transferred to another. This rule applies in cases involving attorneys, painters, artists, authors, doctors, teachers, and the like. If the personal service to be performed is routine, then assignment is usually permitted.

Regarding the second question, a general provision that prohibits assignment in a contract is usually not enforced by the courts. Section 2–210 of the Uniform Commercial Code provides that any party may assign his or her rights to receive benefits under a contract, and that any prohibition of assignment in the contract will be construed as barring only a delegation of duties under the contract. The rule in most states is that an individual may assign a contract despite a provision against assignment, but the nonassigning party may sue for breach of contract. In these cases, there is the power to assign but not the right to assign.

A contract may not be assigned if the assignment is either prohibited by law or violates public policy. If the assignment would substantially modify the nonassigning party's contractual duties, the courts will refuse to enforce the assignment. For example, if you enter into a contract to supply a small grocery store with all the wrapping paper it needs for six months and the store assigns the contract to a major supermarket, the assignment would be invalid because the amount of paper needed differs substantially. Another limitation on the right to assign a contract involves those cases in which the assigned rights would substantially alter the obligor's risk.

In most cases, it is not usually necessary that an assignment be written in order for it to be effective. Written assignments are usually required only when an interest in land, the sale of goods in an amount over $500, wage assignments, and assignments used as security interests are involved. These kinds of assignments are discussed later in this chapter.

Consideration is not necessary for a valid assignment because the assignor (one who assigns the contract) may make a gift of his or her rights under a contract. The assignment must indicate a present intent to transfer rights under the contract. An assignment given for consideration is usually irrevocable. If it is without consideration (i.e., a gift), however, then it is usually revocable.

The person to whom the assignment is made (the *assignee*) replaces the assigning party as a party to the contract, and the assignee can then sue the nonassigning party (the *obligor*) for breach of contract directly.

The implied warranty of title and the right to assign are included in an assignment. If these warranties are violated, the assignee may sue the assignor for breach of contract (the assignment contract). Unless it is specifically warranted in the assignment contract, the assignor does not guarantee that the other party will perform his or her obligations under the contract. Rights and benefits may be assigned under a contract; duties and obligations are not assigned but are delegated.

Delegation of Duties under a Contract

As we have noted, duties are not assignable but are delegated. The key difference is that the party who delegates the duties is still liable to the other parties under the contract if the new party fails to perform the duties. The question as to what duties are delegable is also present. The usual restrictions on the delegation of duties involve personal skill and judgment, special trust, or those restrictions that change the nature of the duties under the contract. For example, a professional baseball player could not assign his duties to play baseball under a major league contract to another player.

Rights under a contract may be assigned without the delegation of the duties to perform. For example, the baseball player could assign his right to receive a salary to another person, but he could not assign his duty to play baseball. Unless otherwise stated, a total assignment of rights also includes the delegation of duties (if the duties are delegable).

Assignment for the Benefit of Creditors

An assignment for the benefit of creditors is usually in the form of a general assignment of the property owned by a debtor to the assignee without the creditors' receiving any additional value. The assignee holds the property in trust and pays creditors a pro rata share of the income from the property. In most states this action is a common law remedy for a creditor who attempts to escape bankruptcy. *Note:* Under the Uniform Partnership Act, all the partners of a partnership must sign any partnership assignment for benefit of creditors. In some states, assignments for the benefit of creditors must be notarized.

Bailments

A *bailment* is a delivery of a thing in trust for some special object or purpose pursuant to an expressed or implied contract. Bailments are either voluntary or involuntary. A *voluntary bailment* is established by a contract between the parties. An *involuntary bailment* is made by the accidental leaving or placing of personal property in the possession of any person. For example, an involuntary bailment occurs if one's property is carried by a flood onto the property of another. This section discusses voluntary bailments.

Under a bailment, the person taking possession of the property, the *bailee*, is normally obligated to return the identical property to the *bailor* (the person who left the property). Bailments are classified according to the benefits derived from the bailment as gratuitous bailments (those for the sole benefit of the bailor), loans for use (those for the sole benefit of the bailee), and storage or hire (those for the benefit of both). A gratuitous bailment would occur when your neighbor keeps your boat for you when you are out of town. In this case, the benefit is solely to you and the neighbor is doing you a favor. If you lend your neighbor your lawn mower so he can cut his lawn, this is a loan for use, because the bailment is for the sole benefit of the neighbor. A storage or hire bailment occurs when someone keeps your personal property but charges you a storage fee. In this case, each of you benefits from the bailment.

Forms in This Chapter

- FORM 6–1: GENERAL ASSIGNMENT. Makes a general assignment of a right to another person or company.

- FORM 6–2: ASSIGNMENT OF ACCOUNTS RECEIVABLE. Assigns accounts receivable.

- FORM 6–3: ASSIGNMENT OF CONTRACT. Assigns rights under a contract.

- FORM 6–4: ASSIGNMENT OF CONTRACT BENEFITS. Assigns only the benefits of a contract and not the duties under the contract.

- FORM 6–5: ASSIGNMENT OF WAGES. Assigns wages.

- FORM 6–6: CONSENT TO ASSIGNMENT OF WAGES. Used by a spouse to consent to the assignment of the wages of the other spouse.

- FORM 6–7: ASSIGNMENT OF COPYRIGHT. Assigns a copyright.

- FORM 6–8: PERMISSION FOR ONE-TIME USE OF COPYRIGHT. Gives a one-time permission to use a copyrighted work.

- FORM 6–9: LICENSE TO USE TRADEMARK. Gives a license to use the trademark of a business.

- FORM 6–10: ASSIGNMENT OF PATENT. Assigns a patent.

- FORM 6–11: ASSIGNMENT OF PENDING PATENT APPLICATION. Assigns a product or process for which a patent is pending.

- FORM 6–12: LICENSE TO USE PATENT RIGHT. Gives a license to use a patent.

- FORM 6–13: ASSIGNMENT OF A REAL ESTATE CONTRACT. Assigns an interest in a real estate contract. Often used to assign an option to purchase real estate.

- FORM 6–14: ASSIGNMENT OF A MECHANIC'S LIEN. Assigns a mechanic's lien. To be valid in many states, it must be recorded in the same manner that the mechanic's lien was recorded.

- FORM 6–15: ASSIGNMENT OF A BANK ACCOUNT. Assigns a bank account. Before using the form, make sure bank will accept assignment.

- FORM 6–16: ASSIGNMENT OF STOCK CERTIFICATES. Assigns stock certificates.

- FORM 6–17: ASSIGNMENT OF MONEY DUE. Assigns a debt that someone owes you.

- FORM 6–18: ASSIGNMENT OF AN UNSECURED NOTE. Assigns an unsecured promissory note.

- FORM 6–19: ASSIGNMENT OF A SECURED NOTE. Assigns a secured note.

- FORM 6–20: ASSIGNMENT OF LIFE INSURANCE POLICY. Assigns a life insurance policy.

- FORM 6–21: ASSIGNMENT OF INSURANCE CLAIM. Assigns an insurance claim.

- FORM 6–22: ASSIGNMENT OF LIFE INSURANCE POLICY AS COLLATERAL. Assigns a life insurance policy that is being used as a collateral for loan(s).

- FORM 6–23: GENERAL ASSIGNMENT FOR THE BENEFIT OF CREDITORS. An assignment for the benefit of creditors as to the use of this form.

- FORM 6–24: GENERAL ASSIGNMENT BY A CORPORATION FOR THE BENEFIT OF CREDITORS. (See discussion on assignments for the benefit of credits as to use.)

- FORM 6–25: ASSIGNMENT OF A PARTNER'S INTEREST IN PARTNERSHIP. Assigns a partnership interest.

- FORM 6–26: ASSIGNMENT OF INTEREST IN JOINT VENTURE. Assigns an interest in a joint venture.

- FORM 6–27: ASSIGNMENT OF INCOME FROM A TRUST. Assigns an interest in a trust.

- FORM 6–28: ASSIGNMENT OF CLAIM FOR DAMAGES. Assigns a claim for damages.

- FORM 6–29: ASSIGNMENT OF A JUDGMENT. Assigns a judgment. It is often necessary to assign a judgment to a collection agency for collection.

- FORM 6–30: NOTICE OF ASSIGNMENT OF CONTRACT. Notifies the other parties to a contract of the assignment.

- FORM 6–31: DIRECTION TO PAY. Directs a debtor to pay someone other than the creditor.

- FORM 6–32: NOTICE OF ASSIGNMENT (BY ASSIGNEE). Used by the assignee to notify the third parties of the assignment.

- FORM 6–33: NOTICE OF ASSIGNMENT (BY ASSIGNOR). Used by the assignor to notify third parties of the assignment.

- FORM 6–34: NOTICE OF ASSIGNMENT FOR BENEFIT OF CREDITORS. Forwarded to creditors to notify them that the assignment has been made.

- FORM 6–35: NOTICE OF CANCELLATION OF ASSIGNMENT. Notification that an assignment has been canceled.

- FORM 6–36: DEMAND FOR PROOF OF ASSIGNMENT. Requires proof of an assignment.

- FORM 6–37: BAILMENT CONTRACT. A short form of a bailment contract.

- FORM 6–38: BAILEE'S NOTICE TO RECOVER PROPERTY. Used by a bailee (holder of the personal property) to give notice to the owner of the property to take possession. Applies only to gratuitous bailments (i.e., when the holder of the property is not being paid by the owner to hold it).

- FORM 6–39: BAILEE'S NOTICE OF INTENT TO SELL PROPERTY. Notifies bailor of intent to sell bailed property unless it is claimed within a certain period.

- FORM 6–40: BAILEE'S NOTICE OF ADVERSE CLAIM ON BAILED PROPERTY. Provides the bailor with notice of an adverse claim on the bailed property.

- FORM 6–41: BAILOR'S DEMAND FOR DELIVERY OF PROPERTY. Demands delivery of property.

- FORM 6–42: BAILEE'S NOTICE OF LOSS TO PROPERTY. Provides owner of property that it was lost or damaged during bailment.

- FORM 6–43: BAILOR'S DEMAND FOR INFORMATION. Demands more information regarding loss of bailed property.

6-1 GENERAL ASSIGNMENT

For good and valuable consideration, the undersigned hereby unconditionally and irrevocably assigns and transfers unto [Assignee] all rights, title, and interest in and to the following:

The undersigned warrants that she/he has full rights and full authority to make this assignment and transfer. The undersigned also warrants that the rights and benefits assigned hereunder are free and clear of any liens, encumbrances, adverse claims, or interest.

This assignment shall be binding upon and inure to the benefit of the parties, their successors, assigns, and personal representatives.

Signed under seal this _____ day of _____, 19____.

_____
Assignor

_____
Address

6-2 ASSIGNMENT OF ACCOUNTS RECEIVABLE

For good and valuable consideration, the undersigned hereby unconditionally and irrevocably assigns and transfers all rights, title, and interest in and to the accounts receivable as annexed to [Assignee] and his/her successors and assigns.

The undersigned assignor warrants that the said accounts are just and due in the amounts stated and that he/she has not received payment for the same or any part thereof and that he/she has full rights and full authority to make this assignment and transfer. The undersigned also warrants that the rights and benefits assigned hereunder are free and clear of any liens, encumbrances, adverse claims, or interest. In addition, the assignor also warrants that he/she has no knowledge of any disputes or defenses thereon. The accounts are sold without warranty or guaranty of collection and without recourse to the undersigned Assignor in the event of nonpayment. Assignee may prosecute collection of any receivable in his/her own name.

This assignment shall be binding upon and inure to the benefit of the parties, their successors, assigns, and personal representatives.

Signed under seal this _____ day of _____, 19_____.

_____
Assignor

_____
Address

6-3 ASSIGNMENT OF CONTRACT

For good and valuable consideration, the undersigned hereby unconditionally and irrevocably assigns and transfers over to [Assignee] and
his/her successors and assigns all rights, title, and interest in and to the
following described contract with _____, dated ____ _____,
19_____.

[describe contract at this point]

The undersigned Assignor warrants that the said contract is in full force
and effect in the form and terms annexed and that the contract is fully
assignable.

The Assignee assumes and agrees to perform all the remaining and
executory obligations of the Assignor under the contract, if any and to
indemnify and hold Assignor harmless from any claim or demand resulting from nonperformance therein by the Assignee.

The Assignee is entitled to all monies and other benefits accrued or
remaining to be paid under the contract, which rights are also assigned
hereunder. Assignor warrants that he/she has full rights and full authority
to make this assignment and transfer. The undersigned also warrants that
the rights and benefits assigned hereunder are free and clear of any liens,
encumbrances, adverse claims, or interest. In addition, the Assignor also
warrants that he/she has no knowledge of any disputes or defenses
thereon.

This assignment shall be binding upon and inure to the benefit of the
parties, their successors, assigns, and personal representatives.

Signed under seal this _____ day of _____, 19_____.

_____
Assignor

_____
Assignee

6-4 ASSIGNMENT OF CONTRACT BENEFITS

For good and valuable consideration, the undersigned hereby unconditionally and irrevocably assigns and transfers over to [Assignee] and his/her successors and assigns all benefits to be received in and from the following described contract with _____, dated _____, 19_____ .

[described contract at this point]

The undersigned Assignor warrants that the said contract is in full force and effect in the form and terms annexed and that the contract is fully assignable.

The Assignee is entitled to all monies and other benefits accrued or remaining to be paid under the contract, which rights are also assigned hereunder. Assignor warrants that he/she has full rights and full authority to make this assignment and transfer. The undersigned also warrants that the rights and benefits assigned hereunder are free and clear of any liens, encumbrances, adverse claims, or interest. In addition, the Assignor also warrants that he/she has no knowledge of any disputes or defenses thereon.

This assignment shall be binding upon and inure to the benefit of the parties, their successors, assigns, and personal representatives.

Signed under seal this _____ day of _____, 19_____ .

_____
Assignor

6-5 ASSIGNMENT OF WAGES

For good and valuable consideration, the undersigned hereby unconditionally and irrevocably assigns and transfers and orders paid to [Assignee] the sum of $_____ per pay period of wages or salary earned or to be earned and payable to me by [employer].

This assignment is given to satisfy a debt of [debtor].

I warrant that I am [unmarried][married] with[out] minor children.

I authorize and direct my employer to pay to Assignee named above until the full amount of the debt has been paid.

The undersigned Assignor warrants that there are no conflicting assignments of wages. The undersigned also warrants that the rights and benefits assigned hereunder are free and clear of any liens, encumbrances, adverse claims, or interest. In addition, the Assignor also warrants that he/she has no knowledge of any disputes or defenses thereon.

This assignment shall be binding upon and inure to the benefit of the parties, their successors, assigns, and personal representatives.

Signed under seal this _____ day of _____, 19_____.

_____
Assignor

6–6   CONSENT TO ASSIGNMENT OF WAGES

I, [name], am the spouse of [Assignor] in the attached assignment of wages. I consent to that assignment.

I also consent to the authorization and direction of my spouse to his/her employer to pay to Assignee the wages agreed to be assigned.

This consent to the assignment shall be binding upon and inure to the benefit of the parties, their successors, assigns, and personal representatives.

Signed under seal this _____ day of _____, 19____.

_____
Spouse

6-7 ASSIGNMENT OF COPYRIGHT

For good and valuable consideration, receipt of which is hereby acknowledged, [name of assignor], Assignor hereby assigns all copyright in [name of work being assigned] the Work, to [person receiving the assignment], Assignee.

Both Assignee and Assignor agree that the Assignee can register and dispose of the copyright in the Work in the Assignee's own name.

Assignor warrants:

1. That he/she is the owner of the copyright in the Work and has the right to assign the copyright.
2. The Work has been copyrighted.
3. There is no dispute or pending dispute over the existence, ownership, or right to assign the Work.

WITNESSED this _____ day of _____, 19_____.

_____
Assignor

_____
Assignee

State of   )

County of   ) SS

On this date, [list names of person(s) who signed above] personally appeared before me and acknowledged that the above signature(s) are valid and binding.

_____
Notary Public

My Commission expires:

6-8

PERMISSION FOR ONE-TIME USE OF COPYRIGHT

For good and valuable consideration, receipt of which is hereby acknowledged, [name of assignor], Grantor hereby grants permission for the one–time use of the below described Work that is copyrighted [name of work], to [person receiving the permission], Grantee.

Grantee agrees to use the Work for the below stated purpose only:

[state purpose]

Grantor warrants:

1. That he/she is the owner of the copyright in the Work and has the right to grant permission to use the copyright.
2. The Work has been copyrighted.
3. There is no dispute or pending dispute over the existence, ownership, or right to use the Work.

WITNESSED this _____ day of _____, 19_____.

_____
Grantor

_____
Grantee

State of   )

County of   ) SS

On this date, [names of person(s) who signed above] personally appeared before me and acknowledged that the above signature(s) are valid and binding.

_____
Notary Public

My Commission expires:

6-9 LICENSE TO USE TRADEMARK

For good and valuable consideration, receipt of which is hereby acknowledged, [Assignor], Licensor hereby allows, permits, licenses [person receiving the right to use the license], Licensee the rights to use the below described trademark:

[describe trademark]

This license to use the described trademark is subject to the below limitations:

[list limitations here]

This license to use the above trademark will expire on [date] or on use of the trademark in violation of the above listed limitations.

Licensor warrants:

1. That he/she is the owner of the trademark and has the right to license the use of it.
2. The trademark has been registered as permitted by state and federal law.
3. There is no dispute or pending dispute over the existence, ownership or right to the trademark.

WITNESSED this _____ day of _____, 19_____.

_____
Licensor

_____
Licensee

State of   )

County of   ) SS

On this date, [list names of person(s) who signed above] personally appeared before me and acknowledged that the above signature(s) are valid and binding.

_____
Notary Public

My Commission expires:

6-10   ASSIGNMENT OF PATENT

For good and valuable consideration, receipt of which is hereby acknowledged, [Assignor], Assignor hereby assigns all patent rights in patent number _____ namely: [describe patent being assigned] the Patent, to [person receiving the assignment], Assignee.

Both Assignee and Assignor agree that the Assignee can register and dispose of the Patent in the Assignee's own name.

Assignor warrants:

1. That he/she is the owner of the said patent and has the right to assign it.

2. The patent is a valid patent.

3. There is no dispute or pending dispute over the existence, ownership or right to assign the patent.

WITNESSED this _____ day of _____, 19_____.

_____
Assignor

_____
Assignee

State of   )

County of   ) SS

On this date, [list names of person(s) who signed above] personally appeared before me and acknowledged that the above signature(s) are valid and binding.

_____
Notary Public

My Commission expires:

6-11 ASSIGNMENT OF PENDING PATENT APPLICATION

For good and valuable consideration, receipt of which is hereby acknowledged, [Assignor], Assignor also referred to as the inventor, hereby assigns all patent rights in pending patent described in and identified by an application for United States Letters Patent, filed [date filed] namely: [describe patent being assigned] the Pending Patent, to [person receiving the assignment], Assignee.

Both Assignee and Assignor agree that the Assignee can register and dispose of the Pending Patent in the Assignee's own name.

Assignor warrants:

1. That he/she is the owner of the said item or process involved in the pending patent and has the right to assign it.

2. The pending patent covered by a valid patent application.

3. There is no dispute or pending dispute over the existence, ownership or right to assign the matter covered in the patent application.

WITNESSED this _____ day of _____, 19_____.

_____
Assignor

_____
Assignee

State of   )
County of   ) SS

On this date, [list names of person(s) who signed above] personally appeared before me and acknowledged that the above signature(s) are valid and binding.

_____
Notary Public

My Commission expires:

6–12 LICENSE TO USE PATENT RIGHT

For good and valuable consideration, receipt of which is hereby acknowledged, [Assignor], Licensor hereby allows, permits, licenses [person receiving the right to use the patent], Licensee the rights to use the below described patent:

[describe patent]

This license to use the described patent is subject to the below limitations:

[list limitations here]

This license to use the above patent will expire on [date] or on use of the patent rights in violation of the above listed limitations.

Licensor warrants:

1. That he/she is the owner of the patent and has the right to license the use of its rights.

2. There is no dispute or pending dispute over the existence, ownership or right to the patent.

WITNESSED this _____ day of _____, 19____.

_____
Assignor

_____
Assignee

State of   )
County of   ) SS

On this date, [list names of person(s) who signed above] personally appeared before me and acknowledged that the above signature(s) are valid and binding.

_____
Notary Public

My Commission expires:

6-13 ASSIGNMENT OF A REAL ESTATE CONTRACT

For good and valuable consideration, receipt of which is hereby acknowledged, on [date], I assigned all my interest and benefit in the following contract for the sale and purchase of:

[legal description of real estate]

to: [person to whom contract was assigned, including address]

WITNESSED this _____ day of _____, 19_____.

_____
Assignor

_____
Assignee

State of   )

County of   ) SS

On this date, [list names of person(s) who signed above] personally appeared before me and acknowledged that the above signature(s) are valid and binding.

_____
Notary Public

My Commission expires:

6-14 ASSIGNMENT OF A MECHANIC'S LIEN

State of   )

County of   ) SS

For good and valuable consideration, receipt of which is hereby acknowledged, on [date], I, [name] of the City of [city], County of [county], State of [state] assigned all my interest and benefit together with all right and interest in and to the debt there secured in the following mechanic's lien:

[describe lien including property covered by lien]

The affidavit and claim for which is dated [date of lien] and which was executed by [name of person executing lien] and which is filed in [location where lien filed] and recorded on Page _____, Volume _____ of the Records of [describe records]

to: [person to whom contract was assigned, including address]

WITNESSED this _____ day of _____, 19_____.

_____

_____

State of   )

County of   ) SS

On this date, [list names of person(s) who signed above] personally appeared before me and acknowledged that the above signature(s) are valid and binding.

_____

Notary Public

My Commission expires:

6-15 ASSIGNMENT OF A BANK ACCOUNT

For good and valuable consideration, receipt of which is hereby acknowledged, on [date], I assigned all my interest and benefit in the following bank account No. _____ in the name of the Assignor in [name and address of bank]

to: [person to whom account is being assigned, including address]

The Assignor irrevocably authorizes Assignee to ask for, demand, collect, and give a receipt for money in such bank account, without any previous demand or notice.

WITNESSED this _____ day of _____, 19_____.

_____
Assignor

_____
Assignee

State of   )

County of   ) SS

On this date, [list names of person(s) who signed above] personally appeared before me and acknowledged that the above signature(s) are valid and binding.

_____
Notary Public

My Commission expires:

6–16   ASSIGNMENT OF STOCK CERTIFICATES

For good and valuable consideration, receipt of which is hereby acknowledged, on [date], I assigned all my interest and benefit in the following stock certificates [describe number of shares, type of stock, e.g., Class A Common Stock] of _____ [corporation], which are represented by certificate number(s) _____

to: [person to whom shares are being assigned, including address]

I warrant that the certificate is genuine and to my knowledge is valid, and that I have the legal right to transfer it.

I appoint the Assignee as my attorney in fact to effect a transfer of the assigned shares on the books of the _____ [corporation] with full power of substitution.

WITNESSED this _____ day of _____, 19_____.

_____
Assignor

_____
Assignee

State of   )

County of   ) SS

On this date, [list names of person(s) who signed above] personally appeared before me and acknowledged that the above signature(s) are valid and binding.

_____
Notary Public

My Commission expires:

6-17 ASSIGNMENT OF MONEY DUE

For good and valuable consideration, the undersigned hereby unconditionally and irrevocably assigns and transfers all rights, title and interest in and to all monies due to [Assignee] and his/her successors and assigns by [name of debtor].

The undersigned Assignor warrants that the said account is correct and due in the amount stated and that he/she has not received payment for the same or any part thereof and that he/she has full rights and full authority to make this assignment and transfer. The undersigned also warrants that the rights and benefits assigned hereunder are free and clear of any liens, encumbrances, adverse claims, or interest. In addition, the Assignor also warrants that he/she has no knowledge of any disputes or defenses thereon. The account is sold without warranty or guaranty of collection and without recourse to the undersigned Assignor in the event of nonpayment. Assignee may prosecute collection of any receivable in his/her own name.

This assignment shall be binding upon and inure to the benefit of the parties, their successors, assigns, and personal representatives.

Signed under seal this _____ day of _____, 19_____.

_____
Assignor

6-18 ASSIGNMENT OF AN UNSECURED NOTE

For good and valuable consideration, receipt of which is hereby acknowledged, on [date], I assigned all my interest, title, ownership, and benefit in the below described promissory note:

[describe the note at this point].

Attached is the original of the said promissory note to: [person to whom account is being assigned, including address].

The Assignor irrevocably authorizes Assignee to ask for, demand, collect, and give a receipt for money that is due or may become due on the said note, without any previous demand or notice except as required by the terms of the attached note.

WITNESSED this _____ day of _____, 19_____.

_____

_____

State of   )

County of   ) SS

On this date, [list names of person(s) who signed above] personally appeared before me and acknowledged that the above signature(s) are valid and binding.

_____

Notary Public

My Commission expires:

6-19 ASSIGNMENT OF A SECURED NOTE

For good and valuable consideration, receipt of which is hereby acknowledged, on [date], I assigned all my interest, title, ownership and benefit in the below described promissory note:

[describe the note at this point].

Attached is the original of the said promissory note to: [person to whom account is being assigned, including address].

The Assignor irrevocably authorizes Assignee to ask for, demand, collect and give a receipt for money that is due or may become due on the said note, without any previous demand or notice except as required by the terms of the attached note.

The Assignor hereby assigns to the Assignee all of the Assignor's rights to the below–described security interest: [list the item, property, or account which secures the note] to secure performance under the terms of the attached note. In the event default as described in the security agreement occurs, the Assignee has the right, authority, and power to take the actions permitted to be taken by the Assignor. For this purpose, the Assignee is appointed the Attorney in fact of the Assignor to enforce the terms of the security agreement and the attached note.

WITNESSED this _____ day of _____, 19_____.

_____
Assignor

_____
Assigner

State of   )

County of   ) SS

On this date, [list names of person(s) who signed above] personally appeared before me and acknowledged that the above signature(s) are valid and binding.

_____
Notary Public

My Commission expires:

6-20

ASSIGNMENT OF LIFE INSURANCE POLICY

For good and valuable consideration, the undersigned hereby unconditionally and irrevocably assigns and transfers all rights, title, and interest in and to the life insurance policy No. _____ with the [insurance company] on the life of _____.

The undersigned Assignor warrants that he/she is the owner of the said life insurance policy and that he/she has full rights and full authority to make this assignment and transfer. The undersigned also warrants that the rights and benefits assigned hereunder are free and clear of any liens, encumbrances, adverse claims, or interest. In addition, the Assignor also warrants that he/she has no knowledge of any disputes or defenses thereon. The Assignee shall have full authority to change the beneficiary, to assign, surrender, or to borrow on the policy. Until a change is made by the assignee, this assignment does not change or affect the interest of the beneficiary.

This assignment shall be binding upon and inure to the benefit of the parties, their successors, assigns, and personal representatives.

Signed under seal this _____ day of _____, 19_____.

_____
Assignor

6-21 ASSIGNMENT OF INSURANCE CLAIM

For good and valuable consideration, the undersigned hereby unconditionally and irrevocably assigns and transfers all rights, title and interest in and to the insurance claim on insurance policy No. _____ with the [insurance company], to wit the claim that is based on the following incident/event:

[describe the incident/event, e.g. automobile accident which occurred on 2–3–1994 involving a 1994 Ford pickup, license number KKL 342]

The undersigned Assignor warrants that he/she is the owner of the said insurance policy and that he/she has full rights and full authority to make this assignment and transfer. The undersigned also warrants that the claim assigned hereunder is free and clear of any liens, encumbrances, adverse claims, or interest. In addition, the Assignor also warrants that he/she has no knowledge of any disputes or defenses thereon.

This assignment shall be binding upon and inure to the benefit of the parties, their successors, assigns, and personal representatives.

Signed under seal this _____ day of _____, 19_____.

_____
Assignor

6-22 ASSIGNMENT OF LIFE INSURANCE POLICY AS COLLATERAL

For good and valuable consideration, the undersigned hereby assigns and transfers, subject to the below restrictions, all rights, title, and interest in and to the life insurance policy No. _____ with the [insurance company] on the life of _____.

The undersigned Assignor warrants that he/she is the owner of the said life insurance policy and that he/she has full rights and full authority to make this assignment and transfer. The undersigned also warrants that the rights and benefits assigned hereunder are free and clear of any liens, encumbrances, adverse claims, or interest. In addition, the Assignor also warrants that he/she has no knowledge of any disputes or defenses thereon.

It is expressly agreed by both parties that the following specific rights are included in this agreement:

1. This assignment is made, and the policy is to be held as collateral security for any and all liabilities of Assignor to Assignee, either now existing, or that may arise between the Assignor and Assignee.

2. In the event of death of the insurer prior to the payment of any debts described in paragraph 1 above, the Assignee has the right to recover the remaining portion of the debts to include all interest, late penalties, and other authorized charges.

3. In the event that any payment of the debts are in default by at least 30 days, the Assignee has the right to surrender the policy to the insurance company and collect the remaining portion of the debts to include all interest, late penalties, and other authorized charges.

4. The Assignee is under no obligation to pay any premium on the said policy. Any premiums paid by the Assignee will be added to and become a part of the liabilities secured.

This assignment shall be binding upon and inure to the benefit of the parties, their successors, assigns, and personal representatives.

Signed under seal this _____ day of _____, 19_____.

_____
Assignor

6-23   GENERAL ASSIGNMENT FOR THE BENEFIT OF CREDITORS

For good and valuable consideration, the undersigned hereby unconditionally and irrevocably assigns and transfers unto _____ all rights, title, and interest in and to the following property:

This assignment is based on the Assignor's financial condition and is to be considered as an assignment for the benefit of creditors. This agreement is made with the hope of avoiding legal proceedings. The creditors who accept this assignment will share in those assets of Assignor that are not exempt by law, without preference or priority except as required by law.

The undersigned warrants that he/she has full rights and full authority to make this assignment and transfer. The undersigned also warrants that the rights and benefits assigned hereunder are free and clear of any liens, encumbrances, adverse claims, or interest except as noted.

This assignment shall be binding upon and inure to the benefit of the parties, their successors, assigns, and personal representatives.

The Assignee shall collect all income, interest, debts, etc. of the property and distribute the proceeds as follows:

1. payment of expenses of administering this assignment;
2. payment of priority, preferred, and secured claims in the priority as established by law; and
3. payment of unsecured claims on a pro rata basis.

The Assignee will not be liable to any unknown creditors or any creditor who failed to receive notice of this assignment. Assignee will not make any payments to creditors who do not accept this assignment unless so ordered by a court or approved by the Assignor.

No bond shall be required of the Assignee.

Signed under seal this _____ day of _____, 19____.

_____
Assignor

Accepted:

Date:

_____
Assignee

Accepted by the below listed creditors:

Signature of creditors accepting: Date accepted:

_____   _____

_____   _____

_____   _____

_____   _____

_____   _____

6-24 GENERAL ASSIGNMENT BY A CORPORATION FOR THE BENEFIT OF CREDITORS

For good and valuable consideration, the undersigned corporation hereby unconditionally and irrevocably assigns and transfers unto _____ all rights, title, and interest in and to the following property:

[describe property]

This assignment is based on the Assignor's financial condition and is to be considered as an assignment for the benefit of creditors. This agreement is made with the hope of avoiding legal proceedings. The creditors who accept this assignment will share in those assets of Assignor that are not exempt by law, without preference or priority except as required by law.

The corporation warrants that it has full rights and full authority to make this assignment and transfer. The corporation also warrants that the rights and benefits assigned hereunder are free and clear of any liens, encumbrances, adverse claims, or interest except as noted.

This assignment shall be binding upon and inure to the benefit of the parties, their successors, assigns, and personal representatives.

The Assignee shall collect all income, interest, debts, etc. of the property and distribute the proceeds as follows:

1. payment of expenses of administering this assignment;

2. payment of priority, preferred, and secured claims in the priority as established by law; and

3. payment of unsecured claims on a pro rata basis.

The Assignee will not be liable to any unknown creditors or any creditor who failed to receive notice of this assignment. Assignee will not make any payments to creditors who do not accept this assignment unless so ordered by a court or approved by the Assignor.

No bond shall be required of the Assignee.

This assignment for the benefit of creditors was duly approved by corporate resolution enacted by the board of directors at the regularly scheduled meeting held on [date].

Signed under seal this _____ day of _____, 19____.

_____

By _____

for the Assignor Corporation

Accepted: _____

Date: _____

_____
Assignee

Accepted by the below listed creditors:

Signature of creditors accepting: Date accepted:

_____   _____

_____   _____

_____   _____

_____   _____

_____   _____

6–25

ASSIGNMENT OF A PARTNER'S INTEREST IN PARTNERSHIP

For good and valuable consideration, receipt of which is hereby acknowledged, on [date], I assigned all my interest in the partnership of [name of partnership] located at [address of partnership]

to: [person to whom the interest is being assigned, including address]

The Assignor warrants that he/she is a general [or limited] partner in the above listed partnership and has the right to assign his/her interest in the partnership.

WITNESSED the hands of said Assignor(s) this _____ day of _____, 19_____.

_____
Assignor

_____
Assignee

State of   )

County of   ) SS

On this date, [list names of person(s) who signed above] personally appeared before me and acknowledged that the above signature(s) are valid and binding.

_____
Notary Public

My Commission expires:

6-26 ASSIGNMENT OF INTEREST IN JOINT VENTURE

For good and valuable consideration, receipt of which is hereby acknowledged, on [date], I assigned all my interest in the joint venture of [description of joint venture] located at [business address of venture]

to: [person to whom the interest is being assigned, including address]

The Assignor warrants that he/she has the right to assign his/her interest in the above described joint venture. The Assignor also warrants that his/her interest in the joint venture is as follows:

WITNESSED the hands of said Assignor(s) this _____ day of _____, 19_____.

_____
Assignor

_____
Assignee

State of   )
County of   ) SS

On this date, [list names of person(s) who signed above] personally appeared before me and acknowledged that the above signature(s) are valid and binding.

_____
Notary Public

My Commission expires:

6-27 ASSIGNMENT OF INCOME FROM A TRUST

For good and valuable consideration, receipt of which is hereby acknowledged, on [date], I assign $_____ of my share in the income from a trust fund established by the Will of _____, deceased, which trust fund is in the custody of [trustee's name and address] to: [person to whom account is being assigned, including address]

I direct the trustee to the above described trust fund to pay to the Assignee the amount named above from the income that is due or may become due until the amount stated above is paid in full.

The Assignor warrants that he/she has the right to assign his/her interest in trust fund.

WITNESSED this _____ day of _____, 19_____.

_____
Assignor

_____
Assignee

State of   )
County of   ) SS

On this date, [list names of person(s) who signed above] personally appeared before me and acknowledged that the above signature(s) are valid and binding.

_____
Notary Public

My Commission expires:

6-28   ASSIGNMENT OF CLAIM FOR DAMAGES

For good and valuable consideration, receipt of which is hereby acknowledged, on [date], I assign and transfer to: [person to whom account is being assigned, including address] Assignee any and all sums of money due or owing to me, and all claims, demands, and cause or causes of action of whatsoever kind and nature that I have had, now have, or may have against _____ of [address] or any other person or persons, whether jointly or severally, arising out of, or for, any loss, injury, or damage sustained by me in connection with: [describe incident or basis of claim].

This assignment is without recourse and assignor does not guarantee payment of the assigned claim.

The Assignor warrants that he/she has the right to assign his/her claim and appoints the Assignee as his or her attorney with power to demand and received satisfaction of the assigned claim and, in the name of the Assignor, but at Assignee's expense, to sue or any other legal process necessary for the collection of this claim.

WITNESSED this _____ day of _____, 19_____.

_____
Assignor

_____
Assignee

State of   )

County of   ) SS

On this date, [list names of person(s) who signed above] personally appeared before me and acknowledged that the above signature(s) are valid and binding.

_____
Notary Public

My Commission expires:

6-29 ASSIGNMENT OF A JUDGMENT

For good and valuable consideration, receipt of which is hereby acknowledged, on [date], I assign and transfer to: [person to whom account is being assigned, including address] Assignee, any and all sums of money due or owing to me, and all claims, demands, and cause or causes of action of whatsoever kind and nature that I have had, now have, or may have from that certain judgment against _____ of [address] to wit; [list court number and court in which judgment was granted].

This assignment is without recourse and Assignor does not guarantee payment of the assigned claim.

The Assignor warrants that he/she has the right to assign his/her judgment and appoints the Assignee as his or her attorney with power to demand and receive satisfaction of the assigned judgment and, in the name of the Assignor, but at Assignee's expense, to sue or any other legal process necessary for the collection of this judgment.

WITNESSED this _____ day of _____, 19_____.

_____
Assignor

_____
Assignee

State of   )
County of   ) SS

On this date, [list names of person(s) who signed above] personally appeared before me and acknowledged that the above signature(s) are valid and binding.

_____
Notary Public

My Commission expires:

6-30   NOTICE OF ASSIGNMENT OF CONTRACT

Certified Mail, Return Receipt Requested

Date:

To: [party to original contract]

on [date], I assigned all my interest and benefit in the following contract:

[describe contract]

to: [person to whom contract was assigned, including address]

Accordingly, any payments to be made under the contract should be addressed to the above named Assignee.

_____
Assignor

6-31   DIRECTION TO PAY

Certified Mail, Return Receipt Requested

Date:

To: [Payor name and address]

You are hereby directed to pay to [name of person who will receive the pay] [Assignee] all sums of money currently due me as the result of:

[describe the account in question]

Accordingly, all payments to be made under the above described account should be addressed to the above named Assignee until you receive directions to redirect said payments.

_____
Assignor

6-32 NOTICE OF ASSIGNMENT (BY ASSIGNEE)

Date:

To: [party to original
contract]

on [date], [name of Assignor] assigned all his/her interest and benefit in the following:

[describe what was assigned]

to: [person to whom contract was assigned, including address]

Accordingly, any payments, rights, benefits to be paid or distributed as the results of the assigned property should be addressed to the above named Assignee.

Attached to this notice is a copy of the assignment.

_____
Assignee

6-33 NOTICE OF ASSIGNMENT (BY ASSIGNOR)

Certified Mail, Return Receipt Requested

Date:

To: [party to original
   contract]

on [date], [name of Assignor] assigned all his/her interest and benefit in the following:

[describe what was assigned]

to: [person to whom contract was assigned, including address]

Accordingly, any payments, rights, benefits to be paid or distributed as the results of the assigned property should be addressed to the above named Assignee.

Attached to this notice is a copy of the assignment.

_____
Assignor

6-34

NOTICE OF ASSIGNMENT FOR BENEFIT OF CREDITORS

Certified Mail, Return Receipt Requested

Date:

To: [Creditors]

On [date], [name of Assignor] assigned all his/her interest and benefits, for the benefit of creditors in the following assets:

[describe what was assigned]

to: [person to whom contract was assigned, including address]

You are requested to inform Assignee within 15 days of the current status of the attached debt or account.

Attached to this notice is a copy of the assignment.

_____
Assignee

6-35 NOTICE OF CANCELLATION OF ASSIGNMENT

Certified Mail, Return Receipt Requested

Date:

To: [party to original
    contract]

on [date], you were notified that [name of Assignor] assigned all his/her interest and benefit in the following:

[describe what was assigned]

to: [person to whom contract was assigned, including address]

Notice is hereby given that the above stated assignment has been canceled by agreement between the parties. A copy of the cancellation agreement is attached.

Accordingly, the undersigned is now the owner of any benefits, income, etc. of the subject of the previous assignment. All payments, etc. should be forwarded to the below person at the below address:

[name and address of person to whom payments should now be made]

_____

6-36 DEMAND FOR PROOF OF ASSIGNMENT

Certified Mail, Return Receipt Requested

Date:

To: [party to giving notice of
    assignment]

on [date], you were notified that [name of Assignor] assigned all his/her interest and benefit in the following:

[describe what was assigned]

to: [person to whom contract was assigned, including address]

Demand is hereby given for reasonable proof that the [account, debt, stock certificate, etc.] was assigned.

_____

6-37 BAILMENT CONTRACT

This storage contract is entered into by [owner of property], Bailor, and [person receiving the property] Bailee, for the storage of the below listed items of property:

Article: _____ Value: _____ Condition: _____

Article: _____ Value: _____ Condition: _____

Article: _____ Value: _____ Condition: _____

Storage Charges: _____

In consideration of the payment of storage charges as listed above, bailee agrees to store the above listed articles of personal property for _____ months. Thereafter, monthly storage charges in the amount of $_____ will be due in advance on the first day of each month. This is a month–to–month contract and may be canceled by either party on a one month's notice.

Date: _____

_____
Bailor

_____
Bailee

6-38

BAILEE'S NOTICE TO RECOVER PROPERTY

Certified Mail, Return Receipt Requested

To: [owner of property]
[address of owner]

You are hereby notified that the [description of property], now on the premises of the undersigned at [address and location of property, including city and state], must be removed on or before [include date and time, including year].

This notice is given to inform you that the bailee's duties cease with respect to the bailed property on your failure to remove the property, after being given notice to remove it.

Dated: _____

_____
Bailee Signature

6-39

BAILEE'S NOTICE OF INTENT TO SELL PROPERTY

Certified Mail, Return Receipt Requested

To: [owner of property]
[address of owner]

You are hereby notified that the [description of property], now on the premises of the undersigned at [address and location of property, including city and state], will be sold at a public auction if the property is not claimed by you prior to [date and time, including year]. You were notified on [date] to remove the subject property. You have not taken any action to that extent. If the property is sold at public auction, the proceeds will first be used to cover the cost of the sale, then storage charges. If any proceeds are remaining, they will be forwarded to you at your last known address.

This notice is given to inform you that the Bailee's duties cease with respect to the bailed property on your failure to remove the property after being given notice to remove it.

Dated: _____

_____
Bailee Signature

6-40

BAILEE'S NOTICE OF ADVERSE CLAIM ON BAILED PROPERTY

Certified Mail, Return Receipt Requested

To: [owner of property]
    [address of owner]

You are hereby notified that the [description of property], now on the premises of the undersigned at [address and location of property, including city and state], is subject to the below described adverse claim:

[describe claim]

This notice is given to inform you that the Bailee's duties cease with respect to the bailed property on your failure to defend any adverse claims against the property.

The undersigned is under no obligation to defend the subject claim.

Dated: _____

_____
Bailee Signature

6-41 BAILOR'S DEMAND FOR DELIVERY OF PROPERTY

Certified Mail, Return Receipt Requested

To: [bailee of property]
    [address]

You are hereby requested to deliver the [description of property], to [address and location, including city and state].

This demand is given to inform you of the Bailor's duty to return the bailed property. Accordingly, unless the property is returned within _____ days, steps will be taken to enforce my legal rights to recover my property.

Dated: _____

_____
Bailor Signature

6-42   BAILEE'S NOTICE OF LOSS TO PROPERTY

Certified Mail, Return Receipt Requested

To: [owner of property]
    [address of owner]

You are hereby notified that the [description of property], now on the premises of the undersigned at [address and location of property, including city and state], was on [date] [lost, damaged, destroyed, etc.] as the result of:

This notice is given to inform you of the loss so that you may file any claims with your insurance company, etc.

Dated: _____

_____
Bailee Signature

6-43   BAILOR'S DEMAND FOR INFORMATION

Certified Mail, Return Receipt Requested

To: [bailee of property]
    [address]

You notified me on [date] that my property that was under your care had been [destroyed, lost, damaged, etc.]. Demand is hereby made for further information as to the circumstance of the [loss or damage].

This demand is given to inform you of the bailor's duty to explain any damage or loss to the bailed property. Accordingly, unless the information is provided within _____ days, steps will be taken to enforce my legal rights regarding this property.

Dated: _____

_____
Bailor Signature

Chapter 7

Sales Forms and Agreements

This chapter discusses contracts and sales and contains the necessary forms and agreements used in the sale of goods and services. The chapter also contains the forms and agreements pertaining to the shipment and delivery of goods.

Contracts

A contract is a promise or set of promises for which the law provides a remedy for their breach. Contracts are classified as to how they were formed. They can be expressed, implied, or in the form of a quasi contract. An *expressed contract* is one formed by the expressed agreement of the parties involved. An *implied contract* is one in which the parties' actions form the manifestations of assent. An implied contract occurs when a customer in a store picks up an item of merchandise and pays for it without making any statements regarding its purchase. The customer's actions in taking the merchandise and paying for it and the business' actions in accepting the payment imply that both agree to the sale and the purchase of the item in question. A *quasi contract* is one that the courts construct to prevent fraud or unjust enrichment on the part of one person.

Contracts may also be classified as to whether they are bilateral or unilateral. In a *bilateral contract*, each party exchanges promises (it's a promise for a promise situation). For example, Frank promises to sell a new car to Gail, and Gail in return promises to pay a sum of money for the car. A *unilateral contract* is one in which one party promises to pay for or perform some obligation when the other party does an act. For example, Joe tells Jerry that he will pay

Jerry $25 to cut Joe's lawn. In this situation, Joe is asking not for a promise from Jerry but an act.

Contracts are also classified as to their validity. A *valid contract* is enforceable by both sides to the contract. A *void contract* is totally without legal effect. A *voidable contract* is one in which one party can either enforce the contract or void it. This type of situation could occur when a contract is entered into with a minor. In most cases, the minor may either enforce the contract or void it because of lacking the capacity to enter into it. Some contracts are valid but unenforceable. For example, if the contract is required to be in writing and is not, it would be valid but unenforceable in most states.

Formation of a Contract

To enter into a contract, the parties must have mutual agreement, or assent, between them. *Mutual assent* means that both parties must agree to the same bargain at the same time. There must be an offer and an acceptance of the offer. An *offer* is a communication to another party that the person making the offer (*offerer*) wants to enter into a contractual relationship with the person to whom the offer is directed (*offeree*). To create a contract, the offer must be accepted by the offeree.

To be a valid offer, an offer's terms must be definite and certain. The essential elements of an offer include the following:

- The identity of the person or persons to whom the offer is directed.
- Identification of the subject matter of the offer.
- The compensation to be paid for the requested performance.
- The time of performance of the contract.

The identity of the person to whom the offer is directed may be determined by the actions of the offerer or by any other evidence indicating to whom the offer is addressed. Only the person to whom the offer is addressed may accept it. If a third person tries to accept an offer that is not addressed to him or her, this attempted acceptance may be accepted by the original offerer as an offer by the third person.

The subject matter of the offer is sufficiently identified if the court can ascertain the subject matter with reasonable accuracy. If the subject matter involves the sale of land, the offer must identify not only which land is involved but also the price being either offered or asked for the land. If the subject matter involves the sale of goods, the quantity must be certain or confirmable.

In many cases unspecified terms in an offer will be assumed. For example, if no time has been set for the performance of the contract, "within a reasonable time" is assumed. If no terms of payment are set forth, then the payment is presumed to be in cash. Uncertain items in the offer may often be cured by an acceptance that includes the missing items. In such a case, the offerer must accept the new items to constitute a meeting of the minds.

Termination of an Offer

An offer must be accepted in order to have a meeting of the minds before it terminates. A rejection of the offer by the person to whom the offer is directed terminates the offer. An answer to an offer that rejects part of the offer and adds new terms is a rejection of the original offer, but it is also considered a counteroffer that may be accepted by the original offerer. For example, when X is offered an opportunity to buy land at $20,000, X may counteroffer with, "Not at that price but at $15,000." This is a rejection of the original offer and thus terminates it. However, it is also a new offer addressed to the original offerer.

A mere inquiry about better terms without rejecting the original offer is not considered a counteroffer. An example is, "I am still thinking about your offer, but would you take $15,000?" In this case, the original offer has not been rejected, and it can be accepted later.

An offer is automatically terminated by the death or incapacity of either of the parties or by the destruction of the subject matter of the contract. An offer may also be terminated if the original offerer withdraws the offer before it is accepted. If the offer states that it will expire within a certain time, the offer is terminated at the end of that time, unless it is accepted sooner.

If no time limit is included in the terms of the offer, it expires after a reasonable time. *Reasonable time* is determined by looking at the subject matter of the contract and considering the customs and usages in business.

Acceptance of an Offer

Acceptance is an overt indication to assent to the terms of the offer. For an acceptance to be effective, it must be communicated to the offerer, and the acceptance must be unequivocal. Under the Uniform Commercial Code, some additional terms may be added to the acceptance. This concept is discussed in the "Sales" section of this chapter. A unilateral contract is accepted by the performance of the act requested.

Consideration

For a contract agreement to be legally enforceable, consideration is required. In most cases, *consideration* is the selling price or the act bargained for. As one court stated, "Consideration is the price for enforceability in the courts." Two elements are essential to constitute consideration. First, there must be a "bargained for exchange," and second, the "bargained for exchange" must be of legal value. If X agrees to buy a car from Y for $5,000, the consideration on X's part is to pay $5,000, whereas the consideration on Y's part is to transfer ownership of the automobile.

In most cases, consideration must be part of a new obligation, not one previously promised or given (which is called *past consideration*). As to legal value, the courts require only that the consideration have some value. Equal value is not required. Some courts, however, have held that items of token value have no legal value and thus are not of sufficient legal value to uphold contracts.

As a general rule, a preexisting duty will not be considered to be valid consideration. If the person promising to do an act already has a preexisting duty to do the act, the promise is not sufficient consideration. The exceptions to this rule are when additional or different consideration is given and when the preexisting duty is owed to a third person. Not all states accept the last exception to the preexisting duty rule. An example of a preexisting duty situation would be one in which a supplier, already under a duty to provide you with supplies at a contract price, refuses to deliver them unless you pay a higher price. Your agreement to pay the higher price would be unenforceable in most states for lack of consideration, because the supplier already had a duty to deliver the supplies at a contract rate.

Contractual Capacity

Certain individuals lack the capacity to enter into valid, enforceable contracts. For example, persons whose mental capacity is such that they are incapable of understanding the nature and effects of their acts are also incapable of entering into a valid contract.

Minors are restricted in their ability to enter into enforceable contracts. The basic rule is that if a contract is not liable for the necessities of life, minors can cancel any contract they enter into. However, if a minor wishes to affirm the contract, the minor may do so and thus force the other party to comply with the terms of the contract.

There is a conflict of authority among the states as to whether intoxication at the time of entering into a contract makes the contract void. In most states, if the other party knew of the state of intoxication, he or she cannot take advantage of the drunken party. If, however, the other party did not know that he or she was dealing with a drunken individual, then the contract is enforceable.

Defenses to Enforcement of Contracts

Several common defenses are used to prevent the enforcement of a contract. The most common is that a valid and enforceable contract was never entered into between the parties.

A mutual mistake that goes to the heart of the agreement prevents the formation of a contract because there is no meeting of the minds between the offerer and the offeree. For the mistake to be sufficient to prevent the existence of a legal contract, the mistake must pertain to an essential part of the contract. For example, I offer to buy Y's car for $500. But Y, having two cars, thinks I am buying one car whereas I intended to buy the other car. There is a mutual mistake here as to which car I am buying, so there is no agreement, and thus no contract.

If the mistake is unilateral (i.e., only by Party 1), it usually does not prevent the formation of a valid contract. If, however, Party 2 knew or should have known about the mistake, Party 2 cannot take advantage of Party 1's mistake. When there is mistake as to the value of an article, the courts usually enforce the contract, because the value of the article is a common risk taken in most contracts.

Generally, the courts set aside a contract if fraud or misrepresentation concerns a material part of the agreement. Contracts that are illegal or that violate public policy are also unenforceable. Typical are gambling contracts, contracts relating to crimes, and contracts that charge an illegal interest rate.

Statute of Frauds

The *statute of frauds* is the common law term given to those state statutes that require certain contracts to be in writing to be enforceable. Verbal contracts are usually valid, but certain agreements must be in writing. Agreements usually required in writing are promises by an executor or administrator of an estate to pay the estate's debts out of his or her own funds, promises to pay the debts of another, promises made in consideration of marriage, contracts that cannot be performed within a year, sales of goods valued at $500 or more, and agreements that transfer an interest in land.

Agreements that transfer an interest in land are the most common type that have to be in writing. Leases in excess of a year are also required to be in writing. Timber, fruit, crops, or similar products are not an interest in land if they are to be severed by the seller. Mortgages and other security devices on real estate are considered as an interest in land.

To determine if a contract by its terms cannot be performed within a year, look at the date the contract was entered into. For example, a contract of employment to run from January 1 until December 30 would have to be in writing if it were entered into prior to December 29 of the prior year. A contract to employ someone for life can be performed within a year because the person might die within the year. This contract is not required to be in writing.

As noted, a promise for the sale of goods valued at $500 or more is required to be in writing by a section of the Uniform Commercial Code. See the discussion on "Sales" in this chapter.

The writing that is required under the statute of frauds is acceptable if it contains the identity of parties involved, the identity of the subject matter, the terms and conditions of the agreement, consideration, and the signature of the party against whom the contract is to be enforced. This writing can involve more than one document if they are logically connected. In addition, the writing may be made after the contract is entered into. A contract that fails to comply with the statute is not void but only unenforceable.

In many states, partial performance of the contract removes the statute's requirement. In other states, many courts allow a reasonable recovery based on the value of the goods rather than on the contract price, to prevent fraud. If the party admits in court that a contract exists, the admission satisfies the statute of fraud.

Third Parties: Rights and Duties

The general rule is that a contract creates rights and duties only on the parties to the contract. There are several situations, however, in which a contract either creates duties or rights on persons not involved in its formation. The most common situations are those in which the contract is primarily to benefit a third person (third–party beneficiary contracts) and those involving the assignments of rights in a contract.

A *third-party beneficiary contract* is one in which one person enters into a contract with a second person, who is to render a benefit to a third person. For example, I want to give a new car to my son. I contract with the automobile dealer to deliver a car to my son, and I pay for it. In this case, my primary motive for entering into the contract is to benefit my son. My son could sue the automobile dealer for breach of contract if the dealer fails, without adequate justification to deliver the car.

To sue for the nonperformance of a contract, the third party beneficiary must be the intended beneficiary. The third party beneficiary cannot sue if he or she is only an indirect or incidental, beneficiary. An *indirect beneficiary* indirectly benefits from the contract, which was not entered into for his or her direct benefit. For example, I enter into a contract to buy you a new car from a local automobile dealer if you will rebuild my building. Although the automobile dealer will indirectly benefit from the contract, it was not intended for his or her direct benefit. Thus, he or she cannot sue for failure of one party to perform under the contract.

Intended third–party beneficiary contracts are grouped under two general classes: creditors and donees. A *creditor beneficiary contract* is one in which the agreement is made to pay a debt to a third person. A *donee beneficiary contract* occurs when the contract's purpose is to give a gift to a third person. The third person may enforce his or her rights under the contract only after he or she learns about it and by conduct or otherwise accepts the benefits of it. Benefits cannot be forced on third persons.

Interpretation of Contracts The courts use several general rules in cases involving contract disputes. Foremost is the rule that a contract will be construed as a whole contract. Specific clauses in the contract will be presumed to make the contract effective as a whole. Words will be presumed to be used in accordance with their ordinary meanings unless they are given special meanings by the parties. If different provisions in the contract are inconsistent, the courts will give preference to written phrases over typed or printed ones, and to typed phrases over printed ones. In cases in which the parties' intentions are unclear, the courts will look to the customs and usage in the particular business and locale involved.

Parole Evidence Rule The Parole Evidence Rule is used in determining the parties' intentions at the time a contract was entered into. The courts do not permit parole evidence (i.e., oral statements) that conflict with the written agreement if the written agreement was intended to be a complete expression of the parties' agreement. For the rule to apply, the courts must first determine that the written agreement was the final expression of the agreement and that it was intended as a complete record of the parties' agreement.

The purpose behind the Parole Evidence Rule is to prevent the parties from disputing the provisions of a written contract and thus to reduce the uncertainty involved in contractual law. Exceptions to the rule are additional agreements made after the written agreement was executed and those agreements that do not vary the terms in the written agreement. The courts will also overlook the rule to prevent fraud.

Discharge of Contractual Duties

The usual method of discharging contractual duties is by performance. Contractual duties are also discharged if the contract becomes illegal because of a change in the law. All the parties to the contract by agreement may cancel the contract or modify the duties under it.

A difficult question in cases of the discharge of performance is when it becomes impossible to perform the duties. If no one can perform the duties, then they are usually discharged (i.e., performance is excused). If the duties are impossible to perform except by the party involved, then they usually are not excusable. Some recent court cases have excused the performance of contractual duties when performance has become impracticable. The test for impracticability is if performance will cause an extreme and unreasonable hardship to require the party to perform it. A discharge by *novation* occurs when the parties substitute a new contract for the current agreement. In this situation, the old contract is discharged, and the new assignment determines the rights, duties, and benefits of the parties.

Account Stated Contract

An *account stated contract* is one in which the parties agree as to the final amount one party owes to the other party. Such a contract occurs when there are several transactions between the parties, such as those in an open account. This agreement merges all the individual transactions between the parties and discharges all rights and duties except those contained in the account stated contract.

To qualify as an account stated contract, there must be more than one previous transaction between the parties, and they must agree on the amount due. This agreement may be presumed by the courts when one party sends the other a statement of balance due on the account and the receiving party does not object within a reasonable period of time (which varies among states). To prevent an account stated contract, immediately object to any incorrect account mailed to you.

Breach of Contracts

To determine the effects of a breach of contract, it first must be decided whether it is a material or a minor breach. A minor breach does not relieve the other party from performing his or her duties under the contract. In cases of minor breach, the only remedy is to sue for damages.

In cases involving material breaches of contract, the other party may treat the contract as ended and sue for damages. The nonbreaching party is not obligated to perform his or her duties under the contract. A minor breach and a statement by the breaching party that she or he does not intend to complete the duties under the contract is an anticipatory repudiation of the agreement. The nonbreaching party may then terminate the contract and sue for damages. Whether the breach is material depends on the following:

- The benefits the nonbreaching party loses as the result of the breach. The larger the loss, the more likely it is to be considered a material breach.
- The extent to which the injured party may be compensated for the loss by the payment of damages.
- Prior failures of the breaching party to perform to the contractual duties.
- The hardship caused to the other party by the breach.
- Whether the breach was negligent or willful.
- The likelihood that the breaching party will perform the remainder of the duties under the contract.

Remedies for Breach of Contract

The most frequent remedy for breach of contract is the payment of damages. Compensatory damages are for reasonably foreseeable losses suffered as the result of the breach. Punitive damages are sometimes awarded by the courts as punishment to the breaching party. Punitive damages are usually not awarded in breach of contract cases. Nominal damages may be given in those cases where a breach of contract is established but no damages are proven.

In certain cases, the courts will order that the breaching party specifically perform the duties under the contract. Most of the time, specific performance is available only when money damages are insufficient.

Sales

A sale is a contract governed by the law of contracts. However, the Uniform Commercial Code (UCC) has established some special rules that apply to the sale of goods by merchants.

Article 2 of the UCC does not apply to the sale of land or intangibles (e.g., stocks, bonds). If you are a merchant involved in the sales of goods or if you buy your supplies from a merchant, you should refer to the provisions of Article 2. In some states, minor provisions of Article 2 were modified when they were enacted into law. Therefore, before relying on the article, check with your local library to see if any modifications are in effect in your state.

Secured Transactions

The term *secured transaction* is used to describe the financing of the sale of goods that occurs when a security interest is retained by the person financing the purchase. A secured transaction includes conditional sales contracts, chattel mortgages, factoring, pledges, and trust receipts. Article 9 of the UCC deals with secured transactions. It does not apply to assignments of wages, state statutory liens such as mechanics' liens (except as to the priorities of the liens), or to transfers by a government or one of its agencies.

Product Warranties

The normal warranties that accompany any products or merchandise your business sells are discussed later in this chapter. Disclaimers of warranties and limited warranties are also discussed. *Warranty* is a contractual term concerning some aspect of a product, such as its title, its quality, and its fitness for a particular purpose.

There are two basic types of warranties: implied and expressed. An *implied warranty* is assumed in the sale of a product unless a specific disclaimer is agreed on when the product is sold. *Expressed warranties* are those agreed on by the parties at the time of the sale.

Words such as *warrant* or *guarantee* are not required in a warranty to validate it. Any promises the seller makes pertaining to the product (and therefore becoming a part of the contractual bargain) establish an expressed warranty that the product conforms to the promises.

A statement of a product's value is not considered to be a warranty but only the personal opinion of the seller. The seller's claim that a product is worth $3,000 is not a guarantee of the value of the product. It will not support a breach of warranty action when the buyer learns that the item is not worth $3,000. A similar situation exists if the seller says the product will "probably" not need repair in the next six months. However, the seller's saying that the item will "not" need repair in the next six months may be considered a warranty.

In many cases, the courts have ruled that promises contained in advertisements are express warranties, especially when the advertisements imply that the products have certain qualities. A seller's description of a product has also been held to be an expressed warranty. One court held that the description of a product as "boned chicken" constituted a warranty that the product was indeed boned chicken.

In cases involving the use of product samples, the courts have stated that an implied warranty exists guaranteeing that the products are of the same type and quality as their samples. This concept also applies to the sale of bulk products by samples. In sales by models, a warranty also exists guaranteeing that the model is an accurate representation of the actual goods.

Uniform Commercial Code

The Uniform Commercial Code (UCC) provides the statutory base for most warranties involving the sale of personal property. For a warranty to exist, there first must be a sale. In one case a shopper was injured by a soft drink bottle that exploded in a self-service supermarket before she reached the cashier to complete the sale. The court held that a warranty did not exist because the sale had not been completed. (*Note:* The shopper recovered damages on other grounds.)

The two primary warranties implied by the UCC are the implied warranty of merchantability and the implied warranty of fitness for a particular purpose. Also, unless there is a disclaimer, there is an implied warranty that the product does not infringe a patent or copyright. Any disclaimer of implied warranties is required to be prominently set forth in clear language.

Fraudulent Representations

There is a key difference between fraudulent representations and warranties. A *fraudulent representation* is a false statement about the condition of the product, whereas a *warranty* is a guarantee as to the fitness or condition of the product. In some cases, a statement by the seller may be both a fraudulent representation and a warranty. For example, in cases involving statements about the ownership or right to sell the product, a false statement that the seller has the right to sell the item is both a warranty of title and a fraudulent representation.

If there is a breach of warranty, the buyer must sue for damages under the contract, and the only recoverable damage is for the monetary loss reasonably foreseeable as the result of the breach of contract. In cases involving fraudulent representation, however, the buyer may sue not only for monetary losses but also for additional money for punitive damages.

Implied Warranty of Title

Any time a product is sold, there is an implied warranty that the seller either owns the product or has the right to sell it, that the product will be free of any security interests or other liens, that the product will be delivered free of the rightful claim of any third person, and that the buyer will receive a marketable title to the product. This implied warranty is considered to be a preferred warranty and is implied in all sales unless clearly waived by the buyer.

Implied Warranty of Fitness

Unless otherwise informed, the buyer has a right to expect that the product is free from defects of materials or workmanship and that the product is reasonably fit for its intended purpose. There is also an implied warranty that the goods are of "merchantable quality" or free from defects rendering them "unmerchantable." Other implied warranties of fitness include promises that the products are adequately contained, packaged, and labeled and that they conform to the promises made on the label.

The implied warranty of fitness does not apply to products manufactured to the buyer's specifications. In these cases, the buyer takes the risk that the product will be fit for its intended purpose. The seller, however, warrants that the product will conform to the buyer's specifications.

Disclaimers

Disclaimers, or *waivers of warranties,* are often called "as is" contracts. In this type of contract, the buyer assumes all risks as to the fitness of the product and accepts the product "as is." The buyer assumes any expense in the product's repair or servicing. To defeat any implied warranties of fitness, the buyer must accept the "as is" statement before the contract is complete. Similar statements, such as "as they stand" and "with all faults," are sufficient if it is clear that the buyer accepts the product in its present condition. *Note:* There is still an implied warranty of title.

The "as is" contract is not a favorite with courts, and they tend to find reasons to ignore the "as is" restriction. If you sell products in this manner, make sure that the buyer is aware that the product is being sold "as is." In one case, a drum of insecticide was labeled, "Seller makes no warranty of any kind, expressed or implied, concerning the use of this product. Buyer assumes all risk in use or handling, whether in accordance with directions or not." The court stated that this statement would be an effective disclaimer of any warranties only if the seller could establish that the buyer was aware of the disclaimer at the time of the purchase.

Any disclaimers regarding the product can be printed on notices, letterheads, labels, and the like, provided that their existence is conveyed to the buyer before the contract is completed. The disclaimer can be verbal, but problems of proof can occur when they are entirely verbal.

If the written contract contains statements excluding other agreements, such as "this contract constitutes the entire agreement of the parties," the courts may not allow the buyer to establish any disclaimers that were not included. This rule is based on the concept that the entire contract is contained in the document and that to allow evidence of any other disclaimers would conflict with the written contract.

The buyer consents only to honest disclaimers of warranties. The courts will ignore any disclaimer that is fraudulent.

Conflicting Warranties

Conflicts sometimes occur in the separate warranties of the products being sold. The courts will try to interpret the terms of the warranties in a manner that wil carry out the parties' intentions when the contract was entered into. If this is not possible, a rule of construction is that specific descriptions or terms override general descriptions or terms.

Limited Warranties

As noted earlier, expressed warranties are made by the seller regarding the fitness and other characteristics of the product. Expressed warranties are in addition to any implied warranties.

If a seller wants to include only certain guarantees in the sale of a product, the seller should give a limited warranty. In a limited warranty, the seller expressly states that the only guarantees applying to the sale are those listed in the contract or in accompanying papers. A sale with a limited warranty also automatically includes the implied warranty of title unless otherwise stated. Limited warranties are often used.

Privity of Contract

Privity of contract is the term the courts use to describe the original parties to the contract. In some jurisdictions, the courts have ruled that for a warranty to be applied, a privity of contract must exist between the seller and the person who suffered an injury or damage because of the breach of a warranty. In these jurisdictions, privity of contract between the plaintiff and the defendant is essential to recovery on a warranty.

In one famous case involving privity of contract, a Mr. McPearson was driving his new Buick when the front wheel failed and he was injured. He sued General Motors for breach of contract and claimed that GM had violated the warranty of fitness in selling him a defective auto. General Motors contended that the auto was sold to a dealer and not to McPearson and that therefore there was no privity of contract and the warranty did not cover McPearson. In rejecting this argument, the court abolished the requirement for privity of contract in warranty cases. The court stated that because the auto was sold to the dealer who, GM knew, would resell it, the warranty extended to the ultimate purchaser. This rule (decided in 1919) has been accepted in almost every state.

The trend is clearly toward eliminating the requirement of privity in warranty cases. In most states, any warranties included in the sale of a product now extend to the buyer's family, household, and guests, and to other persons expected to use the product.

Magnuson-Moss Consumer Warranty Act

The basic federal statute on warranties of consumer goods is the Magnuson–Moss Consumer Warranty Act. That act does not require you as a seller to give any warranties with the sale of goods or products. If you do provide any expressed written warranty, the warranty must have a prominent heading, such as Limited Warranty or Full Warranty. *Note:* Limiting the warranty in any manner makes the warranty a limited warranty. The act applies to all merchants involved in interstate commerce. (*Note:* Refer to the discussion in Chapter 1 regarding the meaning of the term *interstate commerce.*. There are few products or goods sold today that are not considered as part of interstate commerce.)

The expressed warranties must contain in clear and understandable language the following terms:

- The identity of the persons to whom the warranties are extended. *Note:* If this provision is omitted, then the warranties are extended to any person coming into contact with the product. For example, if a warranty will be limited to only the original consumer purchaser, this limitation must be clearly stated in the warranty.

- A description of the products or goods covered by the warranties.

- A description of the products or goods excluded by the warranties.

- Remedial action to be provided by the warrantor (person issuing the warranties) if defects, malfunctions, or failures occur.

- The period covered by the warranties.

- The steps or procedures that the consumer should follow to obtain relief under the warranties.

- Information on any informal procedures for dispute resolution that will be used in case of disputes under the warranties.

- All limitations or exclusions of coverage of the warranties.

- Information regarding the consumer's legal rights—for example, a statement such as: "This warranty is a valid contract and provides you with specific legal rights and other rights, which may vary from state to state."
- Any limitations on the duration and coverage of implied warranties. *Note:* Some states restrict limitations on implied warranties.

The Magnuson–Moss Act does not supersede the rules of the UCC. The UCC applies state remedies, and the Magnuson–Moss Act applies federal remedies.

Uniform Vendor and Purchaser Risk Act

To eliminate some of the difficult questions regarding which warranties apply to the sale of real property (i.e., buildings and land), many states have adopted the Uniform Vendor and Purchaser Risk Act. Its purpose is to establish a uniform law regarding warranties in the purchase of real estate.

The act states that any executed contract for the purchase and sale of real property shall include an agreement giving the parties the following rights and duties unless the contract expressly provides otherwise:

1. If all or a material part of the property is destroyed before legal title and possession have been transferred (without fault of the buyer), the seller cannot enforce the terms of the contract and the buyer has a right to have any portion of the purchase price paid returned.

2. If all or a material part of the property is destroyed without fault of the seller after the buyer has accepted possession or legal title to the property, the buyer is not excused from the duty to pay the agreed price.

The theory behind this act is that, by establishing clear and concise rules as to who will suffer the loss in the event all or a material part of the property is destroyed, the parties can take the necessary steps to get insurance to protect themselves.

Forms in This Chapter

- FORM 7–1: CONTRACT FOR PURCHASE OF PERSONAL PROPERTY. Used for the purchase of personal property.

- FORM 7–2: CONDITIONAL SALES CONTRACT. Used to purchase goods conditionally.

- FORM 7–3: SALE OR RETURN CONTRACT. Used to sell goods on a sale or return basis.

- FORM 7–4: SALE ON APPROVAL. Used to buy or sell goods on approval.

- FORM 7–5: BILL OF SALE (WARRANTY). Used when there are warranties attached to the sale.

- FORM 7–6: BILL OF SALE (WITH ENCUMBRANCES). Used when there are encumbrances.

- FORM 7–7: BILL OF SALE (QUITCLAIM). Used when goods are sold without normal warranties.

- FORM 7–8: BILL OF SALE FOR MOTOR VEHICLE. A bill of sale for a motor vehicle.

- FORM 7–9: RETURN AUTHORIZATION. Authorizes the return of goods.

- FORM 7–10: RETURN OF GOODS RECEIVED ON APPROVAL. Returns goods received on approval.

- FORM 7–11: CONDITIONAL ACCEPTANCE OF NONCONFORMING GOODS. Conditionally accepts nonconforming goods.

- FORM 7–12: NOTICE OF DEFECTIVE GOODS. Notifies seller that goods received are defective.

- FORM 7–13: CONDITIONAL PAYMENT FOR GOODS. Pays for goods but retains the right to return them if they are not acceptable.

- FORM 7–14: DEMAND FOR PARTICULARS ON REJECTED GOODS. Demands more detail on rejected goods.

- FORM 7–15: REPLACING REJECTED GOODS. Notifies the buyer that seller is replacing rejected goods.

- FORM 7–16: INSTRUCTIONS FOR RETURNING REJECTED GOODS. Provides instructions on returning rejected goods.

- FORM 7–17: DELIVERY OF SUBSTITUTED GOODS. Notifies buyer that seller is sending substituted goods.

- FORM 7–18: NOTICE OF WRONGFUL REJECTION. Notifies buyer that goods were wrongly rejected.

- FORM 7–19: LATE DELIVERY OF GOODS. Notifies buyer that goods will be delivered late.

- FORM 7–20: INABILITY TO FILL ORDER. Notifies the buyer that seller is unable to fill buyer's order.

- FORM 7–21: RECEIPT OF GOODS. Acknowledges receipt of goods.

- FORM 7–22: LIMITED WARRANTY CLAUSE. A clause that may be included in a contract for the sale of goods.

- FORM 7–23: LIABILITY EXCLUSION CLAUSE. A clause that may be used to limit liability in a contract for the sale of goods.

- FORM 7–24: CHECKLIST FOR EXPRESS WARRANTY REQUIREMENTS. Can be used to ensure compliance with the Magnuson–Moss Act.

- FORM 7–25: BID REQUEST. Requests bids on goods.

- FORM 7–26: NOTICE THAT SALE OF GOODS WILL BE ON C.O.D. TERMS. Notifies buyer that C.O.D. terms will apply unless buyer can arrange alternative financing.

- FORM 7–27: CONSIGNMENT SALE. Used for sale of goods on consignment.

- FORM 7–28: INVITATION FOR QUOTATION. Requests price quotations on goods.

- FORM 7–29: DEMAND FOR DELIVERY OF GOODS. Demands delivery of goods that have not been delivered by the scheduled delivery date.

- FORM 7–30: CANCELLATION OF PURCHASE ORDER (LATE DELIVERY). Cancels a purchase order that has not been delivered by the due date.

- FORM 7–31: REJECTION OF GOODS (NONCONFORMING). Rejects goods that do not conform to the purchase order.

- FORM 7–32: PARTIAL REJECTION OF GOODS (NONCONFORMING). Rejects that part of a shipment of goods that does not conform to the purchase order.

- FORM 7–33: RETURN OF REJECTED GOODS. Notifies a seller that buyer is still waiting for instruction as to the disposition of rejected goods.

- FORM 7–34: ACCEPTANCE OF NONCONFORMING GOODS. Accepts nonconforming goods.

7–1　CONTRACT FOR PURCHASE OF PERSONAL PROPERTY

This contract is for the purchase of personal property made by and between _____ (Seller) and _____ (Buyer).

For good and valuable consideration the parties agree as follows:

1. Seller agrees to sell and Buyer agrees to buy the below described property:

2. The mutually agreed purchase price is $_____ ; payable as follows: $_____ as a deposit due no later than _____, 19_____. The balance of $_____ will be payable on delivery by cash or certified check.

3. Seller warrants it has good and legal title to the said property and has full authority to sell it. The said property is to be sold by warranty bill of sale free and clear of all liens, encumbrances, liabilities, and adverse claims of any kind.

4. Said property is sold as is. There is no warranty of merchantability, fitness, or working order or condition of the property except that it is sold in its present condition.

5. The parties agree that title to the property will transfer to the Buyer when said property is delivered to the Buyer's address.

6. This agreement shall be binding upon and inure to the benefit of the parties, their assigns, successors, and personal representatives.

IN WITNESS WHEREOF the undersigned have hereunto set their hands this _____ day of _____, 19_____.

_____
Buyer

_____
Seller

7-2 CONDITIONAL SALES CONTRACT

For good and valuable consideration, this conditional sales contract is entered into between _____ (Seller) and _____ (Buyer). Seller agrees to sell and the Buyer agrees to buy the following goods on a conditional sale:

Sale price	$ _____
Sales tax	$ _____
Other charges	$ _____
Finance charges	$ _____
Total purchase price	$ _____

Deductions
    Down payment $ _____
    Other credits $ _____

Total deductions	$ _____
Amount financed	$ _____
ANNUAL INTEREST RATE	_____%

The amount financed is payable in _____ monthly payments of $_____ each, starting on the _____ day of the month of _____, 19____, and continuing on the same day each succeeding month until paid in full.

The title to the goods remain with the Seller until payment of the full purchase price, subject to allocation of payments and release of security interest as required by law. The Buyer agrees to keep the goods free from other liens and encumbrances and not to remove the goods from the below address without the written consent of the Seller.

Buyer agrees to execute all financing statements as may be required of Seller to perfect this conditional sales contract.

The entire balance shall become immediately due upon default on any installment due or other breach of this agreement.

In the event of a default, Seller may enter upon the premises of the Buyer and reclaim said goods. If the Seller retakes the goods he/she has the right to resell them for credit to the balance purchased, and Seller may reacquire same all as further defined and set forth under state law.

On the demand of the Seller, the Buyer shall keep the goods adequately insured with the Seller named as the loss payee. On request, the Buyer shall provide Seller with proof of insurance.

In the event of default, Buyer shall be responsible to pay attorney fees, collection costs, and other fees associated with enforcement of this agreement. This agreement is binding upon and inure to the benefit of the parties, their successors, assigns, and personal representatives.

The full balance shall become due on default. Upon default, Seller will have the further right to retake the goods, hold and dispose of same and collect expenses, together with any deficiency due from the Buyer, but subject to the Buyer's right to redeem pursuant to law and the Uniform Commercial Code.

This agreement shall also be in default upon the death, insolvency, or bankruptcy of Buyer.

Signed under seal and accepted this _____ day of _____, 19_____.

_____
Buyer

_____
Seller

7-3   SALE OR RETURN CONTRACT

To: [buyer,
     address]

Dear Sir/Madam:

As per your order, the goods delivered on the attached invoice are sent to you on a "sale or return" basis. They are sent for examination or inspection only. They remain our property and will be returned to us on our demand.

Until you return the goods to us, you shall assume responsibility for any damages or loss to the goods. Accordingly, you have no right to sell, encumber, or otherwise dispose of the goods unless you accept them and pay for them or you receive our written consent.

Upon acceptance by you, the balance of the purchase price shall be paid within the terms stated on the attached invoice. Until goods are accepted by you, we retain title to them.

Thank you for your business.

Sincerely,

7-4　SALE ON APPROVAL

To: [buyer,
　　address]

Dear Sir/Madam:

As per your order, the goods delivered on the attached invoice are sold on a "sale on approval" basis. Accordingly, you have _____ days after receipt of the goods to return them in good condition and receive full credit or refund, including cost of return. If the goods are not returned within that time period, they will be deemed accepted without right of return.

Upon acceptance by you, the balance of the purchase price shall be paid within the terms stated on the attached invoice. Until goods are accepted by you, we retain title to them.

Thank you for your business.

Sincerely,

7-5 BILL OF SALE (WARRANTY)

For good and valuable consideration, and the payment of the sum of $_____, receipt of which is hereby acknowledged, the Seller hereby sells and transfers to the Buyer the following described personal property:

The Seller warrants to Buyer and its assigns and successors that Seller has good and marketable title to said property and the full authority to sell and transfer the property free of all liens, encumbrances, liabilities, and adverse claims of every nature and description whatsoever. The said property is sold and transferred free of all liens, encumbrances, liabilities and adverse claims of every nature and description whatsoever.

Seller further warrants to Buyer that Seller will fully defend, protect, indemnify, and hold harmless the Buyer and Buyer's lawful successors and assigns from any adverse claim thereto.

Except as noted above, the goods are sold in "as is condition" and where presently located.

Signed under seal and accepted this _____ day of _____, 19_____.

_____
Seller

_____
Address

7-6 BILL OF SALE (WITH ENCUMBRANCES)

For good and valuable consideration, and the payment of the sum of $_____, receipt of which is hereby acknowledged, the Seller hereby sells and transfers to the Buyer the following described personal property:

The Seller warrants to Buyer and its assigns and successors that Seller, that except as noted below, has good and marketable title to said property and the full authority to sell and transfer the property free of all liens, encumbrances, liabilities, and adverse claims of every nature and description whatsoever. Except as noted below, the said property is sold and transferred free of all liens, encumbrances, liabilities, and adverse claims of every nature and description whatsoever.

The said property is sold subject to a certain security interest, lien, or encumbrance on said property in the favor of _____ (lienholder) with a balance owed thereon of $_____. Buyer agrees to assume and promptly pay said secured debt and indemnify and hold Seller harmless from any claim arising thereon.

Seller further warrants to Buyer that, except for claims arising out of above encumbrance, Seller will fully defend, protect, indemnify, and hold harmless the Buyer and Buyer's lawful successors and assigns from any other adverse claim thereto.

Except as noted above, the goods are sold in "as is condition" and where presently located.

Signed under seal and accepted this _____ day of _____, 19_____.

_____
Seller

_____
Address

7-7   BILL OF SALE (QUITCLAIM)

For good and valuable consideration, and the payment of the sum of $_____, receipt of which is hereby acknowledged, the Seller hereby sells and transfers with quitclaim covenants to the Buyer the following described personal property:

The Seller hereby sells and transfers only such rights, title, and interest as Seller may hold. The said property is sold subject to such prior liens, encumbrances, and adverse claims, if any, that may exist, and Seller hereby disclaims any and all warranties thereto.

Except as noted above, the goods are sold in "as is condition" and where presently located.

Signed under seal and accepted this _____ day of _____, 19_____.

_____
Seller

_____
Address

7-8

BILL OF SALE FOR MOTOR VEHICLE

For good and valuable consideration and the payment of the sum of $_____, receipt of which is hereby acknowledged, the Seller hereby sells and transfers to _____ Buyer and his/her successors and assigns the below described motor vehicle:

Make:
Model:
Year:
License Number:
Vehicle Serial Number:
Color:

Seller warrants that he/she is the legal owner of the above described vehicle and that the vehicle is being sold free and clear of all adverse liens, claims, and encumbrances and that Seller has full right and authority to sell and transfer the said vehicle. Seller will protect, defend, save harmless, and indemnify Buyer from any adverse claims thereto.

The said vehicle is sold "as is" without any expressed or implied warranty as to condition or working order.

Signed under seal and accepted this _____ day of _____, 19_____.

_____
Seller

_____
Address

7-9   RETURN AUTHORIZATION

To: [customer,
    address]

Re: Your order no._____;   our invoice no. _____

Dear Sir/Madam:

In regard to the above referenced goods, this letter is your authorization to return the goods. We regret that you are not satisfied with the goods. As per our guarantee, you will be given full credit or a refund when we have received the goods.

Please include a copy of this letter and a copy of our invoice with the goods. To assist us in improving our services, please indicate below the reason(s) that the goods were not acceptable to you:

Sincerely,

7-10   RETURN OF GOODS RECEIVED ON APPROVAL

Date:

To: [seller,
    address]

Re: Our order _____; your invoice no. _____

Dear Madam/Sir:

The above order contained our right to return the goods if we did not approve them. Accordingly, we are electing to return the goods that we received on approval.

[optional]
The reasons we are returning the goods are as follows:

Sincerely,

7-11 CONDITIONAL ACCEPTANCE OF NONCONFORMING GOODS

Date:

To: [seller,
    address]

Re: Our order no._____;   your invoice no. _____

Dear Madam/Sir:

We have received your shipment in response to our above order. The goods received, however, do not conform to the specifications set forth in our order as noted below:

We are prepared to accept the nonconforming goods if you will allow us a credit of $_____, making the total purchase price of the order $_____. Please advise us immediately as to whether this arrangement is satisfactory.

Unless we receive information otherwise within the next 15 days, we will reject the nonconforming goods.

Sincerely,

7-12   NOTICE OF DEFECTIVE GOODS

Date:

To: [seller,
   address]

Re: Our order no. _____; your invoice no. _____

Dear Madam/Sir:

We are in receipt of the goods shipped by you on [date] in response to our purchase order referenced above. Please be advised that the goods received are defective as noted below:

Please advise us as to the action you are going to take to remedy this problem. Unless we receive a satisfactory response within 15 days, we will take the necessary action, to include possible legal action, to protect our rights.

Sincerely,

7-13   CONDITIONAL PAYMENT FOR GOODS

Date:

To: [seller,
   address]

Re: Conditional payment of goods received in accordance
      with our purchase order _____.

Dear Madam/Sir:

We have received goods from you in response to our purchase order. Payment is enclosed pursuant to your request. We have not, however, had the opportunity to inspect the goods to determine if they meet our requirements and specifications. Accordingly, we reserve the right to reject any nonconforming goods discovered after a full and proper inspection. We also expect proper credit for any goods discovered to be nonconforming.

Sincerely,

7–14 DEMAND FOR PARTICULARS ON REJECTED GOODS

Date:

To: [buyer,
    address]

Re: Your letter of _____, 19____.

Dear Madam/Sir:

As per your purchase order, we delivered goods to you. You rejected the shipment without explaining the reasons for the rejection. Please provide us with the particulars regarding the rejected goods.

Unless we received adequate explanation within 15 days, we will take the necessary action, which may include legal proceedings, to protect our rights.

Sincerely,

7–15 REPLACING REJECTED GOODS

Date:

To: [buyer,
    address]

Re: Replacement of Rejected Goods

Dear Sir/Madam:

Your notice of rejection of our goods has been received. Please be advised that we are immediately shipping you replacement goods. Please return the rejected goods to us. We will credit your account with the cost of returning the subject goods.

We regret any inconveniences this may have caused you.

Sincerely,

7–16　INSTRUCTIONS FOR RETURNING REJECTED GOODS

Date:

To: [buyer,
　　address]

Re: Return of Rejected Goods

Dear Sir/Madam:

We are in receipt of your notice of rejected goods. Please return at our cost the goods. Shipment instructions are as follows:

We are sorry for any inconveniences that this may have caused you.

Sincerely,

7–17 DELIVERY OF SUBSTITUTED GOODS

Date:

To: [customer,
     address]

Re: Your purchase order of _____, 19____ .

Dear Sir/Madam:

We have received your purchase order of [date]. Unfortunately, we can not deliver the specific goods that you have ordered because of:

We do have similar goods that appear to meet your requirements. We are shipping the substituted goods for your approval. The substituted goods differ from the ordered goods in the following manner:

The purchase price of the substituted goods is $ _____ .
If the substituted goods are not acceptable to you, please return them as soon as possible. You may return them by the same carrier that delivered them. We will, of course, pay the return shipping charges.
Sorry for any convenience that this may cause you.

Sincerely,

7–18 NOTICE OF WRONGFUL REJECTION

Date:

To: [buyer,
     address]

Re: Your rejection of goods

Dear Sir/Madam:

Pursuant to your purchase order of [date], we shipped goods to you. We have since been notified that you have rejected the subject goods. The goods met or exceeded the specifications contained in your purchase order. Accordingly, your rejection was without legal justification.

In view of the above, unless we receive full payment within 15 days from the date of this letter, we will take the necessary action to protect our interest. The necessary action may include the institution of legal proceedings.

Sincerely,

7–19 LATE DELIVERY OF GOODS

Date:

To: [buyer,
     address]

Re: Notice of late delivery of goods

Dear Sir/Madam:

We have received your purchase order of [date]. We are unable to deliver the ordered goods until [date]. This late delivery is because of:

We regret any inconveniences that this may have caused you.

Sincerely,

7–20 INABILITY TO FILL ORDER

Date:

To: [buyer,
     address]

Re: Notice of inability to fill order

Dear Sir/Madam:

We have received your purchase order of [date]. We are unable to deliver the ordered goods because of:

Enclosed is your check. We regret any inconveniences that this may have caused you.

Sincerely,

7-21 RECEIPT OF GOODS

Date:

To: [seller]

The undersigned hereby acknowledges receipt of the goods described on the attached invoice. They have been inspected and found to be without defect and conforming to the purchase order.

_____

[buyer]

7-22 LIMITED WARRANTY CLAUSE

The goods contained in this shipment are warranted to be free from defects in workmanship and materials on purchase. If the goods are found to be defective, they will be replaced without charge on return to the vendor if returned within [e.g., 90 days] with proof of purchase.

This warranty is given only to the original purchaser and is void if the goods are damaged by negligence or accident after purchase; used for other than intended purpose; altered; repaired at other than an authorized service center; or used with other goods that affect the integrity, performance, or safety of these goods.

This is the only warranty provided with the goods and is given in place of all other warranties, including but not limited to warranties of quality, fitness, and merchantability.

The Seller accepts no liability for any consequential damages or loss suffered by anyone as the result of using or being unable to use the goods.

7-23 LIABILITY EXCLUSION CLAUSE

[Buyer] acknowledges and accepts that [seller] is not liable in tort, contract, or equity for any innocent or negligent misrepresentation made in connection with this contract and/or any breach of any warranty, expressed or implied, including any implied or expressed collateral contract.

7-24 CHECKLIST FOR EXPRESS WARRANTY REQUIREMENTS

The Magnuson–Moss Act

The express warranties must contain in clear and understandable language the following terms:

_____ The identity of the persons to whom the warranties are extended.

_____ A description of the products or goods covered by the warranies.

_____ A description of the products or goods excluded by the warranties.

_____ Remedial action to be provided by the warrantor (person issuing the warranties) if defects, malfunctions, or failures occur.

_____ The period covered by the warranties.

_____ The steps or procedures that the consumer should follow to obtain relief under the warranties.

_____ Information on any informal procedures for dispute resolution that will be used in case of disputes under the warranties.

_____ All limitations or exclusions of coverage of the warranties.

_____ Information regarding the consumer's legal rights. For example, a statement such as: "This warranty is a valid contract and provides you with specific legal rights and other rights, which may vary from state to state."

_____ Any limitations on the duration and coverage of implied warranties. *Note:* Some states restrict limitations on implied warranties.

7-25   BID REQUEST

To: [potential seller]

Please provide us with your bid on the following items:

Item	Quantity	Unit Price	Total Price
1. _____	_____	_____	_____
2. _____	_____	_____	_____
3. _____	_____	_____	_____
4. _____	_____	_____	_____
5. _____	_____	_____	_____

In your price quote, the goods are to be delivered to us free on board (F.O.B.) at the following location:

If your bid prices are not firm for at least 30 days, please tell us when the bid prices will no longer be valid.

Sincerely,

7-26   NOTICE THAT SALE WILL BE ON C.O.D. TERMS

Date:

To: [buyer]

Dear Sir/Madam:

We have received your order for the below listed goods:

Please be advised that we will ship the ordered goods cash on delivery (C.O.D.) ten days from the date of this letter unless we receive instructions otherwise. If you care to make other financing arrangements, please contact [name and telephone number of contact person].

Thank you for your order. We hope we can continue to be of service to you.

Sincerely,

7-27   CONSIGNMENT SALE

Date:

To:

In accordance with your order, we are shipping the goods you ordered on a consignment basis. Any goods not sold within 60 days may be returned to us for credit. You are responsible for the cost of the freight in returning the goods to us. The sale on consignment includes the following terms:

1. Title to the goods remains with us until the goods are paid
2. You are responsible to provide insurance against loss or damage to the goods while they are in your possession or being returned to us
3. You will sign any financing agreements that are needed to protect our interest
4. All items sold by you are subject to the payment terms contained in the attached invoice.

Please indicate your acceptance of the above terms by signing a copy of this letter and returning it to us.

Sincerely,

Date: _____

The above terms are accepted.

_____

Buyer

7-28 INVITATION FOR QUOTATION

Date:

[company,
address]

To:

Re: Price quotations on [goods]

Our company is interested in purchasing the following goods:

[List goods]

Please provide us with a firm quote on the above listed goods. We also need to know the following information regarding the goods:

1. Are delivery costs included in your quotes? Unless otherwise stated, we will assume the delivery costs are included in your price quotes.
2. What is the delivery time from the receipt of our order to receipt of shipment? This time frame will be a condition of any purchase order.
3. Are your quotes inclusive or exclusive of state taxes? Unless they are clearly stated, we will assume that your quotes are inclusive of sales taxes.
4. What are your terms of payment? Are there any discounts for early payment of invoices?
5. What is the expiration date of all price quotes?

Any price quotes received must be firm.

Sincerely,

7–29 DEMAND FOR DELIVERY OF GOODS

Date:

[company,
address]

To:

Re: Demand for the delivery of goods

On [date], our company ordered the following goods:

[List goods]

Even though the delivery date has passed, we have not received the delivery of them.

Unless we receive immediate delivery of the goods, we will cancel the order and seek the return of our payments. If necessary, we will take legal action.

Sincerely,

7-30 CANCELLATION OF PURCHASE ORDER (LATE DELIVERY)

Date:

[company,
address]

Re: Purchase order of [date]; cancellation of

Dear Sir/Madam:

Our company ordered the following goods:

Payment in the amount of $_____ was forwarded to your company on [date] as payment in full for the order. The goods were to be delivered not later than [date].

As of this date, we have not received the above goods. Accordingly, please cancel the order and return our monies. If we have not received a refund within ten days of the above date, we will take the necessary legal action to obtain the refund.

Sincerely,

7-31

REJECTION OF GOODS (NONCONFORMING)

Date:

[company,
address]

Re: Rejection of nonconforming goods

Dear Sir/Madam:

Our company ordered the following goods:

Payment in the amount of $_____ was forwarded to your company on [date] as payment in full for the order. The goods received did not conform to our purchase order as noted below:

[state reason for rejection of goods]

Accordingly, we reject the goods and demand return of our monies. If we have not received a refund within ten days of the above date, we will take the necessary legal action to obtain the refund.

Please advise us as to the disposition of the goods. We do not accept any responsibility for their safekeeping if we do not receive disposal instructions from you within the next ten days.

Sincerely,

7-32 PARTIAL REJECTION OF GOODS (NONCONFORMING)

Date:

[company,
address]

Re: Rejection of nonconforming goods

Dear Sir/Madam:

Our company ordered the following goods:

Payment in the amount of $_____ was forwarded to your company on [date] as payment in full for the order. Part of the goods received did not conform to our purchase order as noted below:

[state reason for rejection of goods]

Accordingly, we reject those goods that do not conform and demand return of our monies that were paid for the goods that have been rejected. If we have not received a refund within ten days of the above date, we will take the necessary legal action to obtain the refund.

Please advise us as to the disposition of the rejected goods. We do not accept any responsibility for their safekeeping if we do not receive disposal instructions from you within the next ten days.

Sincerely,

7–33 RETURN OF REJECTED GOODS

Re: Return of rejected goods

Dear Sir/Madam:

On [date] we notified you that your goods have been rejected and the reasons for the rejection. At that time, we requested instructions regarding the return or other disposition of the goods.

Since we have not received any instructions regarding them, we no longer accept any responsibility for them. Please advise us within the next 10 days as to their disposition.

Sincerely,

7–34 ACCEPTANCE OF NONCONFORMING GOODS

Date:

[company,
address]

Re: Acceptance of nonconforming goods

Dear Sir/Madam:

This letter is to advise you that the goods you shipped pursuant to our purchase order of [date] do not conform to the specifications set forth in the purchase order. The goods do not meet the specifications in that they [state how goods do not conform].

However, we are accepting the goods that you shipped. Because of the nonconformance, we request that you discount the purchase price by _____ percent. In addition, please be advised that we expect all future orders to conform to our specifications.

Sincerely,

_____
Purchasing Agent

Chapter 8

Sale of Business Assets

This chapter discusses the buying and selling of a business and the forms needed for the buying and selling of business assets.

Forms of Ownership

There are three basic forms of business ownership: sole proprietorship, partnerships, and corporations. The situation often dictates the form of business ownership. Too often, however, the form is more a matter of chance than of deliberate planning. At other times, the business climate, the type of business, the financing available, and so on, dictate the form of business ownership. As much thought and planning should go into this decision as any other one connected with the business. There is no preferred form of ownership for every business. Consider the advantages and disadvantages of each form before you make the decision about the form of ownership. this could be the most important decision you make regarding the business. The legal aspects of partnerships are discussed in Chapter 12 and of corporations in Chapter 9. Because the legal aspects of sole proprietorship are discussed throughout the book, an overview of the issues is presented in this section.

Sole proprietorships are the most common form of ownership for small businesses. Approximately 78 percent of all U.S. businesses are of this type. A *sole proprietorship* is a business that is owned entirely by one person, as opposed to ownership by a partnership or a corporation. If any part of the business is owned by others, then it is not a sole proprietorship. For example, if you own 99 percent of the business and someone else owns the other 1 percent, you most likely have a partnership. It is not a sole proprietorship. In 1992, there were more than 9 million sole proprietorships in the United States.

Sole proprietorships are customarily managed by the owners. Absentee ownership in sole proprietorships is very rare. The three key advantages of the sole proprietorship that make this form of ownership so popular are (1) the ease with which the business is formed, (2) the lesser degree of governmental control than that which applies to partnerships and corporations, and (3) the fact that a sole proprietorship is considered but an alter ego of the owner. This last advantage gives owners a greater degree of control over the business and its assets. In fact, owners have the same rights of ownership and control over the business property that they have over their own personal assets.

Many businesses start out as sole proprietorships. Later, because of the need for additional financing, growth, or other factors, they become either corporations or partnerships. Remember that if you transform your business from a sole proprietorship to a partnership or a corporation, you will lose a great measure of control over it.

The main disadvantage of a sole proprietorship is the unlimited financial liability of the owner. Thus, if the business is failing, not only can creditors attach the assets of the business; they can also attach the personal assets of the owner. Any property that a personal creditor of the owner could attach may also be attached by a creditor of the business. Carefully consider this factor of unlimited financial liability before opening a business under this form of ownership.

Many small businesspersons find tax advantages in the sole proprietorship form of business because some legitimate tax deductions can also be used for their personal benefit. The sole proprietor should be careful in this area because any personal expenses charged against the business for tax purposes may constitute tax evasion, which is a crime.

Legal Aspects of Buying or Selling a Business

The legal aspects of planning, capitalization, and financing new and existing businesses are discussed in this section. The legal aspects of buying a franchise are also covered. According to the U.S. Chamber of Commerce, most businesses fail because they lack adequate financial resources. Accordingly, whether your plan is for buying an existing business or starting a new one, make its financial underpinnings your first priority. Give close attention to the financing necessary to start or buy the business and the operating expenses that you must meet until the business is producing revenue.

In this section, conventional and unconventional methods of financing are also discussed. A secondary aspect of developing a business capitalization plan is the effect of taxes. Investigate the way the government will treat the investment expenditures for tax purposes.

Evaluating a Business

Probably the most difficult step in buying or selling a business is determining what it is worth as a going concern. Two basic methods are used to determine the value of the business. The first is based on an expectation of future profits and the return on investment (ROI). This method is preferred by most accountants and attorneys. It forces the buyer and the seller to give at least minimal attention to factors such as trends in sales and profit, the capitalized value of the business, and the expectations of return on investment.

The second evaluation method is based on the appraised value of the business' assets at the time of the negotiation, assuming that these assets will continue to be used in the business. This method gives little consideration to the future of the business, and it determines the value only as it relates to the present. It is more commonly used, not because it is more reliable than the first, but because it is easier to understand.

Whatever method you use to determine the value of the business you propose to buy, make a projection of the income and the profits or losses for at least the next five years by preparing a sales estimate for this period along with a matching estimate of the cost of goods to be sold and the expected operating expenses. The seller should be able to provide you with the historical cost data of the business. At this point, you may want to ask an independent accountant to analyze the actual profits or losses of the business for the past five years. You can then use that analysis to make projections for the future with some degree of certainty. Make a study of the general and local economic changes that may affect the future of the business as part of the analysis. Include any possible competition that may not have been present in the past but may be present in the future.

Looking at Future Profits

Let's assume that you've made a five-year projection of the annual profits of the business and that the profits are estimated to average $40,000 a year for the next five years. How much should you be willing to invest in this business? First, consider the return on investment. If you were to take the money you were going to invest in this business and instead put it into a safe investment such as a bank certificate of deposit that earns 8 percent annual interest, your proposed business should be able to return a profit in excess of that 8 percent. Keep in mind that a high percentage of businesses, almost 50 percent, have financial problems within their first three years of existence or after a change of ownership. Therefore, ensure that any return of investment is sufficiently high to justify the financial risk involved. Unless the business will pay you a 20- to 25-percent return on capital, you should be very leery about investing in it unless it has a low risk factor. Another factor to consider before you invest in a going business, especially a small business, is the trend of profits. If all other factors are equal, a company whose profits are declining is worth much less than one whose profits are increasing.

Appraisals of Assets

As noted earlier, in most cases involving the buying and selling of a business, the price is based on a value established by its assets. The assets most commonly purchased in a small business are its inventory, sales, office supplies, fixtures, equipment, and goodwill. Evaluating the tangible assets, such as inventory, sales, office supplies, fixtures and equipment, will not be too difficult. However, evaluating the goodwill of an existing business is difficult. *Goodwill* is that asset that involves the business' good name, its high financial standing, if any, and its reputation for superior products or customer service, if any. An economist would define goodwill as the ability of a business to realize above-normal profit as a result of its reputation. Don't put too much value in the goodwill of most small businesses. Historically, few small businesses that are for sale produce excess profits.

In determining the merchandise inventory of the business, make sure that its value is not overpriced and that the method used to cost out the inventory items accurately reflects their value.

Negotiating the Contract

One of the major steps in buying a going business is negotiating the purchase contract. The contract should contain details of the price, terms of payment, price allocation, type of transaction, liabilities, and warranties. Be aware that your and the seller's interest may conflict. For example, the seller is interested in getting the best price for the business, getting the money, and getting a favorable tax treatment of the gains from the sale. The seller also wants to eliminate any liability, whereas the buyer is interested in getting the lowest sale price, a favorable tax treatment, and warranty protection against inaccurate financial data and undisclosed or potential liabilities. *Note:* At the present time there are no favorable treatments for capital gains under federal income tax regulations. Do not overlook the possibility that favorable tax treatments for capital gains may be reenacted.

Take care that all essential terms of a purchase contract are in writing. The agreement should include as a minimum a description of the business, all the liabilities and encumbrances on the business, the right to use the trade name of the business, and the purchase price. The purchase price should be broken down into lease or real property involved, fixtures, equipment, inventory, supplies, and goodwill. The method of payment should be set out in detail so that both sides understand their obligations. There should be provisions for making adjustments at the time of the closing in the inventory, insurance premiums, rent, deposit, payroll taxes, and the like. Have a clear understanding of any liabilities you are considering. Make sure that the seller warrants that he or she owns the business and has good and marketable title to its assets. Also be certain that the assets are free from all debts unless specified, otherwise, that all business liabilities are stated, and that the seller has no knowledge of any development or threatened development that would be materially adverse to the business.

Ensure that the contract obligates the seller to conduct the business as usual up to the date of closing. Make sure that the contract requires the seller to use his or her influence to keep available to you the services of the present employees and the goodwill of the business' suppliers, customers, and other persons having a business relationship with the business. The contract should clearly state who is to assume the risk of any loss or obstruction or damage due to fire or other casualties up to the date of closing. In most situations the loss would be on the seller, but this fact should be clearly stated in the contract.

The contract should also contain a covenant not to compete. In the covenant, the seller promises the buyer and the buyer's successors that for a certain period after the sale, the seller will not engage in a similar or competitive business within a reasonable distance. For example, a covenant not to compete for five years and within a radius of 100 miles would usually be considered reasonable.

There should be a clear statement in the contract that the seller will reimburse the buyer on demand for any payments the buyer makes toward liabilities or obligations of the seller not expressly assumed by the buyer. The contract should also state that the seller will reimburse the buyer for any damages or deficiencies resulting from misrepresentation, breach of warranty, or nonfulfillment of the terms of the agreement.

The contract should agree to arbitration of any disputes that arise from it to the selection of neutral parties as arbitrators. The arbitration panel is usually composed of one member selected by the seller, another member selected by the buyer, and a third member chosen by the other two arbitrators. It is always advisable to have an attorney review the final contract before both parties execute it. In some cases, a single arbitrator may be used. Use care in drafting the selection process if an arbitration requirement is in the contract.

Both parties should always sign the contract. Included in the forms for this chapter is a sample buy and sell agreement that can be modified to fit your specific situation.

Franchises

A *franchise* is defined as a contract or agreement allowing the *franchisee* (i.e., the businessperson) to engage in business under a marketing system substantially prescribed by the *franchisor* (i.e., the seller). The business is essentially associated with the franchisor's trademark or other commercial symbol, and the new business-owner is required to pay a franchise fee.

Every 15 minutes, a new franchise store opens in the United States. More than one-third of U.S. retail sales come from franchised businesses. It is predicted that by the year 2000, half of all retail stores will be franchised businesses. The popularity of franchises is based on the general assumption that there is less risk involved in opening a franchise than in opening an independent venture. In many cases, the company selling the franchise finances a portion of the needed start-up capital. It is also easier in some cases to obtain financing for a franchise than for an independent business to do so. For example, Security Pacific Business Finance, Inc., a unit of Secu-

What Should Your Franchise Fee Buy You?

- When you pay a franchise fee, you should expect the following help, services, and support from the franchisor:
- Help in site selection in the form of feasibility studies, demographic analysis, and location.
- Lease negotiation assistance. The franchisor provides help and advice on negotiating a lease.
- Financial help in financing the start-up and initial operating costs. (*Note:* Only about 20 percent of the franchisors provide direct financial assistance; the others should at least provide detailed guidance in obtaining financing.)
- Training.
- Continuing support.
- Advertising and marketing.
- Discounts on products and equipment.
- Research and development.
- On-call assistance.

rity Pacific Corporation of San Diego, California, loaned approximately $25 million in one year to new franchise holders. *Note:* Like many other small businesses, individual franchised stores also fail.

Most states regulate the sale of franchises under the Uniform Franchise Investment Law, which defines a *franchise* as a type of security. Under this law, persons who engage in the business of selling franchises must register with the state just as any securities dealer or broker must.

In most states, it is unlawful to offer for sale or to sell a franchise unless it is registered with the state. The Uniform Franchise Investment Law requires that any prospective buyer be given a copy of a prospectus and a copy of all proposed agreements relating to the sale of the franchise at least 48 hours before the execution of any binding agreement. In addition, the seller (i.e., the franchisor) must maintain a complete set of records of sales that have occurred within the state.

The Federal Trade Commission has published a rule regarding the sale of franchises involved in interstate commerce. The rule requires sellers of franchises to give each prospective buyer a booklet explaining all the important aspects of the franchise in plain English. The booklet also gives the net worth and background of the franchisor. Although there are many reputable companies, such as McDonald's and Midas Muffler, that sell lucrative franchises, there are also many companies that are not as reputable. Several years ago, a national fast-food chain was showing a substantial profit each year. The profit was used to entice investors to buy franchises. The problem was that the company was making its profit from selling franchises and the individual franchises for the most part had a low rate of return for their investment. Therefore, be leery when buying a franchise. Make sure a good market study is done. Get a careful understanding of what you are getting with the franchise fee. Find out what types of assistance will be provided and what the restrictions are. What are your requirements? A good practice is to consult other holders of the same type of franchise. Get their personal experiences on how successful they have been with that particular franchise.

One of the key items that you buy in a franchise is its trade name and the right to use it. Therefore, make sure it is worth the money it will cost you to buy and to operate the franchise under that trade name. Another item you are buying is the expertise of the franchisor in helping you to manage your business. Therefore, get a clear understanding of how a franchisor will help you.

Always check with the Better Business Bureau in your area regarding any prospective franchise before you purchase one. Have an attorney examine the franchise agreement before you sign it.

Business Licenses

A *business license* is the privilege or right to operate a business or to carry on a trade. Unlike the goodwill or trade name of a business, a business license is not property and cannot be transferred. If you purchase an existing business, its license cannot be transferred to you. In these cases, however, it is usually easier to get a license because the city or county will have already approved the operation of that type of business at that location. Before purchasing an existing business, find out if you will have any problems getting the license in your name. Before licenses are issued to certain businesses, checks of police records are required. In some cases, the city or county may require the new owners to post performance bonds. In most states, it is a misdemeanor (i.e., minor crime) to operate a business or carry on a profession without getting the necessary licenses. It is also illegal to continue a business under a license issued to the previous owner. As defined in licensing statutes, a business engages in commerce or trade to make a profit or livelihood. Many local ordinances exempt organizations and activities whose activities are not motivated to profit. Check with your city or county offices to determine if your activities require a license.

In imposing licensing requirements, cities or counties may not discriminate between persons similarly situated and exercising the same privileges. However, they can classify occupations and make different rules regarding each one. Cities or counties can also make different rules regarding merchants who have a fixed place of business and those who do not. In one case, a city was not permitted to place a higher tax on solicitors who had been in business for less than a year than on those who had been in business longer.

Registration of Fictitious Business Name

State laws require a businesses that operates under a fictitious business name to register and maintain an up-to-date statement of that name. These laws give public access to records of businesses that are operated under names other than those of the owner or owners. The statements are usually filed with the city or county where the business operates. Most states have standard forms for filing fictitious names. Check with your local city or county clerk for specifics.

Partnerships and sole proprietorships must file statements of fictitious names unless the businesses are conducted in the surnames of all owners. A partnership must file a statement of fictitious business name unless the business name consists of the surnames of all general partners. A corporation has to file a statement unless it does business under the exact corporate name stated in its articles of incorporation.

A sole proprietorship that operated under the name of W.F. Fields and Co. was determined by one court to have a fictitious name. The name was considered to be fictitious because it implied the existence of additional business owners.

Words describing the type of business are not considered fictitious names—for example, John Brown's Meat Market or Joe Brown's Car Repair Shop.

Business owners who fail to file the required statement cannot maintain any legal actions or transactions made under its fictitious name. The businessowners, however, can still be sued in their own names or in the business' name. Filing a false statement is a criminal offense.

Filing is usually required 30 to 60 days from the time that business transactions begin. In most states, businessowners must publicize the fictitious name in a local newspaper, either before filing the statement with the clerk or shortly thereafter. Owners have to refile every three to five years, depending on the state, or whenever changes occur in ownership or business address. A person who withdraws from or abandons a business is required to file a statement of withdrawal or modification of ownership.

Bulk Sales of Inventory

Article 6 of the Uniform Commercial Code (UCC) covers the bulk sales of the stock or inventories of businesses. Bulk sales are commonly regulated by the bulk transfers or bulk sales acts of the states. Although the laws in each state may vary, they all have the main purpose of preventing fraud. The two most common types of fraud are the following:

1. The businessowner, owing debts he or she is unable or unwilling to pay, sells the inventory for less than its value and still cannot pay the debts. Although the owner is still liable for the balance, the businessowner has no other assets and is either bankrupt or without resources that creditors can attach.

2. The businessowner, being in debt, sells the stock in trade for any price, takes the proceeds, and disappears, leaving the creditors unpaid.

To prevent these types of fraud, bulk transfer statutes provide methods by which creditors may obtain advance notice of the sale of a merchant's stock. Once the creditors know of a pending sale, they can investigate the circumstances of the sale before it occurs and take steps to protect their rights. If creditors suspect that fraud is present, they may take court action either to halt the sale or to impound the proceeds of the sale if necessary to protect their rights. The objections to the bulk sales acts are that they delay sales and cause additional red tape on legitimate sales.

Bulk Transfers

A *bulk transfer* is any sale or change of ownership of a large portion of the inventory, materials, supplies, or merchandise of a business that are not ordinarily a part of the original owner's business.

It is necessary to determine whether the purchase of a business that also includes its inventory is subject to regulation by the bulk transfer act. If it is and the necessary requirements are not met, the new owner of the business may be liable for the debts of the previous owner. The liabilities of the buyer for the debts of the seller are usually limited to the value of the bulk sale items purchased.

A transfer of a substantial part of a businessowner's equipment is a bulk transfer if it is made in conjunction with a bulk transfer of inventory. Bulk transfers do not include transfers of investment securities, money, accounts receivable, contract rights, negotiable instruments, or mortgages. The transfer of these items is covered under other regulations.

Bulk transfers do not include sales by executors, administrators, receivers, trustees in bankruptcy, or any public officer acting under judicial process. Excluded from the act are sales made in the course of any judicial proceeding. Not included are transfers to a person who agrees to accept liability for the seller's business debts and who remains solvent after becoming liable for the debts. Both the seller and buyer are liable for payment of the debts. A transfer to a new business organized to take over and continue the business under a business reorganization is also excluded. In this last situation, the new business must agree to assume liabilities for the debts of its predecessor and give public notice of the reorganization.

Certain transfers are exempted from the provisions of the act. The general exclusions are those made to give security for the performance of an obligation, general assignments for the benefit of all creditors, and those in settlement of a lien or security interest on the inventory.

Schedule of Property

In those sales subject to a bulk sales act, the new owner must obtain from the seller a schedule of property to prevent the new businessowner from being liable for the debts of the previous owners. The schedule of property must include a list of existing creditors and a description of the property sufficient to identify it.

The list of creditors must be signed and sworn to by the seller or the seller's agent and contain the names and business addresses of all the creditors of the seller and the amounts of the debts owed to each. The seller must also list the names and business addresses of all persons who are known to assert claims against him or her, including those people with claims the seller disputes.

As noted previously, the owner's failure to comply with the requirements of the act enables the creditors of the business to ignore the sale and to levy on the property for the amount of the debts. The submission of a false schedule by the seller is a criminal offense. A buyer who accepts a false schedule of property in good faith and complies with other aspects of the acts is usually protected from creditors' attempts to levy on the property.

Because failure to comply with the act makes the buyer liable for the debts of the seller, the noncompliance can be resolved by the buyer's paying the unpaid creditors. If the debts of the seller are paid as they mature, then no liability occurs.

Notice to Creditors

The requirement to notify creditors is another major condition of the bulk transfer act. Creditors must be notified by seller or buyer at least 10 days before the buyer takes possession of the goods or pays for them, whichever comes first. The notice shall contain the following:

- A statement that a bulk transfer is about to be made.

- The names and business addresses of both the seller and the buyer, and of all other business names and addresses used by the seller in the past three years.

- Whether or not, as a result of the transfer, all the seller's debts are to be paid in full by the buyer as they fall due. If so, the address to which creditors should send their bills must be included.

- If the debts of the seller are not to be paid in full as they fall due or if the buyer is in doubt on that point, then the notice shall further state the location and general description of the property to be transferred, the estimated total of the seller's debts, and an address where the schedule of property and list of creditors may be inspected.

- Whether the transfer is to pay existing debts of the seller and if so the amount of those debts and to whom owing.

- The amount of value to be paid by the buyer and the time and place of payment.

- The place where creditors of the seller are to file claims or objections to the sale.

This notice must be in writing and delivered personally or by registered or certified mail to all persons on the list of creditors the seller furnished by the seller, and to all other persons who assert claims against the seller. In most states, it is also required that a shortened form of the notice be published in a newspaper of general circulation in the county in which the business is located.

Auction Sales

A bulk sale at auction is subject to the bulk transfer act, but the reporting requirements are different, and failure to comply subjects the auctioneer to payment of an amount equal to the proceeds of the sale. Neither the validity of the sale nor the title of the buyer is affected by the auctioneer's failure to comply. In a recent case, one court concluded that an auctioneer is liable only if he or she knows that the auction constitutes a bulk transfer. If goods are received on consignment for sale, the auctioneer may not know that a bulk transfer is involved.

Protected Creditors

All business creditors of the seller with claims based on transactions occurring before the bulk transfer are protected under the bulk sales or transfer act. Previous creditors with unliquidated claims (claims in which the amounts due are disputed) are also protected. Creditors whose claims are based on transactions occurring after a notice to creditors is given are not included.

Limitations of Actions and Levies

Unless the bulk transfer has been concealed, court action or levies must be made within six months after the date the buyer takes possession of the goods. When the transfer has been concealed, court action must be taken or levies made within six months after its discovery by the creditor.

Levy means not only levies of execution orders of a court judgment but also attachment, garnishment, trustee process, receivership, or any other proceeding used by the state courts to apply a debtor's property toward payment of the debts.

If the buyer sells the goods in a situation in which the bulk sales or transfer act was not obeyed, a question arises whether the subsequent buyer takes the goods subject to the claims of the first seller's creditors. Generally, if the second buyer takes the goods without knowing the defect and pays a reasonable price for them, the second buyer takes a good title to them and is not liable to the original seller. If the second buyer either knows of the defect in sale or does not pay a reasonable price for the goods (i.e., receives them as a gift), the second buyer may be liable to the original seller's creditors. In addition, if the buyer fails to ensure that the bulk sale requirements have been met, he or she may be held liable for the debts.

Forms in This Chapter

- FORM 8–1: BUSINESS PURCHASE PROPOSAL. Communicates a proposal to purchase a business.

- FORM 8–2: AGREEMENT FOR THE PURCHASE AND SALE OF BUSINESS ASSETS. Purchases and sells business assets.

- FORM 8–3: BUSINESS PURCHASE PROPOSAL (REGULATED BUSINESS). Communicates a proposal to purchase a business.

- FORM 8–4: AGREEMENT FOR THE PURCHASE AND SALE OF BUSINESS ASSETS (REGULATED BUSINESS). Purchases or sells business assets.

- FORM 8–5: SALE OF PARTNERSHIP. Sells a partnership.

- FORM 8–6: PROVISION FOR EMPLOYMENT OF SELLER. Employs the seller as a management consultant.

- FORM 8–7: ASSUMPTION OF COLLECTIVE BARGAINING AGREEMENT. Used to have the buyer assume the collective bargaining agreement.

- FORM 8–8: ASSUMPTION OF EMPLOYEE BENEFIT PLANS. Used to have the buyer assume the employee benefit plans.

- FORM 8–9: STATEMENT OF FICTITIOUS BUSINESS NAME. Records a fictitious business name.

- FORM 8–10: ABANDONMENT OF FICTITIOUS BUSINESS NAME. Used to abandon a fictitious business name.

- FORM 8–11: NOTICE OF INTENDED BULK TRANSFER. Notification of an intended bulk transfer.

- FORM 8–12: NOTICE OF INTENDED BULK TRANSFER (AUCTION). Notification of an intended bulk transfer by auction.

- FORM 8–13: BULK SALES AFFIDAVIT. A bulk sales affidavit to assure buyers that the bulk sale of the goods is valid.

8-1 BUSINESS PURCHASE PROPOSAL

[company,
address]

[date]

Re: Proposal to Purchase Business

Dear _____:

Our company is interested in purchasing the [name and address of business]. The purchase would include fixtures, equipment, furniture, stock in trade, parts, supplies, leasehold interests, and goodwill.

Subject to a formal contract, we are prepared to offer $_____ for the business subject to the below listed terms:

[include suggested terms here]

If you are interested in selling the above stated business at the quoted price, please contact us and we will submit a formal offer to purchase.

Sincerely,

_____

8-2

AGREEMENT FOR THE PURCHASE AND SALE OF BUSINESS ASSETS

This agreement for the purchase and sale of business assets is between [name of buyer] (the Purchaser) and [name of seller] (the seller) for the business being carried on under the name of [name and address of business], which is a going concern.

1. The business being sold and purchased includes but is not limited to:
   furniture, fixtures, and equipment listed in Schedule A [not shown];
   all stock in trade;
   all parts and supplies;
   all leasehold interests involving the business; and
   the goodwill of the business.

2. The below assets are excluded from the purchase and sale:

   [list any assets not included in the sale]

3. The purchase price for the business is $_____. The purchase price is allocated as follows:

   a. for equipment, furniture and fixtures $ _____

   b. for stock in trade $ _____

   c. for goodwill $ _____

   d. for parts and supplies $ _____

   e. for all other assets being purchased and sold $ _____

4. The purchase price paid for the stock in trade and for parts and supplies will be adjusted based on an inventory of those items on the day after the close of the sale. Items will be valued at the direct costs to seller. The selling price will be adjusted up or down based on the results of the inventories. Purchaser may exclude from the inventories any items the Purchaser reasonably considers as unsalable or unusable. Seller shall furnish Purchaser proof of direct costs of items.

5. Terms of payment: [insert terms of payment at this point].

6. Warranties, conditions, and representations: The following warranties, conditions, and representations in favor of the Purchaser are incorporated into this agreement:

   a. That Purchaser obtain the necessary financing on satisfactory terms;

   b. That the business may continue to be carried on at its present location;

   c. That all lessors consent to assignment of the leases to purchase;

d. That Seller provide Purchaser with at closing, all the closing documents; and

e. That Purchaser is permitted to obtain all permits and licenses required to carry on the business.

7. Warranties, conditions, and representations: The following warranties, conditions, and representations are made and given by the Seller and are incorporated into this agreement.

a. That Seller owns and has the right to sell the business, assets, supplies, materials, goodwill, and the items contained in Schedule A.

b. That the equipment is in good operating condition except as follows:

c. Seller will continue to carry on the business in the usual manner until closing and will not do anything to the prejudice of the business or the goodwill;

d. That the financial statements provided by the Seller are accurate, fair, and prepared in accordance with generally accepted accounting standards and principles;

e. That the assets agreed to be bought and sold are sold free and clear of all liens, encumbrances, and charges except as noted: _____
_____

f. That all leases are in good standing and that the Seller has fulfilled all of its obligations under the leases;

g. That Seller has made a full and fair disclosure in all material aspects of any matter that could reasonably be expected to affect the Purchaser's decision to purchase the business;

h. That Seller will execute the necessary documents, make the necessary assignments, clearances, and assurances to assure that the Purchaser can assume ownership of the business and conduct business in the normal course of affairs.

8. The risk of loss or damage of the business and business assets remains with the Seller until the time of closing.

9. The Seller shall pay all sales taxes payable or collectible in connection with carrying on the business prior to closing. Seller shall provide Purchaser at closing, proof that the applicable sales taxes have been paid. The Purchaser shall pay any and all sales taxes payable in respect to the sale pursuant to this agreement.

10. The Seller covenants with the Purchaser that, as part consideration for closing of this agreement, the Seller will not operate a [type of business] or in any way aid or assist others to operate such a business within a 25-mile radius of the location of present business for a period of five years.

11. Seller shall comply will all applicable laws governing the bulk sales or any other assets pursuant to this agreement.

12. The Seller shall deliver to the Purchaser in proper form the following documents:

    a. bill of sale

    b. all records and financial data, including but not limited to, a list of customers, vendors, etc., relevant to the carrying on of the business

    c. executed assignments of leases

    d. clearance, consents, and assurances reasonably necessary to carry on the business

    e. title documents on equipment and assets

    f. executed notice required to be filed under any business name registration law; and

    g. any other documents needed to carry on the business.

13. This agreement is governed by the law of the state in which the business is located.

14. Time is of the essence in this agreement.

15. This agreement binds and benefits the parties and their respective heirs, executors, administrators, personal representatives, successors, and assigns.

16. If any provision or part of this agreement is void for any reason, it shall be severed without affecting the validity of the balance of this agreement.

17. There are no warranties, conditions, terms, or collateral contracts affecting the transaction contemplated in this agreement except as noted in this agreement.

This agreement constitutes an offer to purchase and may be accepted only by the Seller. If the offer is not accepted by [date], this agreement becomes null and void. Acceptance may be only by the receipt by the Purchaser of a properly signed copy of this agreement.

EXECUTED under seal on this _____ day of _____, 19_____.

_____   _____
    Seller   Purchaser

8-3

BUSINESS PURCHASE PROPOSAL (REGULATED BUSINESS)

[company,
address]

[date]

Re: Proposal to Purchase Business

Dear _____:

Our company is interested in purchasing the [name and address of business]. The purchase would include fixtures, equipment, furniture, stock in trade, parts, supplies, leasehold interests, and goodwill.

Subject to a formal contract, we are prepared to offer $_____ for the business subject to the below listed terms:

[include suggested terms here]

This proposal is continuant on Purchaser's qualifying by the regulatory authority to operate said business.

If you are interested in selling the above stated business at the quoted price, please contact us and we will submit a formal offer to purchase.

Sincerely,

_____

AGREEMENT FOR THE PURCHASE AND SALE OF BUSINESS ASSETS (REGULATED BUSINESS)

This agreement for the purchase and sale of business assets is between [name of Purchaser] (the Purchaser) and [name of Seller] (the Seller) for the business being carried on under the name of [name and address of business], which is a going concern.

1. The business being sold and purchased includes, but is not limited to: furniture, fixtures, and equipment listed in Schedule A; all stock in trade; all parts and supplies; all leasehold interests involving the business; and the goodwill of the business.

2. The below assets are excluded from the purchase and sale:

   [list any assets not included in the sale]

3. The purchase price for the business is $_____. The purchase price is allocated as follows:

   a. for equipment, furniture and fixtures $ _____

   b. for stock in trade $ _____

   c. for goodwill $ _____

   d. for parts and supplies $ _____

   e. for all other assets being purchased and sold $ _____

4. The purchase price paid for the stock in trade and for parts and supplies will be adjusted based on an inventory of those items on the day after the close of the sale. Items will be valued at the direct costs to Seller. The selling price will be adjusted up or down based on the results of the inventories. Purchaser may exclude from the inventories any items the Purchaser reasonably considers as unsalable or unusable. Seller shall furnish Purchaser proof of direct costs of items.

5. Terms of payment: [insert terms of payment at this point].

6. Warranties, conditions, and representations: The following warranties, conditions, and representations in favor of the Purchaser are incorporated into this agreement:

   a. That Purchaser obtain the necessary financing on satisfactory terms;

b. That the business may continue to be carried on at its present location;

c. That all lessors consent to assignment of the leases to purchase;

d. That Seller provide Purchaser with at closing, all the closing documents; and

e. That Purchaser is permitted to obtain all permits and licenses required to carry on the business.

7. Warranties, conditions, and representations: The following warranties, conditions, and representations are made and given by the Seller and are incorporated into this agreement:

a. That Seller owns and has the right to sell the business, assets, supplies, materials, goodwill, and the items contained in Schedule A.

b. That the equipment is in good operating condition except as follows: _____.

c. Seller will continue to carry on the business in the usual manner until closing and will not do anything to the prejudice of the business or the goodwill.

d. That the financial statements provided by the Seller are accurate, fair, and prepared in accordance with generally accepted accounting standards and principles.

e. That the assets agreed to be bought and sold are sold free and clear of all liens, encumbrances, and charges except as noted: _____.

f. All leases are in good standing and that the Seller has fulfilled all of its obligations under the leases.

g. That Seller has made a full and fair disclosure in all material aspects of any matter that could reasonably be expected to affect the Purchaser's decision to purchase the business.

h. That Seller will execute the necessary documents, make the necessary assignments, clearances, and assurances to assure that the Purchaser can assume ownership of the business and conduct business in the normal course of affairs.

8. The risk of loss or damage of the business and business assets remains with the Seller until the time of closing.

9. The Seller shall pay all sales taxes payable or collectible in connection with carrying on the business prior to closing. Seller shall provide Purchaser at closing proof that the applicable sales taxes have been paid. The Purchaser shall pay any and all sales taxes payable in respect to the sale pursuant to this agreement.

10. The Seller covenants with the Purchaser that, as part consideration for closing of this agreement, the Seller will not operate a [type of business] or in any way aid or assist others to operate such a business within a 25-mile radius of the location of present business for a period of five years.

11. Seller shall comply with all applicable laws governing the bulk sales or any other assets pursuant to this agreement.

12. The Seller shall deliver to the Purchaser in proper form the following documents:

    a. bill of sales

    b. all records and financial data, including but not limited to, a list of customers, vendors, etc., relevant to the carrying on of the business

    c. executed assignments of leases

    d. clearance, consents, and assurances reasonably necessary to carry on the business

    e. title documents on equipment and assets,

    f. executed notice required to be filed under any business name registration law; and

    g. any other documents needed to carry on the business.

13. This agreement is governed by the law of the state in which the business is located.

14. Time is of the essence in this agreement.

15. This agreement binds and benefits the parties and their respective heirs, executors, administrators, personal representatives, successors, and assigns.

16. If any provision or part of this agreement is void for any reason, it shall be severed without affecting the validity of the balance of this agreement.

17. There are no warranties, conditions, terms, or collateral contracts affecting the transaction contemplated in this agreement except as noted in this agreement.

18. This agreement is continuant on Purchaser's qualifying by the regulatory authority to operate said business.

This agreement constitutes an offer to purchase and may be accepted only by the Seller. If the offer is not accepted by [date], this agreement becomes null and void. Acceptance may be only by the receipt by the Purchaser of a properly signed copy of this agreement.

EXECUTED under seal on this _____ day of _____, 19_____.

_____   _____
Seller   Purchaser

_____   _____
Title   Title

_____   _____
Address   Address

8–5   SALE OF PARTNERSHIP

This agreement for the purchase and sale of [name of partnership] doing business under the name of _____ , a general partnership, is made between [name of Purchaser] (the Purchaser), and [name of partnership] (the Sellers), which is a going concern.

1. The business being sold and purchased includes but is not limited to:
   furniture, fixtures, and equipment listed in Schedule A;
   all stock in trade;
   all parts and supplies;
   all leasehold interests involving the business; and
   the goodwill of the business.

2. The below assets are excluded from the purchase and sale:

   [list any assets not included in the sale]

3. The purchase price for the business is $_____. The purchase price is allocated as follows:

   a.   for equipment, furniture, and fixtures $ _____

   b.   for stock in trade $ _____

   c.   for goodwill $ _____

   d.   for parts and supplies $ _____

   e.   for all other assets being purchased and sold $ _____

4. The purchase price paid for the stock in trade and for parts and supplies will be adjusted based on an inventory of those items on the day after the close of the sale. Items will be valued at the direct costs to sellers. The selling price will be adjusted up or down based on the results of the inventories. Buyer may exclude from the inventories any items the Purchaser reasonably considers as unsalable or unusable. Sellers shall furnish Purchaser proof of direct costs of items.

5. Terms of payment: [insert terms of payment at this point].

6. Warranties, conditions, and representations: The following warranties, conditions, and representations in favor of the Purchaser are incorporated into this agreement:

   a. That Purchaser obtain the necessary financing on satisfactory terms;

   b. That the business may continue to be carried on at its present location;

   c. That all Lessors consent to assignment of the leases to purchase;

d. That Sellers provide Purchaser with, at closing, all the closing documents; and

e. That Purchaser is permitted to obtain all permits and licenses required to carry on the business.

7. Warranties, conditions, and representations: The following warranties, conditions, and representations are made and given by the Sellers and are incorporated into this agreement:

a. That Sellers are the sole partners of the general partnership and they own and have the right to sell the business, assets, supplies, materials, goodwill, and the items contained in Schedule A.

b. That the equipment is in good operating condition except as follows: _____.

c. Sellers will continue to carry on the business in the usual manner until closing and will not do anything to the prejudice of the business or the goodwill;

d. That the financial statements provided by the Sellers are accurate, fair, and prepared in accordance with generally accepted accounting standards and principles;

e. That the assets agreed to be bought and sold are sold free and clear of all liens, encumbrances, and charges except as noted: _____.

f. All leases are in good standing and that the Sellers have fulfilled all of their obligations under the leases;

g. That Sellers have made a full and fair disclosure in all material aspects of any matter that could reasonably be expected to affect the Purchaser's decision to purchase the business;

h. That Sellers will execute the necessary documents, make the necessary assignments, clearances, and assurances to assure that the Purchaser can assume ownership of the business and conduct business in the normal course of affairs.

8. The risk of loss or damage of the business and business assets remains with the Sellers until the time of closing.

9. The Sellers shall pay all sales taxes payable or collectible in connection with carrying on the business prior to closing. Sellers shall provide Purchaser at closing proof that the applicable sales taxes have been paid. The Purchaser shall pay any and all sales taxes payable in respect to the sale pursuant to this agreement.

10. The Sellers covenant with the Purchaser that, as part consideration for closing of this agreement, the Sellers will not operate a [type of business] or in any way aid or assist others to operate such a business within a 25-mile radius of the location of present business for a period of five years.

11. Sellers shall comply with all applicable laws governing the bulk sales or any other assets pursuant to this agreement.

12. The Sellers shall deliver to the Purchaser in proper form the following documents:

    a. bill of sales

    b. all records and financial data, including but not limited to, a list of customers, vendors, etc., relevant to the carrying on of the business

    c. executed assignments of leases

    d. clearance, consents, assurances reasonably necessary to carry on the business

    e. title documents on equipment and assets,

    f. executed notice required to be filed under any business name registration law; and

    g. any other documents needed to carry on the business.

13. This agreement is governed by the law of the state in which the business is located.

14. Time is of the essence in this agreement.

15. This agreement binds and benefits the parties and their respective heirs, executors, administrators, personal representatives, successors, and assigns.

16. If any provision or part of this agreement is void for any reason, it shall be severed without affecting the validity of the balance of this agreement.

17. There are no warranties, conditions, terms, or collateral contracts affecting the transaction contemplated in this agreement except as noted in this agreement.

This agreement constitutes an offer to purchase and may be accepted only by the Sellers. If the offer is not accepted by [date], this agreement becomes null and void. Acceptance may be only by the receipt by the Purchaser of a properly signed copy of this agreement.

EXECUTED under seal on this _____ day of _____, 19_____.

_____   _____
Seller   Purchaser

_____
Seller

8-6 PROVISION FOR EMPLOYMENT OF SELLER

As part of the sale and purchase of the business, the Buyer shall employ the Seller in a principal executive capacity and the Seller shall enter into the employ of the Buyer in said capacity. The employment shall commence on the closing date of the sale and shall last for a period of _____ months. The salary shall be $_____ per month. A completed employment contract is attached to the agreement as Exhibit ____ [not shown].

8-7 ASSUMPTION OF COLLECTIVE BARGAINING AGREEMENT

The only collective bargaining agreements that the Seller is a party to or is bound by are as follows:

[list union agreements here]

A true and complete copy of each agreement is attached to the agreement as Exhibit(s) _____[not shown]. The Buyer agrees to assume and will be bound by the attached contracts and will hold Seller harmless from any expense or liability arising out of any breach of the said collective bargaining contracts.

8-8 ASSUMPTION OF EMPLOYEE BENEFIT PLANS

The Buyer is familiar with the attached employee benefit plans, Exhibits _____ [not shown]. The Buyer hereby adopts and assumes the pension, profit-sharing, and retirement plans and any other employee benefit plans attached to this agreement. Buyer will take such action as is required to continue in effect all such employee benefit plans substantially in their present forms.

8-9   STATEMENT OF FICTITIOUS BUSINESS NAME

The following persons [list names, partnership, or corporation] is/are conducting business as [set forth fictitious name] at [address including street, city, county, and state]. The complete names and addresses of the individuals or of each general partner or name of corporation are as follows:

   The business is conducted as [individual, general partnership, limited partnership, unincorporated association, corporation, or business trust].

Dated: _____

_____
Signature

Statement filed with the County Clerk of _____ County, State of _____ on _____, 19_____.

8-10   ABANDONMENT OF FICTITIOUS BUSINESS NAME

The following persons [list names, partnership, or corporation] were conducting business as [set forth fictitious name] at [address including street, city, county, and state].

   The undersigned person hereby certifies that [name of business] has ceased to use the fictitious name in transacting business within the State of _____.

   The complete names and addresses of the individuals or of each general partner or name of corporation who conducted business under that name are as follows:

   The above fictitious name is hereby abandoned.

Dated: _____

_____
Signature

Statement filed with the County Clerk of _____ County, State of _____ on _____, 19_____.

8-11 NOTICE OF INTENDED BULK TRANSFER

To: [creditor name,
      address]

Notice is hereby given that:

1. [name of seller], Transferor, is about to make a bulk transfer or sale of the property of [business name].

2. The transfer is being made to: [name and address of Purchaser], Transferee.

3. The Transferor has not used any other business name except the one listed above in the last three years.

4. All debts of the Transferor will be paid in full as they come due. Creditors are to send all bills to: _____.

5. The property to be transferred is located at: _____.

6. The total debts of the transferor is estimated to be $_____.

7. A list of the creditors and the schedule of the property to be transferred may be inspected at [address].

8. The transfer is [or is not] being made to pay existing debts.

9. Creditors of the transferor must file their claims in writing with the transferee at the [address] on or before [date].

Dated:

_____

                    Transferee

Dated:

_____

                    Transferor

8-12

NOTICE OF INTENDED BULK TRANSFER (AUCTION)

To: [creditor name,
address]

Notice is hereby given that:

1. [name of auctioneer] is about to sell at a public auction certain property of [business name and address].
2. The auction will start at [date and time] at [location of auction].
3. As far as the auctioneer knows, the Transferor has not used any other business name except the one listed above in the last three years.
4. Creditors are to send all bills to:
5. The property to be transferred is located at:
6. The total debts of the Transferor is estimated to be $_____.
7. A list of the creditors and the schedule of the property to be transferred may be inspected at [address].
8. Creditors of the Transferor must file their claims in writing at [address] on or before [date].

Dated:

_____
Auctioneer

8–13   BULK SALES AFFIDAVIT

State of   )
County of   ) SS

The undersigned individual residing at [address], being duly sworn, deposes:

1. I am the [owner, president, or managing partner] of the business known as [name of company], hereinafter "Company" and I am the person who executed the attached bill of sale on behalf of the Company.

2. The Company is the sole owner of the property described in the attached bill of sale and has full right to sell and transfer the property involved.

3. All of the property described in the attached bill of sale is free and clear of all obligations and encumbrances.

4. There are no existing court judgments, nor any liens, replevin, attachments or executions, nor any petition in bankruptcy, nor has any arrangement proceeding been filed by or against the Company. In addition, the Company has not taken advantage of any law relating to insolvency.

This affidavit is made to induce the Purchaser to accept the transfer of the goods described in the attached invoice. It is also to assure compliance with the bulk transfer provisions of the UCC as enacted in the State of _____ and to assure the Purchaser that there are no creditors of the Company who are entitled to the statutory notice of sale.

_____

[signature]

State of   )
County of   ) SS

On this date, [list names of person(s) who signed above] personally appeared before me and acknowledged that the above signature(s) are valid and binding.

_____

Notary Public

My Commission expires:

Chapter 9

Corporate Forms and Agreements

This chapter contains a general discussion on the legal aspects of corporations and includes the forms and agreements used by small corporations, including forms involved in the transfer of stock, record of meetings, and stockholder notices.

Corporations

The corporate form of business ownership is the second most popular form of business ownership in the United States. Approximately 14 percent of all businesses are in this category. Although large corporations predominate in terms of dollar volume and gross annual sales, most businesses operating under the corporate form are small, closely held corporations.

In every state, corporations are recognized as separate legal entities having the authority to enter into contracts, to sue, and to own land. For practical purposes, a corporation is treated as an artificial person that is completely separate from its stockholders. A court may disregard this fiction to protect from fraud or injustice innocent persons who deal with the corporation.

Corporations are formed as either profit or nonprofit organizations. A *public corporation,* also classified as a *general corporation,* is publicly traded on the New York Stock Exchange, among others. A general corporation that is not publicly traded is classified as a *close corporation.* Most small- and medium-sized business corporations are close corporations.

In a close corporation, the ownership of stock is restricted by the articles of incorporation to a small group of people. The stock cannot be sold to the public without approval of the other share-holders.

A corporation must be organized under the laws of the state in which it is formed. A corporate name is required, and all acts on behalf of the corporation must be in the corporate name. Its name must indicate that it is operated under a corporate form of business—for example, The Blue Company, Inc.

Advantages and Disadvantages of the Corporate Form

The best-known advantage of the corporate form of business ownership is the limited personal liability of its stockholders. Stockholders usually are not personally liable except for the loss of their investments and for the debts or other obligations of the corporation. A *second* advantage of this form of ownership is that the shares of stock can be freely transferred or traded to others unless transfer or trade is restricted by provisions in the corporate charter. A *third* advantage is that a corporation has perpetual life. Unlike a partnership or sole proprietorship, the corporation continues when a principle investor dies. *Fourth*, a corporation has a regular form of management, and its profits, when distributed to its stockholders, are taxed as dividends, not as ordinary income.

Two disadvantages of the corporate form of ownership, first, are the more elaborate and expensive formalities of organization and management and, second, the fact that a corporation is a tax-paying entity, which may result in double taxation of its profits. Double taxation occurs because the corporation is required to pay taxes on its profits. Then the stockholder receives dividends, the dividends may be taxable as income.

Depending on the circumstances, the tax aspects of a corporation may be advantageous to individual shareholders. Unlike those of a partnership, the profits of a corporation are not taxable until the individual taxpayer receives dividends. If the dividends are reinvested in the corporation, the stockholder is not required to pay the individual taxes. In addition, the tax rate a corporation pays is usually lower than are personal income tax rates.

Foreign Corporations

A state uses the term *foreign corporation* to describe any corporation not organized under its laws. Thus, a corporation chartered in Delaware is a foreign corporation in New York. In an 1869 U.S. Supreme Court decision, *Paul v. Virginia*, the court ruled that a state has unlimited power to regulate foreign corporations because foreign corporations are not protected by the privileges and immunities clause in the Constitution. Under this authority, most states require foreign corporations to register with either the secretary of state or the commissioner of corporations before regularly doing business within the state.

Regularly doing business within the state means engaging in transactions within the state on a recurring basis. Infrequent sales to residents in the state from outside the state is not considered as doing business within the state.

Foreign corporations that are required to register with a state must also appoint an agent who resides within the state. The agent has the authority to accept the service of court or other legal papers on behalf of the corporation. The foreign corporation must also file a certified copy of its articles of incorporation with the secretary of state's office. Foreign corporations may be taxed only on business it has carried on within the state. In the case of real estate taxes, only the portion of corporate property located within the state is taxable.

Rules, regulations, and tax rates affecting corporations vary among the states. Because of this, states with favorable corporate laws, such as Delaware, become known as corporate havens. Businesses are incorporated within those states with the intention of operating in different states. These advantages help large, well-financed corporations, but they usually aren't cost effective for small closely held corporations because a resident agent and registration are required.

Ownership and Control of a Corporation

The business affairs of a corporation are managed by the board of directors. In small, close corporations they are managed by a chief executive officer (CEO). Because shareholders own the corporation's stock, they elect the board of directors and the chief executive officer. However, they do not manage the corporation. Not all stockholders have the right to vote, but there must be at least one class of stockholders with voting rights.

The board of directors and the chief executive officer of the corporation establish its general policies. Neither the members of the board nor the CEO is required to be stockholders, but in most cases they hold substantial portions of the voting stock. The board of directors or chief executive officer appoint the officers of the corporation, who are considered agents of the board or the CEO. They are obligated to enforce the policies of the board or CEO.

Stockholders' meetings must be held at least once a year in most states. All states require that the minutes of stockholders' meetings be kept as part of the corporation's records. Other meetings may be called as provided for in the corporation's articles of incorporation. Advance notice must be given to all shareholders prior to any special meetings. How special meetings are to be called and the notification requirements should be specified in the articles. Unless required by the articles, the stockholders' meetings need not be held in the state where the corporation was formed or is doing business. An unusual number of annual shareholders' meeting are held in resort areas such as Las Vegas.

Shareholders usually have one vote for each share of voting stock that they own. Shares may be voted in person or by proxy. A *Proxy* is the written authority shareholders give to another person to vote on their behalf.

Corporate Minutes

State statutes require that corporations (especially closely held ones) keep minutes of corporate meetings. Failure to keep the minutes may subject the directors to civil and criminal penalties. In addition, the shareholders often can be held liable for the debts of the corporation if adequate minutes are not kept. Common items required by state statutes to be included in corporate minutes include the following:

- Approval of acquisitions and sales of the business
- Ratification of actions taken by directors and officers
- All dividend declarations
- Election and reelection of officers
- All authorizations to issue stocks or other securities
- Approval of loans between the corporation and directors or officers of the corporation
- Approval of all major investments by the corporation
- Approval of all corporate reorganizations.

Management of the Corporation

As noted earlier, the directors and chief executive officer are responsible for the daily management of the corporation. Although stockholders own the corporation and are responsible for electing the board of directors and chief executive officer, they do not manage or directly control the corporation. They have no voice in the day-to-day management of the business. If the shareholders are unhappy with the management of the company, a majority of them can replace the directors or chief executive officer at a regular, scheduled meeting.

The directors and chief executive officer are obligated to manage the corporation using their best business judgment. Any shareholder may bring a stockholder's suit to enforce a corporate right or to protect corporate property that officers of the corporation have failed to protect. A stockholder's suit may also hold the directors and officers personally liable for any losses that result from unauthorized or illegal acts they commit. Before bringing suit, however, the shareholder must first demand that the directors take corrective action. Courts will not interfere with the actions of the directors or CEO unless the shareholder can establish the presence of bad faith, gross negligence, or illegal conduct. If the shareholder wins the suit, in most states the corporation must pay the legal expenses. If the shareholder loses, however, he or she may be required to pay the corporation's legal costs.

Because directors are in a position of trust, they owe a duty of loyalty to the corporation and are not permitted to make a profit at the company's expense. They are obligated to exercise "due care and prudence" in the management of the corporate business.

Dividends

The directors have the authority to declare dividends that may be payable in cash, property, or corporate stock. The stockholders can not force the directors to declare dividends unless they can establish that the directors are acting in bad faith. In most states, if at least one-third of the stockholders request it, the board must provide written justification for not declaring dividends. Usually, dividends can be paid only from the profits of the corporation. If cash or property dividends are paid in excess of the profits, the directors who declare the dividends may be personally liable for the excessive dividends when innocent third persons suffer damage.

The Corporation's Basic Documents

The corporation's structure and organization are set forth in its articles of incorporation, which contain a general statement of the corporation's purposes. The articles are drafted by the founders of the corporation (i.e., the incorporators) and are approved by the secretary of state or the commissioner of corporations of the state where the corporation is created. Any modifications to the articles must be approved by the state.

The second basic document of the corporation is its bylaws, which are the basic operating procedures of the corporation. Bylaws cannot conflict with the articles of incorporation. The articles of incorporation should provide procedures for self-amendment and stipulate any restrictions on the directors' ability to amend the bylaws. If the articles do not include the restrictions, the directors or the CEO may revise the bylaws without shareholder approval. The state will not approve a corporate charter until the articles of incorporation have been approved. By state law, certain provisions must be included in the articles.

Formation of the Corporation

Incorporators of a business may be individuals, partnerships, or other corporations. Incorporators do not have to live in the state where the corporation is formed. If they do not live in the state, then the incorporators authorize a resident of the state to accept the service of notices, court orders, and the like, on behalf of the corporation. This requirement gives the state a certain degree of control over the corporation.

The incorporators must file proposed articles of incorporation with the appropriate state office and pay the required fees. When the state accepts the articles and issues a charter, the corporation is born. The original corporation officers must be listed in the articles of incorporation. Although an individual may hold more than one office, most states require that at least two individuals serve as corporate officers. In many states, the positions of corporate secretary and corporate treasurer must be held by different individuals.

Self-Incorporation

The easiest and most convenient way to incorporate your business is to hire an attorney to do it for you. This isn't the most economical method because attorneys aren't cheap. The average businessperson can form a corporation without consulting an attorney, however.

If you decide to take this route, first get a copy of the regulations on incorporating from the office of the commissioner of corporations or the office or the secretary of state in the state where you wish to incorporate. Make sure you request the regulations for a corporation for profit, not a nonprofit one. If they don't give you enough help, buy a how-to-do-it book. If you follow this approach, find a book about incorporating in your state, because each state differs. The forms included in this chapter contain sample articles of incorporation. If you use them as guides, modify them to meet your state requirements.

In many states, private individuals may establish "closed" corporations that have broad general powers. The individuals sell all of the corporation's stock to businessowners who transfer their business to the corporation. They then have a corporate form of business ownership. When you use this method make sure the articles of incorporation fit your particular needs.

Dissolution of a Corporation

A corporation may be ended voluntarily by its shareholders or involuntarily by the state in which it was chartered. If a corporation fails to pay taxes or violates the statutes under which it was created, the secretary of state can take legal action either to suspend its operations or to dissolve it. Involuntary bankruptcy can also be grounds for dissolution. While it is suspended, a corporation cannot carry on any activities except those leading to dissolution.

Shareholders can voluntarily dissolve the corporation by filing articles of dissolution with the state and winding up the corporation's affairs. When voluntary dissolution occurs, the state corporation office will issue a certificate of dissolution after the state approves the shareholder's articles of dissolution.

If the state or the shareholders take no formal action, the corporation becomes dormant, but it isn't formally dissolved. Dormant corporations can be reactivated by the payment of back taxes, fees, or assessments.

Prior to the state's approving its voluntary dissolution, a corporation must send notices of intent to dissolve to all its creditors, authorize an agent to collect its assets, pay all its debts, and distribute its remaining assets.

Piercing the Corporate Veil

In some circumstances, to prevent fraud from occurring or to achieve equity, the courts disregard corporate status and hold the shareholders and directors liable. There are three situations in which the courts disregard corporate statutes, which is known as piercing the corporate veil:

1. When corporate goals and formalities are ignored, the shareholders treat the corporation's assets as their own property, and the corporation's officers fail to keep the necessary records.

2. When the corporation is undercapitalized. The general rule is that the shareholders must forward enough capital to cover any liabilities that may occur in carrying on the business.

3. When the corporation is organized for fraudulent purposes. For example, the corporate statutes are for fraudulently taken advantage of by an individual shareholder who transfers all of his or her property to the corporation to avoid paying personal debts.

If the court pierces the corporate veil, only active shareholders or those who participated in the fraud are held personally liable. Passive investors who have acted in good faith are usually not held personally liable. When shareholders are held liable, the entire amount of their investment is liable. Their personal assets are also subject to attachment and sale. Usually, only creditors or persons who have been defrauded by the corporation may pierce the corporate veil.

Piercing the veil is a drastic step and is not usually ordered by the courts except in situations where justice clearly requires it.

Professional Corporations

Professional corporations are established by doctors, lawyers, accountants, and other professional persons to gain such for tax advantages such as pension plans and deferred income programs. (Recent changes in federal income tax laws have made professional corporations less attractive than formerly. State statutes permitting professional corporations do not change the basic relationship between the professional practitioner and the client.)

Professional corporations are formed much as are usual corporations except that they can be formed by only one person. Professional corporations may engage in only one category of professional service, such as law or medicine, and only individuals licensed in the particular profession can own shares in them. Unlike those of standard corporations, the shares of professional corporations cannot be transferred without the permission of the secretary of state or the commissioner of corporations. The professional shareholder is personally held liable for malpractice but cannot be held liable for the malpractice of others.

Chapter S Corporations

Chapter S corporations are small, closely held corporations that have elected for federal income tax purposes to be taxed as partnerships. Under the Tax Reform Act of 1986, they were renamed—from "Sub-Chapter S corporations" to "S corporations." To qualify as a Chapter S corporation, the corporation must meet the following conditions:

- Be a domestic corporation.
- Have no more than a specified number of stockholders. (normally 35).
- Have only individuals, estates, or trusts as stockholders.
- Have no nonresident aliens as stockholders.
- Have only one class of stock.

If the corporation meets these requirements, it can elect to receive the special tax treatment by filing a Form 2553 with the IRS. The special status is automatically terminated when the corporation is no longer qualified to be treated as a Chapter S corporation. For example, if the corporation acquires more than 35 stockholders, its status as an S corporation is automatically terminated and the corporation must file and pay normal corporate taxes to the federal government.

Corporate Records

Corporations, including those wholly owned by one person, are required by state statutes or regulations to maintain certain records. The normal penalty for failure to maintain the required records is loss of corporate status protection for the shareholders (owners). The general requirements include articles of incorporation, bylaws, register of stock transactions, minutes of all stockholders' meetings, and copies of stockholders' resolutions.

Forms in This Chapter

- FORM 9–1: ARTICLES OF INCORPORATION. Used to incorporate those corporations in which there is only one class of stock and the stockholders are closely associated with one another. Most small businesses can use these sample articles as the basic guide in incorporating their business.

- FORM 9–2: ARTICLES OF INCORPORATION (WITH MORE THAN ONE CLASS OF STOCK). Used when there are two or more classes of stock.

- FORM 9–3: ARTICLES OF INCORPORATION FOR PROFESSIONAL CORPORATION. Used to incorporate a professional corporation.

- FORM 9–4: ARTICLES OF INCORPORATION (CHAPTER S). Used to incorporate a Chapter S Corporation.

- FORM 9–5: ACTION OF INCORPORATOR. Records the adoption of the by-laws.

- FORM 9–6: WAIVER OF NOTICE AND CONSENT TO HOLDING FIRST MEETING OF DIRECTORS. Records the waiver of notice and consent to holding the first meeting of the directors.

- FORM 9–7: MINUTES OF FIRST MEETING OF DIRECTORS. Records the first meeting of the directors.

- FORM 9–8: LETTER TO SECRETARY OF STATE (NONPROFIT). Forwards the necessary documents for filing to incorporate a nonprofit corporation.

- FORM 9–9: AVAILABILITY OF CORPORATE NAME. Requests information about the availability and reservation of a corporate name. Most states require that a fee be submitted with the request, which can be determined by calling the office of the secretary of state in the state where incorporation is proposed.

- FORM 9–10: REVOCABLE PROXY TO VOTE SHARES. Used by a stockholder who wishes to allow another person or business to vote his or her corporate shares.

- FORM 9–11: IRREVOCABLE PROXY TO VOTE SHARES. A proxy to vote shares of stock that cannot be cancelled.

- FORM 9–12: CORPORATE RESOLUTION. Records a corporate resolution.

- FORM 9–13: AFFIDAVIT OF SERVICE OF NOTICE OF MEETING (BY MAIL). Records the notice of a meeting of the board of directors meeting when notice is given by mail.

- FORM 9–14: CERTIFICATION OF BOARD OF DIRECTORS' MEETING. Certifies the minutes of a board of directors' meeting.

- FORM 9–15: NOTICE OF ANNUAL STOCKHOLDERS' MEETING. Gives notice of annual stockholders' meeting.

- FORM 9–16: NOTICE OF SPECIAL ACTIONS TO BE CONSIDERED AT ANNUAL MEETING. Notifies stockholders that special business actions are to be considered at the annual meeting. *Note*: Certain actions, such as the sale of the majority of assets of a corporation, require special notice.

- FORM 9–17: NOTICE OF SPECIAL MEETING OF MEMBERS. Notifies members of a special meeting of head members of nonprofit corporation.

- FORM 9–18: WAIVER OF NOTICE OF ANNUAL MEETING. Used when all stockholders waive notice of annual meeting. *Note:* All stockholders must sign a waiver for the waiver to be effective. They need not all sign the same piece of paper, so long as the content of each waiver is substantially the same.

- FORM 9–19: STOCK CERTIFICATE. Establishes proof of stock ownership.

- FORM 9–20: AFFIDAVIT OF LOST STOCK CERTIFICATE. Used to obtain replacement of a lost stock certificate.

- FORM 9–21: SUBSCRIPTION TO CORPORATE STOCK. Used to subscribe to corporate stock.

- FORM 9–22: ARTICLES OF INCORPORATION (SMALL, CLOSELY HELD CORPORATION). An alternate form of the articles that may be used for small, closely held corporations.

ARTICLES OF INCORPORATION

ARTICLES OF INCORPORATION
OF
[name of new corporation]

ONE: The name of this corporation is [name]

TWO: The purpose of the corporation is to engage in any lawful act or activity for which a corporation may be organized under the Laws of the State of _____ other than the banking business, the trust company business, or the practice of a profession permitted to be incorporated.

THREE: The name and address in this state of the corporation's initial agent for service of process are [list individual name and address here who can accept service on behalf of the corporation].

FOUR: This corporation is authorized to issue only one class of shares, which shall be designated "common" shares. The total number of such shares authorized to be issued is _____.

Dated this _____ day of _____, 19_____.

_____[signature of incorporator]
I declare that I am the person who executed the above Articles of Incorporation, and that this instrument is my act and deed.

_____ [signature of incorporator]

ARTICLES OF INCORPORATION (WITH MORE THAN ONE CLASS OF STOCK)

ARTICLES OF INCORPORATION
OF
[name of new corporation]

ONE: The name of this corporation is _____.

TWO: The purpose of the corporation is to engage in any lawful act or activity for which a corporation may be organized under the General Corporation Law of [state] other than the banking business, the trust company business, or the practice of a profession permitted to be incorporated.

THREE: The name and address in this state of this corporation's initial agent for service of process are [name and address of individual who can accept service on behalf of the corporation].

FOUR: (a) This corporation is authorized to issue two classes of shares, to be designated common and preferred, respectively. The corporation is authorized to issue _____ shares of common stock and _____ shares of preferred stock.

(b) The rights, preferences, privileges, and restrictions granted to or imposed on the respective classes or series of shares or on their holders are as follows: [insert a statement of the dividend rights, redemption provisions, (including a sinking fund, if any), conversion provisions (including antidilution protection), liquidation rights, voting rights, and the like, for the respective classes, and the protective provisions for rights of preferred shares] .

(c) The [name of preferred class] shares may be issued in any number of series, as determined by the board of directors. The board may by resolution fix the designation and number of shares of any such series.

(d) The board may determine, alter, or revoke the rights, preferences, privileges, and restrictions pertaining to any wholly unissued class or series of shares. The board may thereafter in the same manner increase or decrease the number of shares of any such series (but not below the number of shares of that series then outstanding).

_____
[signature of individual incorporator] [typed name]
Incorporator

By: _____
[signature of authorized individual; typed name and title below]

_____
[signature of initial director; typed name below]
Director

    I declare that I am the person who executed the above instrument and that this instrument is my act and deed.

_____
[signature of incorporator or director; typed name below]

    State of   )
    County of   )

    On [date], before me [insert name and title of officer] a notary public for the State of [identify], personally appeared [name(s)], personally known to me (or proved to me on the basis of satisfactory evidence) to be the person(s) whose name(s) [is/are] subscribed to the within instrument and acknowledged to me that [he/she/they] executed the same in [his/her/their] authorized capacity(ies), and that by [his/her/their] signatures on the instrument the person(s), or the entity on behalf of which the person(s) acted, executed the instrument.

WITNESS my hand and official seal.

      [seal]

                              _____
                              [notary's signature; typed name below]

                              _____

9-3

ARTICLES OF INCORPORATION FOR PROFESSIONAL CORPORATION

ARTICLES OF INCORPORATION OF
[name of new corporation]
A PROFESSIONAL CORPORATION

ONE: The name of this corporation is [name]

TWO: The purpose of the corporation is to engage in the practice of the profession of [law, medicine, or other profession]. The corporation shall have the authority to carry on any activities permitted by a profession corporation under the laws of the State of _____.

THREE: The name and address in this state of the corporation's initial agent for service of process are [list individual name and address who can accept service on behalf of the corporation].

FOUR: This corporation is authorized to issue only one class of shares, which shall be designated "common" shares. The total number of such shares authorized to be issued is _____.

FIVE: Only persons admitted in the State of _____ to practice the profession of _____ may own shares of stock or hold office as an officer in the corporation.

Dated this _____ day of _____, 19____.

_____
[signature of incorporator]

I declare that I am the person who executed the above Articles of Incorporation, and that this instrument is my act and deed.

_____
[signature of incorporator]

WITNESS my hand and official seal.

[seal]

_____
[notary's signature; typed name below]

_____

9–4
ARTICLES OF INCORPORATION (CHAPTER S)

ARTICLES OF INCORPORATION OF
[name of new corporation]
(CHAPTER S CORPORATION)

ONE: The name of this corporation is [name].

TWO: The purpose of the corporation is to engage in any lawful act or activity for which a corporation may be organized under the Law of the State of _____ other than the banking business, the trust company business, or the practice of a profession permitted to be incorporated.

THREE: The name and address in this state of the corporation's initial agent for service of process are [list individual name and address who can accept service on behalf of the corporation].

FOUR: This corporation is authorized to issue only one class of shares, which shall be designated "common" shares. The total number of such shares authorized to be issued is _____.

FIVE: This corporation is formed under the regulations for Chapter S corporations and will seek Chapter S designation with the Internal Revenue Service. Accordingly, only persons who qualify as stockholders under Chapter S requirements may hold stock in the corporation.

Dated this _____ day of _____, 19_____.

_____

[signature of incorporator]

I declare that I am the person who executed the above Articles of Incorporation, and that this instrument is my act and deed.

_____

[signature of incorporator]

WITNESS my hand and official seal.

　　　　[seal]

　　　　　　　　　　　　　　　　_____

　　　　　　　　　　　　　　　　[notary's signature; typed name below]

　　　　　　　　　　　　　　　　_____

9–5   ACTION OF INCORPORATOR

ACTION OF INCORPORATOR
OF
[name of corporation]

The undersigned, sole incorporator of _____, a [state] corporation, hereby adopts the following resolutions:

1. ADOPTION OF BYLAWS. The bylaws of the corporation as presented to the incorporator are adopted. The Secretary is hereby authorized and directed to execute a certification of the adoption of the bylaws and to file the bylaws as so certified in the minute book of the corporation, and to see that a copy of the bylaws, similarly certified, is kept at the principal office of the corporation in accordance with the Corporations Code.

2. ELECTION OF DIRECTORS. The following persons are elected directors of the corporation, to hold office until the next annual meeting and until their successors have been elected and qualified: [list names].

3. APPOINTMENT OF OFFICERS. The following persons are hereby appointed to the indicated offices, to serve at the pleasure of the board of directors:[list names and offices].

Dated: _____

_____
[signature of incorporator]

WITNESS my hand and official seal.

[seal]

_____
[notary's signature; typed name below]

_____

9–6   WAIVER OF NOTICE AND CONSENT TO HOLDING FIRST MEETING OF DIRECTORS

WAIVER OF NOTICE AND CONSENT TO HOLDING
FIRST MEETING OF DIRECTORS
OF
[name of corporation]

We, the undersigned, all the directors of [name of corporation] hereby waive notice of the first meeting of the board of directors on [date] at [location] and consent to the holding of this meeting at the time and place stated above and to the transaction of any and all business, including electing officers, adopting a corporate seal and form of share certificate, providing for the issuance of stock, and any other action that may be necessary or appropriate to complete the organization of the corporation.

Dated: _____

_____

_____

_____

_____

9-7

MINUTES OF FIRST MEETING OF DIRECTORS

MINUTES OF FIRST MEETING OF DIRECTORS
OF
[name of corporation]

This is a record of the minutes of the first meeting of directors of [name of corporation] corporation.

The board of directors of [name of corporation] held its first meeting on [date], at [time], at [address], [city and state] .

The undersigned, all the directors of _____, acting by unanimous written consent without a meeting pursuant to the bylaws of the corporation, consent to their election as directors, accept the resignation of the incorporator(s), and adopt the following resolutions:

The following directors were present: [list names]. The following directors were absent: [list names, or state "None"]. Also present at the meeting were: [list names and titles of other persons present].

[Name] acted as chair of the meeting, and [name] acted as secretary of the meeting.

The chair presented to the meeting the written waiver of notice and consent to the holding of the first meeting of directors signed by each director of the corporation. The chair instructed the secretary to make it a part of the records of the meeting and to insert it in the minute book immediately preceding these minutes.

The chair announced that the corporation was incorporated on [date], the date on which the articles of incorporation were filed by the Secretary of State. The chair presented a certified copy of the articles and directed the secretary to insert it in the corporation's minute book.

The chair informed the board that the corporation is required by statute to designate an agent for service of process in the State of _____, and that [name of agent] had been designated as that agent in the corporation's articles filed with the Secretary of State. On motion duly made, seconded, and unanimously carried, the board adopted the following resolutions:

RESOLVED, that [name], a resident of (state), whose [business/residence] address is [address], is [approved/appointed] as this corporation's agent for service of process.

RESOLVED, that [name of corporate agent], a corporation incorporated under the laws of [state], appointed as this corporation's agent for service of process in State of _____ as required by the Corporations Code.

The chair presented a copy of the corporation's bylaws, as adopted by the incorporator. The board reviewed the general provisions of the bylaws and adopted the following resolutions:

RESOLVED, that the bylaws adopted by the incorporator of this corporation are approved; and

RESOLVED FURTHER, that the secretary of this corporation is authorized and directed to execute a certificate of the adoption of those bylaws, to insert those bylaws as so certified in the minute book of this corporation, and to cause a copy of those bylaws, as they may be amended from time to time, to be kept and maintained at the principal executive office of this corporation.

The board appointed officers for the corporation. The following persons were appointed to the offices set forth opposite their names:

Name	Office
_____	President
_____	Vice President
_____	Secretary
_____	Chief Financial Officer

to serve at the pleasure of the board.

The board also adopted the following resolution authorizing the chief financial officer to act as the corporation's treasurer:

RESOLVED, that for purposes of giving any reports or executing any documents requiring the signature of the "treasurer," the chief financial officer is also deemed to be the treasurer of this corporation.

The chair presented to the board for its approval a proposed seal of the corporation, and the board adopted the following resolutions:

RESOLVED, that the corporate seal presented to this board of directors is adopted as the seal of this corporation; and

RESOLVED FURTHER, that the secretary is directed to affix an impression of the corporate seal of this corporation to the minutes of this meeting in the margin opposite this resolution.

The chair presented to the board of directors for its approval a proposed form of share certificate for the corporation. The board adopted the following resolution.

RESOLVED, that the form of share certificate presented to this board of directors is adopted for use by this corporation, and the secretary is directed to insert a copy of that form of share certificate in the corporation's minute book immediately following the minutes of the meeting.

The chair informed the board of directors that the accounting year should be fixed for the corporation, and the board adopted the following resolution:

RESOLVED, that the first fiscal year of this corporation shall commence on [date of filing of articles by Secretary of State] and shall end on the next succeeding [month and day], and thereafter the corporation's fiscal year shall end on [month and day] of each year.

The chair noted the desirability of designating a principal executive office for the corporation, and the board adopted the following resolution:

RESOLVED, that [address of principal executive office], is designated as the principal executive office of this corporation.

The chair advised the board that, within 90 days after its articles were filed, the corporation must file an annual informational statement with the State Secretary. The board adopted the following resolution:

RESOLVED, that the secretary of this corporation is authorized and directed to prepare and to file or cause to be filed with the Secretary of State the necessary statement; and

RESOLVED FURTHER, that the secretary is directed to insert a copy of that statement in the minute book following the minutes of this meeting.

The chief financial officer informed the board that it would be necessary to establish one or more bank checking and savings accounts and to select a depositary for the corporation's employment taxes trust funds. The board was informed that an SS–4 form had been submitted to the Internal Revenue Service, applying for an employer identification number. The board adopted the following resolutions:

RESOLVED, that this corporation establish in its name one or more deposit accounts with [name of bank], and that the [title, e.g., president] and the [title, e.g., secretary] of this corporation are authorized to establish such an account or accounts, on terms and conditions as agreed on with the bank.

RESOLVED FURTHER, that the corporation's employment taxes trust funds shall be deposited with [name, branch, and address of financial institution].

RESOLVED FURTHER, that the [title, e.g., president] and [title, e.g., secretary], acting together, are authorized to designate as depositaries of this corporation's funds one or more other banks, trust companies, or other financial institutions, and to open, keep, and close general and special accounts in such depositaries.

RESOLVED FURTHER, that any officer of the corporation is authorized to endorse checks, drafts, or other evidences of indebtedness made payable to the corporation, but only for the purpose of deposit; and

RESOLVED FURTHER, that all checks, drafts, and other instruments obligating the corporation to pay money, including instruments payable to officers or other persons authorized to sign them, shall be signed on the corporation's behalf by any of the following officers: [titles of officers authorized to sign checks]; provided, however, that if the amount of the check is in excess of [insert amount], the signature of any two of the following officers [titles] shall be required.

RESOLVED FURTHER, that the standard form of corporate resolution required by [name of financial institution] for opening a corporate account, as presented to this meeting, a copy of which is attached to these minutes, is adopted as the resolution of the board of directors, and the secretary is directed to obtain the necessary signatures, execute the necessary certifications, and take such other steps as needed to open this account.

The meeting then considered the payment of the expenses of incorporation and organization. The chair reported on the fees and expenses that had been incurred to date in this connection [totaling approximately $_____, and the board approved the following resolution:

RESOLVED, that the chief financial officer is authorized and directed to pay the expenses of incorporation and organization and to reimburse the persons advancing funds to the corporation for this purpose, as stated in the report presented to this meeting.

The board considered the applicability of section 1244 of the Internal Revenue Code to the corporation's [common] stock. Section 1244 entitles shareholders to ordinary loss tax treatment of losses from stock that qualifies as "section 1244 stock." The board noted that the corporation is a small business corporation as defined in Internal Revenue Code Section 1244(c)(3)(A). The board adopted the following resolutions:

RESOLVED, that this corporation intends to qualify its [common] stock for treatment under Section 1244 of the Internal Revenue Code, under which the corporation plans that its total equity capital and paid-in surplus shall not in any event exceed $1,000,000, that it shall be largely an operating company, with less than 50 percent of its gross receipts coming from passive sources (royalties, rents, dividends, interest, annuities, and sales or exchanges of stocks or securities), and that it shall conform in all other respects to the requirements necessary to qualify its [common] stock for treatment under section 1244 of the Internal Revenue Code.

RESOLVED FURTHER, that the secretary of this corporation is authorized and directed to keep all records, prepare all reports and returns, and take all other steps as may be necessary to qualify this corporation's [common] stock for treatment under Section 1244 of the Internal Revenue Code.

The board next discussed the issuance of shares. It noted that a total of [number] shares of its [class, e.g., common] stock are authorized by the articles of incorporation of which [number/no.] shares are currently issued and outstanding. It adopted the following resolutions:

RESOLVED, that the corporation issue and sell a total of [total number] shares of its authorized [class, e.g., common] stock to the following persons, in the number and for the consideration set forth opposite their names, respectively:

Name	Number of Shares	Consideration and (if other than cash) Fair Value
[fill in]	[fill in]	[fill in]
[fill in]	[fill in]	[fill in]
[fill in]	[fill in]	[fill in]

RESOLVED FURTHER, that the officers of the corporation are authorized, empowered, and directed to take all actions that may be necessary and proper for this corporation to issue and sell the above-listed shares to the persons named, in accordance with applicable laws, and that those actions shall include, when necessary: (i) filing with the Commissioner of Corporations an appropriate notice or obtaining qualification of the offer and sale of such shares from the Commissioner of Corporations; (ii) doing all acts that may be necessary under the federal securities laws and the applicable securities laws of any other state; and (iii) doing all acts necessary to expedite these transactions or conform them, or any of them, to the requirements of any applicable law.

RESOLVED FURTHER, that each of the officers of this corporation is authorized and directed to execute all documents and to take any other action necessary or advisable to carry out the purposes of this resolution.

The board considered the advantages of electing to be taxed as "an S corporation" under Internal Revenue Code Subchapter S, Sections 1361-1379. It was noted that the corporation comes within the definition of an "S corporation" contained in Section 1361(b) of the Internal Revenue Code in that it is not a member of an affiliated group, it does not have more than 35 shareholders, it has no shareholders who are not individuals and has no shareholders who are nonresident aliens, and it has only one class of stock. After discussion, the following resolutions were adopted:

RESOLVED, that this corporation elects, subject to the unanimous consent of all shareholders, to be an "S corporation" for federal income tax purposes as provided in Section 1362(a) of the Internal Revenue Code. This election is made for the year ending [date], and for each succeeding year until this election is revoked.

RESOLVED FURTHER, that the officers of this corporation are authorized and directed to prepare the documents indicating this election, execute them on behalf of the corporation, obtain the necessary signatures or consents of all shareholders, file the documents with the appropriate authorities, and take any other actions necessary or desirable to effect the purposes of the foregoing resolution.

There being no further business to come before the meeting, the meeting was adjourned by the presiding officer at [time].

_____

[signature of secretary]

9-8

LETTER TO SECRETARY OF STATE (NONPROFIT)

To: Secretary of State
   Corporate Filing Section
   [address]

Re: [name of corporation]

Dear Secretary of State:

   I am enclosing an original and five copies of the proposed Articles of Incorporation of _____, Inc., a proposed [name of state], nonprofit public benefit corporation, together with the Franchise Tax Exemption Application, application fee, and its attachments, fastened separately.

   Please forward the exemption application materials to the Franchise Tax Board and, upon exemption approval, file the enclosed original Articles of Incorporation. After filing, please return to me, at the above address, two of the enclosed copies of the Articles, compared and certified by your office. A check in the amount of $_____ payable to your office is also enclosed.

Sincerely,

9-9   AVAILABILITY OF CORPORATE NAME

Office of the Secretary of State
[street address]
[city, state, and zip code]

Attention: Availability of Corporation Name Division

Dear Sir or Madam:

I am forming a new corporation to be incorporated in the state. The preferred names of the corporation are listed in order of preference:

[List three or four names in order of preference]

Please reserve for 90 days the first available name from the above list, and send the certificate of reservation to my above listed address. If none of the names is available, please notify me of this fact.
Enclosed is the required fee for your service.
Thank you for your cooperation.

Sincerely,

_____
[requesting person's signature]

REVOCABLE PROXY TO VOTE SHARES

REVOCABLE PROXY TO VOTE SHARES
OF
(name of corporation)

The undersigned, being the owner of _____ shares of voting stock of the [name of corporation] do hereby grant to _____ a proxy and appoint him/her my attorney-in-fact to vote on behalf of the undersigned all shares of said stock at any future general or special meeting of the stockholders of the Corporation, and said proxy holder is entitled to attend said meetings and act on my behalf and vote shares personally or through mail proxy, to the same extent as if I voted the shares personally.

During the life of this proxy, all rights to vote the shares shall be held by the proxyholder with full power of substitution or revocation, until this authority is revoked in writing by the undersigned.

The undersigned may revoke this proxy at any time by providing written notice of termination by certified mail, return receipt requested to both the proxy holder and the corporation.

The proxyholder shall be entitled to reimbursement for reasonable expenses incurred hereunder, but otherwise is not entitled to compensation for services rendered under this proxy.

This agreement is binding on and inures to the benefit of the parities, their successors, assigns, and personal representatives.

IN WITNESS WHEREOF, I have signed and executed this proxy on this _____ day of _____, 19_____ .

_____
Stockholder

Accepted on this date:

_____
Proxyholder

State of   )
County of   )

On this date, the above stockholder appeared personally before me and acknowledged that his/her above signature was valid and true.

SEAL   _____
                                                       Notary Public
                                                       My commission expires:

9–11   IRREVOCABLE PROXY TO VOTE SHARES

IRREVOCABLE PROXY TO VOTE SHARES
OF
(name of corporation)

The undersigned, being the owner of _____ shares of voting stock of the (name of corporation) for and in consideration of one dollar, do hereby grant to _____
a proxy and appoint him/her my attorney-in-fact to vote on behalf of the undersigned all shares of said stock at any future general or special meeting of the stockholders of the Corporation, and said proxy holder is entitled to attend said meetings and act on my behalf and vote shares personally or through mail proxy, to the same extent as if I voted the shares personally.

During the life of this proxy, all rights to vote the shares shall be held by the proxyholder with full power of substitution or revocation, until this authority is revoked in writing by the undersigned.

The undersigned may not revoke this proxy, however, the proxy shall not extend beyond the shareholders' meeting, or any extension thereof, to be held on [date].

The proxyholder shall be entitled to reimbursement for reasonable expenses incurred hereunder, but otherwise is not entitled to compensation for services rendered under this proxy.

This agreement is binding on and inures to the benefit of the parties, their successors, assigns, and personal representatives.

IN WITNESS WHEREOF, I have signed and executed this proxy on this _____ day of _____, 19_____.

_____
Stockholder

Accepted on this date:

_____
Proxyholder

State of   )
County of   )

On this date, the above stockholder appeared personally before me and acknowledged that his/her above signature was valid and true.

SEAL   _____
                                                        Notary Public
                                                        My commission expires:

9-12 CORPORATE RESOLUTION

I, the undersigned person, Secretary to the [name of corporation] do hereby certify that at a meeting of the Board of Directors of the [name of corporation] that was duly held at [city and state where meeting was held] with a quorum being present, the following resolution was duly adopted and that the said resolution has not been amended, changed, annulled or revoked, and is not in conflict with any provisions of the Charter or Bylaws of the corporation:

RESOLVED, That [at this point insert wording of the corporate resolution]

IN WITNESS THEREOF, I have subscribed my name and affixed the corporate seal on this _____ day of _____, 19____.

_____
Secretary

9-13 AFFIDAVIT OF SERVICE OF NOTICE OF MEETING (BY MAIL)

State of   )
County of   )

I, [insert name], an adult, having been duly sworn and under oath state: I am the duly qualified secretary of [name of corporation].

That in my duties as secretary, on [date of mailing] I caused to be mailed, notice of the meeting of the board of directors in the said corporation in the form attached [attach copy of notice with document], to be held at the [location of meeting] on [date and time of meeting]. The said notice was dispatched by delivery to the U.S. Postal Office in sealed envelopes, postage prepaid, addressed to each of the directors of the board of said corporation at his or her address as their addresses appear on the official records of the corporation.

Dated this _____ day of _____, 19____.

_____
Secretary

9–14

CERTIFICATION OF BOARD OF DIRECTORS' MEETING

State of   )
County of   )

    [Your name] being duly sworn, deposes and says that he/she is the Secretary of the [name of corporation], organized under the laws of the State of [state in which corporation organized] and having its principle place of business at [location of principal place of business]; that he/she has official custody of the books of said corporation; and that the foregoing is a full, true and correct copy of the minutes of a regular meeting of the Board of Directors of said corporation, held on [date], at (location of meeting).

Witness my hand and seal of the Corporation this _____ day of _____, 19_____.

_____
Secretary

Corporate Seal

Sworn to before me on this

_____ day of
_____ 19_____.

_____
Notary Public

My Commission expires:

NOTICE OF ANNUAL STOCKHOLDERS' MEETING
[name of corporation]
[address of corporation]

You are cordially invited to attend the annual meeting of stockholders of [name of corporation] to be held on the _____ day of _____, 19_____.

The meeting will be held at [address of meeting].

The meeting will start promptly at [time].

If you plan to attend, please return the enclosed attendance card. This will assist the staff in making the necessary arrangements. Please be advised that as a stockholder, you have a right to attend the annual meeting without submitting the attendance card.

If you do not plan to attend, you may wish to complete the enclosed proxy form.

[Optional paragraph]

The following matters will be discussed, actions may be taken and may be voted on:

Only stockholders of record on the stock transfer books of the corporation at the close of business on [date] will be allowed to vote.

Dated: _____

_____
Secretary

9–16 NOTICE OF SPECIAL ACTIONS TO BE CONSIDERED AT ANNUAL MEETING

NOTICE OF SPECIAL ACTIONS TO BE CONSIDERED
AT ANNUAL MEETING
[name of corporation]

Special Notice to Stockholders:

As required by the laws of the State of _____,
and by direction of the Board of Directors of the [name of corporation]
corporation, notice is hereby given that in addition to the usual business
matters to be discussed at the annual meeting of the stockholders of the
[name of corporation] to be held on [date and time of meeting] at [place
of meeting], the said meeting will also discuss and action may be taken on
the following special business:

[include description of special business to be conducted]

_____
Secretary

9–17 NOTICE OF SPECIAL MEETING OF MEMBERS

To members of [name of corporation]:

Notice is hereby given that pursuant to the provisions of the state law
dealing with nonprofit corporations, a special meeting of members of
[name of corporation] will be held on [date and time of meeting] at
[location of meeting].

The purpose of the meeting will be for the purposes of: [insert purposes
here, e.g. for the purposes of amending the By-Laws of the [name of
corporation] as set forth below.

_____
President

WAIVER OF NOTICE OF ANNUAL MEETING

WAIVER OF NOTICE OF ANNUAL MEETING
OF STOCKHOLDERS
[name of corporation]

We, the undersigned stockholders of [name of corporation], constitute all the stockholders of [name of corporation] corporation. We do hereby waive notice and publication of said annual meeting of the stockholders to be held on [date and time of meeting] at [place of meeting]; and we agree that any business transacted shall be valid and legal of the same force and effect as though the said meeting was held after notice given and published.

Witness our hand this _____ day of _____ 19_____.

Stockholders

_____

_____

_____

_____

_____

_____

9–19   STOCK CERTIFICATE

No. [number of certificate]

[par value $ _____ /without par value]

[number] Shares

[Name of issuing corporation]
a [insert state name here] corporation

This certifies that [name of shareholder] is the owner of [number] shares of [describe] stock, [par value $_____ /without par value], _____ of [name of issuer] transferable on the books of the corporation only by the holder in person or by attorney, on surrender of this certificate properly endorsed.

IN WITNESS WHEREOF, the corporation has caused this certificate to be signed by its duly authorized officers and to be sealed with the seal of the corporation this [date].

[Seal]

_____
[signature; typed name below]
[President/Vice President]

_____
[signature; typed name below]
[Secretary/Assistant Secretary]

9-20 AFFIDAVIT OF LOST STOCK CERTIFICATE

State of   )
County of   )

I, _____, residing at _____,
being duly sworn hereby depose that:

1. I am the owner of _____ shares of stock in
   _____ corporation, hereinafter referred to as the corporation. The shares are represented by stock certificate number: _____.

2. The said stock certificate has been lost or mislaid.

3. I have not sold or transferred said certificate.

4. That I agree to indemnify the corporation for any loss as a result of a
   claim by any holder in due course of the said certificate.

Dated:

State of   )
County of   ) SS

On this date, [list names of person(s) who signed above] personally
appeared before me and acknowledged that the above signature(s) are
valid and binding.

                                    _____
                                    Notary Public

                                    My Commission expires:

9-21   **SUBSCRIPTION TO CORPORATE STOCK**

FOR VALUABLE CONSIDERATION RECEIVED, I hereby agree to purchase _____number of shares of the [name of company]. The shares shall be [common] [preferred] stock in the corporation. The price shall be _____per share for a total amount of $_____.

It is my understanding that the shares that I am purchasing have the same rights and privileges of all shares of the same class of stock. The shares that I am purchasing equals _____ percent of all issued and outstanding stock of the same class and _____ percent of all of the issued and outstanding stock of the corporation, regardless of class.

The purchase price will be paid on or before _____, 19_____.

Dated: _____

_____
Purchaser

Agreed to and accepted:

_____

By _____
for the above mentioned corporation

9–22   ARTICLES OF INCORPORATION (SMALL, CLOSELY HELD CORPORATON)

ARTICLES OF INCORPORATION
OF
ALL BUSINESS COMPANY, INC.

We, the undersigned incorporators, hereby certify and file this Certificate of Incorporation under the provisions and subject to the laws of the State of _____, particularly [at this point insert the specific state statute under which the corporation is incorporated] for the purposes of the transaction of business and conduct and promotion of the objects and purposes stated in this document.

The name of the incorporation (hereinafter called the Corporation) is ALL BUSINESS COMPANY, INC.

The Corporation's principal place of business is located in the City of _____, in the County of _____, in the State of _____, at the street and number of _____. [If the principal place of business is outside the state include this phrase: The address of resident agent of the Corporation is _____]

The nature of the business and the purposes to be conducted and promoted by the Corporation are _____. In addition, to the authority to promote any lawful purpose and to engage in any lawful activity for which corporations may be organized under the General Corporation Laws of the State of _____.

The names and addresses of each of the incorporators:

The names and addresses of the original directors are:

The Corporation shall have perpetual existence.

The total number of shares of stock which the corporation is authorized to issue is _____with a par value of $_____ each. All shares of stock shall be of one class and are Common Stock. The number of shares of stock originally issued is _____.

The effective date of the articles of incorporation of the Corporation, and the date upon which the existence of the corporation shall commence is _____, 19____.

IN WITNESS WHEREOF, we, the undersigned incorporators, do hereby further certify that the facts hereinabove stated are truly set forth and have set our respective signatures and seals.

Dated at [place] [month, day, year]:

_____ (seal)

_____ (seal)

_____ (seal)

State of   )
County of   )

On the below listed date, the following persons personally appeared before me [list names of incorporators], all incorporators who sign the foregoing Articles of Incorporation, known to me personally to be such and are familiar with the provisions and contents of the Articles of Incorporation, they acknowledged the act of signing their names and state that the facts of the above document are truly set forth.

Given under my hand and seal of office this _____ day of _____, 19____.

_____
Notary Public

My Commission expires:

Chapter 10

Independent Contractors and Subcontractors

This chapter discusses independent contractors and subcontractors and all the common forms and agreements used by businesses in dealing with them. This chapter also contains a checklist for determining whether an individual is a subcontractor or an employee.

Using Independent Contractors

Whereas most employees work for wages under the direct control of the employer or supervisors, an independent contractor usually does the job for a set fee and retains control over the project. The advantages of using independent contractors rather than employees include the following:

- Generally, the Fair Labor Standards Act (FLSA), which requires the payment of overtime pay (in certain circumstances) and of minimum wages and contains child labor and other restrictions on employers does not apply to the use of independent contractors.
- Workers' disability and compensation insurance requirements do not apply to independent contractors.
- Employers are not required to provide any fringe benefits to independent contractors.
- Employers are not required to pay Social Security or employment taxes (payroll) on wages paid to independent contractors.
- Employers do not withhold income taxes on monies paid to independent contractors.

Contractor or Employee?

There are no clear rules as to when a government agency will determine that the individual is an employee, not an independent contractor. Generally, a person is considered to be an employee if the individual is subject to an employer's control and supervision.

Restatement of Agency

The *Restatement of Agency, 2d ed.,* defines an employee as follows:

An employee is a person employed to perform in the affairs of another and who with respect to the physical conduct in the performance of the services is subject to the other's control or right to control.

The *Restatement* lists the following factors to assist in determining whether a person is an employee or independent contractor, which are often referred to as the *common law* factors that distinguish an independent contractor from an employee:

- The extent of control the employer may exercise over the individual. (An employer has extensive control over the manner in which the employee carries out a job.)

- Whether the individual is engaged in a distinct business or occupation. (An independent contractor is normally engaged in a distinct business or occupation different from that of the employer.)

- The skill required to do the particular job in question. (Independent contractors normally have certain special skills or training.)

- The supplier of the tools and place of work for the individual doing the work. (An employer normally supplies the tools and the place of work for an employee, whereas independent contractors provide their own tools and place of work.)

- The method of payment, whether by time or by job. (An employee is normally paid by the amount of time expended working whereas an independent contractor is paid by the job.)

- Whether the work is part of the regular business of the employer.

- Custom or tradition area as to whether the individual is an independent contractor or an employee.

The Fair Labor Standards Act

The U.S. Supreme Court uses six factors in determining whether an individual is an employee or contractor for purposes of the Fair Labor Standards Act. The court also held that the definition of *employee* was broader for FLSA purposes than under the usual common law definition. The court indicated that there was no single definition of employee that would solve the question in all cases. Of the six factors that the court listed as significant in determining the employment relationship, no one factor was considered to be controlling. The factors listed by the court are the following:

1. *Control.* The nature and degree of control by the principle (employer) over the individual doing the job.
2. *Integral part.* Are the services performed by the individual an integral part of the employer's business?
3. *Investment.* The amount of the investment in facilities and equipment by the worker. Whose tools and equipment are being used?
4. *Permanency.* How permanent is the relationship between the worker and the employer? Is the relationship an ongoing concern or of short duration? If the relationship is a continuing one, the more likely it is that the individual is an employee rather than a contractor.
5. *Initiative and judgment.* The amount of initiative and judgment placed on the individual. The more initiative and judgment, the more likely it is that the individual will be considered a contractor rather than an employee.
6. *Opportunity for loss.* If the worker has no opportunity to lose money on the arrangement, it is an indication that he or she is an employee.

The View of the IRS

The Internal Revenue Service takes a dim view of the use of independent contractors because of the potential loss of tax revenue when an individual is treated as a contractor rather than an employee. Section 3121(d) of the *Internal Revenue Code* defines an employee for purposes of the tax code as follows: "Any individual who, under the usual common law rules applicable in determining the employer–employee relationship, has, the status of an employee." The loss of tax revenue results when the employer fails to withhold taxes and the employee/contractor never pays or never files a return.

The common law factors considered by the IRS include the following:

Is the worker required to follow instructions of the employer? Normally contractors are given job specifications rather than instructions on how to do the job.

Is the worker required personally to do the actual work? Generally, contractors are hired to complete a job and may hire subcontractors to do the actual work, whereas an employee must personally do the job.

Is the worker required to work set hours? Normally, a contractor sets the work hours.

Who controls the worker's assistants? A contractor hires his or her own assistants and has control over them.

Does the worker pursue work from others? Normally, a contractor seeks work from more than one business.

Who decides where the work will be accomplished? Generally, a contractor controls where the work is accomplished.

Who provides training for the worker? Normally, a contractor does not receive training from the employer.

Is the work relationship a continuing one? Contractors do not usually have a continuing relationship with the hiring company.

Does the worker make interim reports? Employees are usually required to make interim reports, whereas contractors are not.

Does the worker work for other firms. Contractors normally work for more than one firm, whereas employees do not.

Who pays incidental expenses? Contractors normally pay their own incidental expenses whereas employees do not.

Does the worker have a significant investment in the business? Contractors normally perform their services without the use of company property.

Can the worker be fired at will? Contractors have contracts to complete the product or do the service and thus cannot be terminated without cause.

Does the worker get any pay if the job is not completed? Contractors normally do not get paid unless they complete the job.

Does the worker offer services to the general public? Contractors usually make their services available to the general public by having an office or place of business, advertising, owning a business license, and listing their services in a business directory.

IRS Audits   During the past several years, the IRS auditors have cracked down on companies that classified their workers as independent contractors to avoid the payment of payroll taxes. At one time, it was estimated that the IRS had 400 field agents assigned to audit this practice. A recent General Accounting Office report estimated that 38 percent of the businesses that it studied had misclassified their employees as independent contractors.

The penalties for misclassifying an employee as a contractor include the requirement to pay all back payroll taxes plus a 100 percent penalty with interest. In addition, if the employer should have withheld income taxes on the salaries of these individuals but did not, the employer may be required to pay to the government an amount equal to all the withholding taxes that should have been withheld from the workers' pay. For example, if you paid a worker $15,000 and listed him or her as a contractor rather than an employee and the IRS says that the individual is an employee, the employer could owe approximately $6,500 in back taxes, penalties, and fines.

One reason that the IRS does not like the classification of *independent contractor* is that it feels that contractors voluntarily report only about 80 percent of their income compared to employees, who report over 95 percent of their earned income.

If the IRS determines that the employer was acting in good faith when the worker was misclassified as an contractor rather than as an employee, normally they will collect only back taxes and interest. In addition, employers may be protected under the "safe harbor" concept. This concept is a special exemption for workers who do not qualify as contractors if one of the following conditions exists:

- They have been consistently treated as contractors since December 31, 1977.
- They have never been treated as an employee, and you have filed the required Form 1099s since December 31, 1978.
- There was a reasonable basis for treating the workers as contractors: You relied on an IRS ruling or written advice from the IRS in response to a request for technical advice; or in a past IRS audit on this subject, the IRS did not reclassify the workers as employees. (*Note:* IRS Procedure 85–18 states that IRS agents should liberally construe what constitutes a "reasonable basis" in favor of the employer.)

IRS Form 1099– Miscellaneous

As noted earlier, in some cases the filing of a Form 1099 on the worker helps to establish that the employer was acting in good faith in classifying the worker as a contractor. The IRS regulations require that a Form 1099 be filed by employers on payments of $600 or more per calendar year made to contractors. There is a penalty for failure to file the required forms. One copy is given to the contractor, and one is filed with the IRS. Most states also require that a copy be filed with the state.

Correcting the Problem

An employer should correct the misclassification as soon as possible. If, however, an employer has five independent contractors on Friday and on the following Monday reclassifies them as employees, this action could be a red flag to the IRS. The best time to reclassify is at the start of a new tax year. Another method is to lease the employees from an employee-leasing company. The leasing firm hires them, pays all required taxes, and passes the cost on to the employer.

Written Contract

The fact that there is a written contract between the business owner and the independent contractor is evidence that the relationship is that of client and contractor rather than employer and employee.

Forms in This Chapter

- FORM 10–1 CONTRACT WITH INDEPENDENT CONTRACTOR. A guide for drafting a contract with an independent contractor.
- FORM 10–2: NOTICE OF PRELIEN. Provides a notice of a prelien.
- FORM 10–3: NOTICE OF CONTRACTOR'S LIEN. Provides notice of a contractor's lien.
- FORM 10–4: RELEASE OF LIEN. Releases a lien.
- FORM 10–5: AGREEMENT TO EXTEND PERFORMANCE DATE. Extends performance date on a contract with independent contractor.
- FORM 10–6: ARBITRATION AGREEMENT (BINDING). Used for a binding arbitration agreement.
- FORM 10–7: ARBITRATION AGREEMENT (NONBINDING). Used for a nonbinding arbitration agreement.

10-1
CONTRACT WITH INDEPENDENT CONTRACTOR

*SAMPLE CONTRACT BETWEEN A BUSINESS
OWNER AND INDEPENDENT CONTRACTOR*

This agreement made between the _____ (Client) and _____ (Contractor) whereas the Contractor intends to perform certain tasks for the Client.

The Client's principal place of business is located at the following address.

_____

_____

The Contractor's principal place of business is located at the following address.

_____

_____

The Contractor declares that he/she is engaged in an independent business and will comply with all state and federal laws regarding taxes and licenses. In addition, Contractor declares that he/she is engaged in the same business for other clients and that the Client is not the only customer of the Contractor.

The Parties to this contract agree as follows:

1. The Contractor will perform the following services for the Client:

_____

_____

2. The Client shall pay the Contractor according to the following terms and conditions:

_____

_____

3. The Contractor shall furnish all equipment, tools, and supplies to accomplish the tasks except:

_____

_____

4. The Contractor maintains control over the manner in which the tasks are to be performed and the products made. The Client agrees to accept and pay as set forth above all products, tasks, etc. that meet the agreed specifications.

5. Contractor understands that no payroll taxes or worker's compensation taxes will be withheld by the Client. That these items are the responsibility of the Contractor.

6. The agreement will terminate on _____.

_____   _____
Client   Contractor

_____   _____
Dated   Dated

10-2 NOTICE OF PRELIEN

Certified Mail, Return Receipt Requested

Date:

To: [owner of property]

By this Notice, you are hereby advised that in accordance with the laws of the State of _____, the undersigned intends to file a mechanic's or materialsman's lien on the real property owned by you and located at:

This lien will be to insure payment of $_____ which is past due for labor performed or materials provided by the undersigned within the last _____ days.

Dated: _____

_____

State of   )   Date: _____

County of   ) SS

On this date, [list names of person(s) who signed above] personally appeared before me and acknowledged the foregoing.

_____

Notary Public

My Commission expires:

10–3   NOTICE OF CONTRACTOR'S LIEN

Certified Mail, Return Receipt Requested

Date:

Notice is hereby given that the below described individual has provided labor and or materials for the construction and/or improvements on the real property known as:

[street address, including city and state]

Said real estate is more particularly described in Book or Volume _____, page _____ of the County Registry of Deeds.

_____ is listed as the owner of the said property.

This lien is to insure payment of $_____ which is past due for labor performed or materials provided by the undersigned within the last _____days.

Dated: _____

                              Date: _____

State of   )
County of   ) SS

   On this date, [list names of person(s) who signed above] personally appeared before me and acknowledged the foregoing.

                              _____
                              Notary Public

                              My Commission expires:

10-4 RELEASE OF LIEN

Date:

Notice is hereby given that the below described lienholder has released the lien filed on the real property known as:

[street address, including city and state]

Said real estate is more particularly described in Book or Volume _____, page _____ of the County Registry of Deeds.

_____ is listed as the owner of the said property.

The notice of lien was duly recorded in Book _____, Page _____of the Lien Records of_____ County.

The Lienholder releases the above described property and owner from all liability arising from the labor performed or the materials furnished by the unsigned lienholder. The Lien is hereby discharged.

Dated: _____

                            Date: _____

State of   )

County of   ) SS

On this date, [list names of person(s) who signed above] personally appeared before me and acknowledged the foregoing.

_____

Notary Public

My Commission expires:

10-5
AGREEMENT TO EXTEND PERFORMANCE DATE

For good and valuable consideration, [individual having work accomplished], First Party and [name of independent contractor] Contractor in and to a certain agreement to: [indicate service to be performed] dated [date of original agreement] do hereby agree:

1. That the original performance date was on or before [date].

2. That the parties agree that the said performance cannot reasonably be completed by that date.

3. The parties hereby mutually agree to extend the date of performance to [new date]. Time being of the essence, and there are no other changes in terms or additional time allowed.

This agreement shall be binding on and inures to the benefit of the parties, their assigns and successors.

Signed this _____ day of _____, 19_____.

Date: _____

State of   )
County of   ) SS

On this date, [list names of person(s) who signed above] personally appeared before me and acknowledged that the above signature(s) are valid and binding.

_____
Notary Public

My Commission expires:

10–6   ARBITRATION AGREEMENT (BINDING)

The undersigned parties hereby acknowledge that there is a conflict, dispute, or controversy between the Company and the Contractor as follows:

[briefly describe dispute]

The parties hereby agree to resolve this conflict, dispute, or controversy and any future disputes, conflicts, or controversies between them by binding arbitration.

The arbitration will be conducted according to the rules of the American Arbitration Association for the City of _____ , which rules and procedures for arbitration are incorporated herein by reference and the decision or award made by the arbitrator shall be final, binding, and conclusive upon each of the parties and enforceable in a court of law.

SIGNED this _____ day of _____, 19___.

State of   )
County of   ) SS

On this date, [list names of person(s) who signed above] personally appeared before me and acknowledged that the above signature(s) are valid and binding.

_____
Notary Public

My Commission expires:

10-7 ARBITRATION AGREEMENT (NONBINDING)

The undersigned parties hereby acknowledge that there is a conflict, dispute, or controversy between the Company and the Contractor as follows:

[briefly describe dispute]

The parties hereby agree to attempt to resolve this conflict, dispute, or controversy and any future disputes, conflicts, or controversies between them by nonbinding arbitration.

The arbitration will be conducted according to the rules of the American Arbitration Association for the City of _____, which rules and procedures for arbitration are incorporated herein by reference and the decision or award made by the arbitrator shall be advisory only and not binding or conclusive upon each of the parties.

SIGNED this _____ day of _____, 19_____.

State of   )
County of   ) SS

On this date, [list names of person(s) who signed above] personally appeared before me and acknowledged that the above signature(s) are valid and binding.

_____
Notary Public

My Commission expires:

Chapter 11

Loans and Security Forms and Agreements

This chapter discusses the legal aspects of loans and securities and the generally used forms and agreements involving loans, both secured and unsecured. It also contains security notes and bonds that may be used.

Loans

The traditional approach to financing a business is to obtain a business loan from either a bank or from a commercial finance company. Bank loans are usually more difficult to obtain and require a greater degree of creditworthiness. On the other hand, bank loans usually carry a cheaper interest rate than do finance company loans.

This distinction between banks and finance companies is not as clear as it once was. More and more banks are adopting "asset-based lending programs" to compete with finance companies. And more finance companies are lowering their interest rates, eliminating the distinction that once existed between them and banks. The net result to the average businessperson is that business loans are generally easier to get, but finance charges or interest rates are somewhat higher than in the past.

SBA Guaranteed Loans

The federal government's Small Business Administration (SBA) guarantees bank loans to qualified small businesses. In an average year, the SBA guarantees about $2.8 billion in loans to small businesses. It has traditionally been very difficult for small businesses to obtain loans. The SBA was empowered to provide financing to alleviate this problem. If your business qualifies, you could find it advantageous to take out an SBA loan rather than another type of financing. The SBA loans are for a fairly lengthy period 6 to 10 years—and are at a relatively low interest rate, usually about 2 percentage points below the going bank rate. In many circumstances, SBA loans provide financing for a person who otherwise would not qualify.

The SBA has an Office of Minority Small Business and Capital Ownership Development to assist minority owners of small businesses. *Note:* This office also provides free management and technical assistance, such as setting up accounting systems, training employees and developing marketing programs. Many of their services are available for both minority and nonminority persons.

The disadvantages of applying for an SBA loan are that the application process usually takes several months, collateral and personal guarantees are sometimes required, and, because of restrictions imposed by SBA, additional financing may be difficult to obtain. If you feel you qualify for a Small Business Administration loan, check with your local SBA office. There is an office in most major cities.

Factoring

Factoring is another unconventional method many businesspersons use to obtain additional financing. Generally speaking, factoring is not an appropriate method of financing a new business, but it can be used to provide added cash for an existing one. Basically, *factoring* is the selling of accounts receivable. If your business has a large volume of accounts receivable, you can turn them into ready cash by factoring, or selling, them to a third person or to a bank. A hybrid type of factoring is one in which the bank lends a percentage of the value of the accounts receivable to the business and, in turn, takes a security interest in the accounts receivable.

Inventory Loans

An *inventory loan* is a short-term loan for which the products inventory is used as collateral. As the inventory is sold, a percentage of the proceeds are required to be paid to the lender. Normally these loans are for short periods that do not exceed one year.

Letters of Credit

A *letter of credit* is issued by a bank or other financial institution to a supplier or other individual creditor with which your business is dealing. It states that the bank or other institution will advance credit on presentation of an invoice from the creditor or supplier. Therefore, instead of your making C.O.D. purchases, the supplier delivers supplies to your business and invoices the bank. The bank pays the supplier direct. At the time the bank makes the payment, the payment becomes a loan from you to the bank. Letters of credit were once used almost exclusively in trade between foreign countries. They are becoming more common in domestic commercial arrangements.

Presenting Your Loan Request

In presenting your loan request, always keep in mind that you are selling your ability to repay the loan to the bank or the finance company. Therefore, make sure you have thoroughly documented your company's financial position and your plans for using and repaying the money. It may help to hire an accountant to prepare the necessary documents and participate in the meetings with the bank or commercial finance company. Above all, remember that you are selling yourself as a person with whom it will be profitable for the bank or the finance company to do business.

Checks and Other Negotiable Instruments

In this section we discuss the rules and regulations regarding checks, bonds, and other negotiable instruments. In today's modern, hectic, and complex business world, it is impossible not to get involved with negotiable instruments. Therefore, it is essential that a businessowner, manager, or supervisor understand the rules and regulations regarding them. The failure to comply with the law regarding negotiable instruments law could result in severe financial hardship to the businessowner.

Unlike most business issues the average businessperson is involved in, there is a high degree of uniformity among the states and the District of Columbia when checks, bonds, and other negotiable instruments are concerned. All states, including the District of Columbia, have adopted Article III of the Uniform Commercial Code (UCC). The Uniform Commercial Code is one of the most comprehensive statutes enacted in U.S. history. It replaced several previous popularly accepted uniform laws, including the one dealing with commercial instruments—the Uniform Negotiable Instruments Law. The rules and regulations discussed in this chapter are taken from Article III of the UCC. There are some variances among the states, but differences are minor compared to the other areas of the law.

The two types of negotiable instruments that Article III of the UCC regulates are notes and drafts. A *note* is a simple promise by one person (the maker) to pay money to the order of another person or the bearer of the note (the payee). A *draft* is an order by one person (the drawer) to a second person (the drawee) that orders the second person to pay money to yet a third person (the payee). The most common form of draft is a check. Basically, a check is an order by the drawer (the person who writes the check) to the bank (the drawee) directing the bank to pay money to a third person (the payee).

The most common types of notes are *promissory notes* and *certificates of deposit.* A note is usually considered a time instrument in that it is due at a future time fixed in the instrument. It is not payable until that date. A draft, (i.e., a check) is an instrument payable on demand and is basically subject to being paid from the day it is issued.

Negotiability

The concept of negotiability allows the instrument to be traded among persons. It allows you to take a check and by endorsement transfer full rights and ownership of it to another person.

Negotiability refers to the form of an instrument. If an instrument is not negotiable, then the rules stated in Article III of the UCC do not apply, and the instrument is merely a contract. To determine whether it is negotiable, the UCC requires that it must:

- Be in a written form.
- Be signed by the maker or drawer.
- Contain an unconditional promise or order to pay a certain sum of money.
- Be payable either on demand or at a definite time.
- Be payable to the order of a certain person or to the bearer.

If the instrument does not meet all these requirements, it is not negotiable; therefore, it cannot be a check or a bond or a certificate of deposit. It could be at the most a formal contract between the parties involved. And, of course, a formal contract is governed not by Article III of the UCC but by the law of contracts in each state. Therefore, variances exist as to the rules, rights, obligations, and privileges affecting the maker of the contract and the holder (the person to whom the obligation under the contract is due).

As noted earlier, the negotiable instrument must be in *a written form*. The UCC, however, is liberal as to what constitutes a writing. For example, printing, typing, or any other intentional reduction to a tangible form is considered writing. Several cases are pending that are trying to determine whether a video tape can constitute a writing under this section of the code.

The second requirement is that it must *be signed by the maker* (i.e., the drawer). The UCC is liberal as to what constitutes a signature. A signature may be made by the use of any name, trade or assumed, or any mark that is intended to be a signature. It is acceptable to use a stamp. The signature does not have to be at the bottom of the instrument. Signing the instrument with a trade name or an assumed name is sufficient. In each case, however, the maker or drawer must intend that the mark or whatever is used, be the maker's signature on the instrument. If the requisite intent is there along with the mark, the signature, the stamp, or whatever, it fulfills the requirement that the note or check be signed by the maker or drawer.

An unauthorized signature, forgery, or the like., does not bind a person who did not sign the instrument. For example, if someone stole one of your checks and signed it, you would not be liable for it unless you ratified or approved the signature. However, the unauthorized signer (the person who forged your name) is liable on the check or instrument as if the person had signed his own or her name.

Third, the *promise* or *order to pay* must be unconditional. An instrument is not negotiable if it states that its promise is subject to or governed by the terms of another agreement, no matter what the substance of the other agreement is.

The promise or order must also be free of any expressed conditions. To include, for example, the phrase, "This promise to pay or this order to pay is conditioned upon a presidential election being held every four years," would make the promise conditional. Therefore, it would not be a negotiable instrument.

The full credit of the maker or drawer behind the document is necessary for it to be an unconditional promise. For example, a draft with the statement that the obligation incurred under the document is to be taken out of a certain fund and no other would make it a conditional promise. Although a check is an order to the bank to pay out of only one fund, the full credit of the maker or drawer is behind that check. If there are insufficient funds in that account to pay the check, the maker or the drawer is obligated to make good the check.

An exception to the requirement that the full credit of the maker or the drawer must be behind the check is in those cases in which a person executes a check on behalf of a partnership, corporation, trust, or the like. In such a case, the full credit of the partnership, association, trust, or other entity, must be behind the instrument to make it negotiable.

As noted earlier, there must be either a promise or an order to pay. A *promise* is an affirmative undertaking to pay. Merely acknowledging the existence of a debt is not sufficient. The maker must actually promise to pay a certain amount. For example, "I owe you $150" is not negotiable; whereas, "I promise to pay you $150," if it meets the other requirements, is negotiable.

The UCC defines an *order* as a direction to someone to pay to the order of a person or to the bearer of the document. It does more than authorize you to pay. For example, "I hereby authorize you to pay *A*" is insufficient. The order must be in words that tell the individual with reasonable certainty that a payment should be made. The words most commonly used are, "I order you to pay" or "pay to the order of."

A fixed amount—that is, a certain sum of money—must be shown on the instrument. It is sufficient if you can look at the instrument and ascertain the exact amount of money due. For example, an instrument that says, "I will pay the amount I owe you within 60 days" does not show a certain sum. Therefore, it is not negotiable. A note that says, "I will pay $5,000 plus 10 percent" is negotiable because you can determine the amount due by looking at the instrument.

If there is any interest included in the transaction, the interest rate must be stated on the note to make the amount certain. In one recent case, the court held that a note with the statement "payable with interest at prime rate" was not negotiable because the rate of interest could not be determined from the note. The amount due was uncertain.

An additional requirement of negotiability is that the instrument must be *payable on demand* or *at a certain time*. An instrument is considered payable on demand if it contains the words "payable on demand," "payable at sight," or "payable on presentation." If the instrument states something such as "payable 60 days after the first snowfall," it is not payable at a definite time and is therefore not negotiable.

A further requirement of negotiability is that it must be payable to *the order of [a certain person]* or *to the bearer.* An instrument is considered payable to the order of a certain person when it states "pay to the order of Jerry Smith," "pay to Jerry Smith on order," or "pay to Jerry Smith or assigns." If the instrument simply says "pay to John Smith" without any of the phrases noted, it is not negotiable. The concept of negotiability means that it should be transferable. Therefore, an instrument that provides "pay to Jerry Smith," does not on the face of it give Jerry Smith the authority to transfer the document.

An instrument may also be made payable "to the bearer," which means that it is payable to whoever possesses the instrument. An instrument is considered payable to the bearer if it is written "payable to the bearer," "payable to whoever has possession," "whoever possesses this note," "payable to John Smith or bearer," "payable to cash," or payable to a fictitious person. If the instrument says "pay to the order of" and that order is blank after these words, the instrument is considered a bearer instrument and whoever possesses it may fill in his or her own name. It is then payable to that person.

Negotiation

Under Article III of the UCC, negotiation is the physical transfer of a commercial paper with the rights of ownership to another person. It is the process by which the instrument is transferred to another party who qualifies as a holder. The term *holder* has a technical meaning under the UCC. The holder is the person who possesses the instrument and has a good title to it. To be a holder, the person must have received it by proper endorsement and without notice of any fraud.

Bearer instruments can be negotiated or transferred merely by passing them from one person to the next. Order instruments (i.e., instruments made payable to Jerry Smith or Order) require an endorsement in addition to a physical transfer of the document. For the holder of the document to have the basic rights, the payee's signature must be valid. For example, if you find a check made payable to the order of Jerry Smith and fraudulently endorse Jerry Smith's name to the back, this action is an invalid transfer of the document.

Endorsement

To affect an endorsement of a negotiable paper, it is not necessary that the endorsement be written on the reverse side of the instrument. It may be placed anywhere on the instrument as long as it is firmly affixed to or written on the instrument and becomes a part of it. A signature anywhere on the document that is not that of the maker or the payee is considered by law as an endorsement.

Words of negotiability, such as "pay to the order of, "are not required in an endorsement. A blank endorsement occurs when the payee merely signs her or his name to the document. A blank endorsement changes an order paper into a bearer paper. Then it may be transferred by delivery alone. A typical blank endorsement occurs when a check is made payable to the order of Jerry Smith. Then Jerry Smith endorses the check with only his name "Jerry Smith." This is a blank endorsement, and the instrument has now become a bearer instrument transferable by mere delivery alone. If Jerry Smith had written on the instrument, "pay to the order of Paul Smith," that would be a special endorsement. Unlike a case involving a blank endorsement, Paul Smith must endorse it to transfer ownership of it. *Note:* There is no requirement to include the term "pay to order of," because it is assumed that Paul Smith would have the right to transfer it. Any blank or special endorsement includes the implied warranty that the instrument will be paid upon demand or when due, that the instrument is valid, and that there are no forgeries on it.

If the check or instrument is not paid, the individual who holds it may collect the amount due from any of the endorsees but cannot collect the amount when the endorser adds the words *without recourse.* This type of endorsement is considered a qualified endorsement. The words "without recourse" mean that the endorser does not guarantee payment of the document. The implied warranty of title, however, is still present.

Holders In Due Course

Holder in due course is a technical term used by the courts to describe a person who in good faith possesses a check or other negotiable instrument that is free and clear of any forgery of those names necessary in the chain of title. According to the UCC, a *holder in due course* is one who in good faith takes the instrument for value without notice that it is overdue or that it has been dishonored, or that there is any defense against it or a claim on the part of any person.

Value merely refers to the fact that the note or the check was received not as a gift but for something of value that was given in exchange for a promise of goods or other consideration.

Good faith means honesty in fact, the test of which is subjective. It also means what the individual actually believes. It does not have to be reasonably good faith, only good faith. Thus, as long as the individual honestly believes something, regardless of the reasonableness of the belief, it would qualify as a good faith belief.

The third requirement is that the check or instrument be taken without notice that it is overdue or has been dishonored. If a check is presented within a reasonable time after it is made and if there is no indication that it has been refused payment by the bank, then it is not considered overdue. If, however, it is a note with a payment date and the date has passed, then the note is considered overdue.

Defenses

To promote the negotiability of checks, bonds, and other instruments, and therefore, the transferability of negotiable instruments, the courts have established two types of defenses when the legality of negotiable paper is challenged: personal defenses and real defenses. *Personal defenses* cannot be used to defeat the claim of a holder in due course. Personal defenses are effective only between the maker and the original payee. If the check or other negotiable instrument has been transferred to a holder in due course, a personal defense may not be used to prevent the holder from collecting the note. Only a real defense may be set up.

The only *real defenses* are the following:

- Infancy, in (that the individuals who made the check or negotiable instrument were not old enough to enter into a contract.
- Incompetency to contract, in that the individual has been declared judicially incompetent.
- Illegality in the underlying transaction, which renders the entire obligation void.
- Duress, in that the check or negotiable instrument occurred in a situation in which one party acted involuntarily because of duress.
- Forgery of the signature of a necessary party to the document or a material alteration in the terms of the document. If any name not necessary to the chain of title is forged, it is immaterial. However, to be a holder in due course, an individual must take good title. Therefore, the names of the persons required to transfer the title cannot be forged.

A material alteration of a document occurs when its terms are changed without the maker's approval. If the document is materially altered, a holder in due course may enforce the document in its original terms but not in its materially altered forms. For example, if a check is written for $100 and is altered illegally by someone to read $1,000, a holder in good course can still enforce the instrument for $100 but not for $1,000. All other defenses that may be set up to prevent payment of a negotiable instrument are personal defenses and cannot be used against holders in good course to justify non-payment.

Collecting on a Negotiable Instrument

The Uniform Commercial Code specifies certain procedures that operate in the trial of cases involving the collection of, or in attempts to collect, negotiable instruments. Production of an instrument by a holder entitles the holder to a directed verdict or a verdict in her or his favor unless the defense establishes a defense. Under the UCC, a holder is not required to prove that he or she is a holder in due course unless that defense is raised. Unless the defendant specifically denies the validity of any signatures in the pleadings, the signatures are considered to be genuine. If the defendant denies the validity of the signature, it is nevertheless presumed to be valid and the defendant must establish that it is invalid.

Liability

No person is liable on a negotiable instrument unless that person's signature clearly appears on it, or unless the signature is placed on it by an agent that the person has authorized to sign for it. By signing an instrument in the proper form, its maker agrees to pay it according to its tenure when it is due. If the check or other instrument is dishonored (i.e., not paid when presented), the maker then has guaranteed that she or he will pay the amount due.

If an authorized agent signs the principal's name without putting his own name on an instrument, only the principal is liable. If the agent was not authorized to sign the principal's name and does, the agent is held personally liable just as if he had signed it with his own name. If an authorized agent signs his and his principal's name and discloses the agency relationship, only the principal is liable. If an agent signs only his own name and doesn't disclose the fact of the agency or of the principal's name, the agent is liable on the instrument whether he was authorized to sign it or not.

An endorser is one who usually signs on the back of the instrument. However, a signature anywhere on the document that cannot be accounted for otherwise is considered to be an endorsement. Under usual circumstances, an endorsement transfers all the rights of the transferor to the recipient. An endorser is liable if the check is returned for insufficient funds or if it is otherwise dishonored.

To hold the endorser liable, he or she must be notified within a certain period of time that the check was dishonored. Signing a negotiable instrument with a general endorsement in effect guarantees that it will be paid. If you endorse the note or check "without recourse," the only things you are guaranteeing are that the title is genuine and that there are no forgeries. You are not guaranteeing payment of the instrument at the time it is presented for payment.

Financial Statements

General accounting practice is that most businesses should keep two basic financial statements: the balance sheet and the income statement. A *balance sheet* is a record of assets, liabilities, and capital. It is a statement of the condition of your business on a given day—for example, December 31. The income statement is a profit and loss statement. It is a summary of your earnings and expenses over a given period, usually monthly, quarterly, and yearly.

Tax Records

The IRS requires that certain records be kept. Failure to keep those records often results in adverse tax consequences for the business. The general theme that IRS operates on is that all monies received by a business are profit and that the burden is on the businessperson to establish the validity of any deductions or subtractions from the gross income. [For a detailed discussion of record keeping for tax purposes, see Cliff Roberson, *How to Fight the IRS and Win* (New York: McGraw-Hill, 1985.)] If during a tax audit, the IRS determines that the business fails to keep adequate records, in addition to disallowing a claimed deduction or expense, the IRS can issue a Notice of Inadequate Records, which directs the taxpayer to keep certain records in the future.

Most tax records are required to be kept for at least three years. The IRS can, however, contend that the business has underreported its income by more than 25 percent or committed fraud, and it can require you to produce records for a six-year period. If the records pertain to the basis of property (adjusted cost of the property), the business should keep the records for at least six years after the property has been disposed of. As a rule of thumb, all records should be kept for ten years.

The required tax records that a business should retain include the following:

The date and description of each transaction in which the business engages.

The date and amount of each item of gross income received.

The date and amount of each payment made.

A description of the nature of each payment.

Payroll records.

Any correspondence to anyone regarding taxes, income, or profits.

Receipts journal.

Expense journal.

Forms in This Chapter

- FORM 11–1: PROMISSORY NOTE (TIME). A promissory note used when the principal and interest are due at a stated date.

- FORM 11–2: PROMISSORY NOTE (DEMAND). A promissory note used when the principal and interest are due on demand.

- FORM 11–3: PROMISSORY NOTE (INSTALLMENT). A promissory note used when the principal and interest are to be paid by installments.

- FORM 11–4: PROMISSORY NOTE (WITH BALLOON PAYMENT). A promissory note used when the principal and interest are to be paid by installments, with the last payment being a higher payment of the balance due.

- FORM 11–5: UNLIMITED GUARANTY. Guarantees the debt of a debtor. Under an unlimited guaranty, the debt may be modified without losing the guaranty.

- FORM 11–6: LIMITED GUARANTY. Guarantees the debt of a debtor. Under a limited guaranty, there are limits as to the nature of the guaranty. It is important that any intended limits be described in the document.

- FORM 11–7: SPECIFIC GUARANTY. Guarantees a specific debt of a debtor.

- FORM 11–8: REVOCATION OF GUARANTY. Notifies a creditor of the termination of a guaranty.

- FORM 11-9: AGREEMENT TO ASSUME OBLIGATION. Used to assume an obligation.

- FORM 11-10: SECURITY AGREEMENT. Obtains a security interest in an item of personal property to secure a debt.

- FORM 11–11: PLEDGE OF PERSONAL PROPERTY. Formalizes a pledge of personal property to secure a debt.

- FORM 11–12: PLEDGE OF STOCK. Formalizes a pledge of shares of stock to secure a debt.

- FORM 11–13: INDEMNIFICATION AGREEMENT. Resolves disputes between two or more persons. Note: Some states require that the agreement be notarized. Under the indemnification agreement, neither party will complain about matters which are settled under this agreement.

- FORM 11–14: ASSIGNMENT OF NOTE. Assigns a promissory note to a third person.

- FORM 11–15: SUBORDINATION AGREEMENT (FULL). Used by a creditor to subordinate (take a lower priority) to another creditor.

- FORM 11–16: SUBORDINATION AGREEMENT (PARTIAL). Used by a creditor to subordinate some but not all claims to those of another creditor

- FORM 11–17: CHECKLIST FOR NEGOTIATING A LOAN. Used as a checklist when negotiating a loan.

- FORM 11–18: NOTIFICATION OF DEBT ASSIGNMENT. Notifies a debtor that his/her account has been assigned to your company.

11–1 PROMISSORY NOTE (TIME)

For good and valuable consideration, the undersigned promises to pay to the order of _____, the sum of _____ dollars ($____). All principal and earned interest shall be due and payable on _____, 19_____, time is of the essence. Interest shall be at the annual rate of _____% on the unpaid balance.

The failure to make full payment with all accrued interest on the above stated due date shall constitute a default on the note, and the defaulted note will be turned over for collection. In the event of default, the undersigned shall be responsible to pay attorney fees, collection costs, and other fees associated with collection of the note.

All parties to the note waive presentment, demand, notice of nonpayment, protest, and notice of protest. Parties also agree to remain fully bound on the note notwithstanding the release of any party or an extension or modification in the terms of the note. The undersigned parties shall be jointly and severally liable under this note.

Signed under seal this _____day of _____, 19_____.

_____
Maker

_____
Maker

11-2 PROMISSORY NOTE (DEMAND)

For good and valuable consideration, the undersigned promises to pay to the order of _____, the sum of _____ dollars ($ _____,). The unpaid principal and any earned interest are due and immediately payable upon demand of the holder of this note. Interest shall be at the annual rate of _____% on the unpaid balance.

The failure to make full payment with all interest due within _____ days after demand shall constitute a default on the note, and the defaulted note will be turned over for collection. In the event of default, the undersigned shall be responsible to pay attorney fees, collection costs, and other fees associated with collection of the note.

This note may be prepaid in whole or in part, without penalty.

All parties to the note waive presentment, demand, notice of nonpayment, protest, and notice of protest. Parties also agree to remain fully bound on the note notwithstanding the release of any party or an extension or modification in the terms of the note. The undersigned parties shall be jointly and severally liable under this note.

Signed under seal this _____day of _____, 19_____.

_____
Maker

_____
Maker

Signed this_____day of _____ , 19_____.

_____

_____

State of   )
County of   )

On this date, [list names of person(s) who signed above] personally appeared before me and acknowledged that the above signature(s) are valid and bindig.

_____
Notary Public

My Commission expires:

11-3

PROMISSORY NOTE (INSTALLMENT)

For good and valuable consideration, the undersigned promises to pay to the order of _____, the sum of _____ dollars ($_____). Interest shall be at the annual rate of _____% on the unpaid balance.

The principal with interest, shall be paid in _____ installments of $____ ___, each, with the first installment due on _____, 19____, and the same amount on the same day of each month thereafter until the principal and earned interest is fully paid. Payments shall be first applied to earned interest and then the balance to the principal.

The note shall be fully payable including earned interest upon the demand of any holder in the event that the undersigned defaults on any payment due by _____ days of its due date or upon death, insolvency, or bankruptcy of the undersigned.

In the event of default, the undersigned shall be responsible to pay attorney fees, collection costs, and other fees associated with collection of the note.

All parties to the note waive presentment, demand, notice of nonpayment, protest, and notice of protest. Parties also agree to remain fully bound on the note notwithstanding the release of any party or an extension or modification in the terms of the note. The undersigned parties shall be jointly and severally liable under this note.

Signed under seal this _____ day of _____, 19____.

_____
Maker

_____
Maker

11-4

PROMISSORY NOTE (WITH BALLOON PAYMENT)

For good and valuable consideration, the undersigned promises to pay to the order of _____, the sum of _____ dollars ($ _____). Interest shall be at the annual rate of _____% on the unpaid balance.

The principal with interest, shall be paid in ____installments of ____ each, with the first installment due on _____, 19____, and the same amount on the same day of each month thereafter for the next ____ consecutive months. The remaining balance with accrued but unpaid interest shall be fully paid on or before _____, 19 ___.

Payments shall be first applied to earned interest and then the balance to the principal.

The note shall be fully payable including earned interest upon the demand of any holder in the event that the undersigned defaults on any payment due by _____ days of its due date or upon death, insolvency, or bankruptcy of the undersigned.

In the event of default, the undersigned shall be responsible to pay attorney fees, collection costs, and other fees associated with collection of the note.

All parties to the note waive presentment, demand, notice of nonpayment, protest, and notice of protest. Parties also agree to remain fully bound on the note notwithstanding the release of any party or an extension or modification in the terms of the note. The undersigned parties shall be jointly and severally liable under this note.

Signed under seal this _____day of_____, 19____.

_____
Maker

_____
Maker

11-5 UNLIMITED GUARANTY

For good and valuable consideration, and as an inducement for [name of Creditor], Creditor, to extend credit time to [name of Borrower], Borrower, the undersigned jointly and severally and unconditionally guarantee to the Creditor the prompt and full payment of all sums due from Borrower to Creditor.

The undersigned agrees to remain fully bound on this guaranty notwithstanding any extension, modification, waiver, release, discharge, or substitution of any collateral or security for the debt. In addition, the undersigned consents to and waives all notice of the same. In the event of default, the Creditor may seek payment directly from the undersigned without need to proceed first against the Borrower. All suretyship defenses are waived by the undersigned.

In the event of default, the undersigned shall be responsible to pay attorney fees, collection costs, and other fees associated with collection of the note.

The guaranty is unlimited as to amount or duration, but may be terminated as to future credit by delivery of notice of termination to Creditor by certified mail, return receipt requested. Termination does not discharge Guarantor's obligations as to debts incurred prior to delivery of notice of termination.

This guaranty is binding upon and inures to the benefit of the parties, their successors, assigns, and personal representatives.

Signed under seal this _____ day of _____, 19_____.

_____
Guarantor

_____
Guarantor

11-6 LIMITED GUARANTY

For good and valuable consideration, and as an inducement for [name of Creditor], Creditor, to extend credit time to [name of Borrower], Borrower, the undersigned jointly and severally and unconditionally guarantee to the Creditor the prompt and full payment of all sums due from Borrower to Creditor. This limited guaranty is limited to the sum of $ _____.

The undersigned agrees to remain fully bound on this guaranty notwithstanding any extension, modification, waiver, release, discharge, or substitution of any collateral or security for the debt. In addition, the undersigned consents to and waives all notice of the same. In the event of default, the Creditor may seek payment directly from the undersigned without need to proceed first against the Borrower. All suretyship defenses are waived by the undersigned.

In the event of default, the undersigned shall be responsible to pay attorney fees, collection costs, and other fees associated with collection of the note.

The guaranty is limited as to amount and may also be terminated as to future credit by delivery of notice of termination to Creditor by certified mail, return receipt requested. Termination does not discharge Guarantor's obligations as to debts incurred prior to delivery of notice of termination.

This guaranty is binding upon and inures to the benefit of the parties, their successors, assigns, and personal representatives.

Signed under seal this _____ day of _____, 19_____.

_____
Guarantor

_____
Guarantor

11-7 SPECIFIC GUARANTY

For good and valuable consideration, and as an inducement for [name of Creditor], Creditor, to extend credit to [name of Borrower], Borrower, the undersigned jointly and severally and unconditionally guarantee to the Creditor the prompt and full payment of the below stated debt with accrued interest due from Borrower to Creditor. This guaranty is limited to following debt:

[describe the debt at this point]

The undersigned agrees to remain fully bound on this guaranty notwithstanding any extension, modification, waiver, release, discharge, or substitution of any collateral or security for the debt. In addition, the undersigned consents to and waives all notice of the same. In the event of default, the Creditor may seek payment directly from the undersigned without need to proceed first against the Borrower. All suretyship defenses are waived by the undersigned.

In the event of default, the undersigned shall be responsible to pay attorney fees, collection costs, and other fees associated with collection of the note.

This guaranty is binding upon and inures to the benefit of the parties, their successors, assigns, and personal representatives.

Signed under seal this _____ day of _____, 19_____.

_____
Guarantor

_____
Guarantor

11-8   REVOCATION OF GUARANTY

To: [creditor,
    address]

Please consider this formal notice of the termination of our guaranty of [date] on behalf of [debtor]. Effective on receipt of this notice, we will not be obligated under the guaranty for any future credit extended to [debtor].

Please advise us as to the present amount due and also notify us when that balance has been paid.

Please confirm below receipt and acknowledgment of this revocation of guaranty by return acknowledgment below.

Sincerely,

_____
Guarantor

_____
Guarantor

Acknowledged: Date: _____   Present balance $ _____

_____
Creditor

11–9 AGREEMENT TO ASSUME OBLIGATION

For good and valuable consideration, the _____Creditor and _____Debtor _____ and _____ the Undersigned enter into this agreement, whereby all parties acknowledge and agree to the below terms, facts and conditions:

1. Debtor currently owes to Creditor the sum $_____, (Debt), which sum is currently due and payable.
2. Undersigned agrees unconditionally and irrevocably to assume and fully pay the Debt and guarantees to Creditor the prompt payment of the Debt on terms as set forth below, and to fully indemnify and save harmless both Creditor and Debtor from any loss thereof.
3. The terms of the Debt repayment are as follows:
4. This agreement does not release or discharge the Debtor's obligations to the Creditor regarding the Debt. The Creditor will, however, forbear in commencing collection action as long as the Undersigned promptly makes the payments as outlined above. In the event of default, Creditor will have full rights, jointly, and severally, against both the Debtor and the undersigned for any sums owed on the Debt.
5. This agreement extends only to the Debt described above.
6. In the event of default, the Undersigned and or the Debtor shall be responsible to pay attorney fees, collection costs, and other fees associated with collection of the note.
7. This agreement is binding upon and inures to the benefit of the parties, their successors, assigns, and personal representatives.

Signed under seal this_____day of _____, 19_____.

_____
Guarantor

_____
Guarantor

_____
Creditor

State of   )
County of   )

On this date, [list names of person(s) who signed above] personally appeared before me and acknowledged that the above signature(s) are valid and binding.

_____
Notary Public

My Commission expires:

11-10 SECURITY AGREEMENT

For good and valuable consideration of [describe the debt, e.g., the loan of $1,000], [name of Debtor], the Debtor, grants to [name of person who is receiving the security interest] the Secured Party, and his/her successors and assigns a security interest as per the Uniform Commercial Code, Article 9 in the following property,

[describe property covered by security interest] which also includes all after acquired property of a like nature and description and proceeds and products thereof, Collateral.

The security interest is granted to secure payment and performance on the following obligations now or hereinafter owed Secured Party from Debtor:

The Debtor makes the below acknowledgments:

1. He/She is the owner of the collateral and that it is free of any liens, encumbrances, security interests, or mortgages except as noted herein.

2. The collateral will be kept at the following address and shall not be moved or relocated without written consent of Secured Party:

   [address where collateral will be kept]

3. Debtor will execute the necessary financing statements as are reasonably required by Secured Party to perfect the security interest in accordance with state law and the Uniform Commercial Code.

4. On a default of any obligation for which the security interest is granted, or the breach of any term of this security agreement, the secured party may declare all obligations immediately due and payable and shall have all the remedies of a secured party as set forth in the Uniform Commercial Code as enacted in Debtor's state. These rights are to be considered as cumulative and not necessarily successive with any other right or remedy.

5. Debtor will maintain insurance on the collateral as the secured party may require, with the secured party named as loss payee.

6. In the event of default, Debtor shall be responsible to pay attorney fees, collection costs, and other fees associated with enforcement of this agreement.

7. This agreement is binding upon and inures to the benefit of the parties, their successors, assigns, and personal representatives.

8. This agreement shall also be in default upon the death, insolvency, or bankruptcy of any party who is obligated under this agreement or on the material decrease in the value of the collateral.

Signed under seal this _____ day of _____, 19____.

_____
Debtor

_____
Secured Party

11–11 PLEDGE OF PERSONAL PROPERTY

For good and valuable consideration of [describe the debt, e.g., the loan of $1,000], [name of Pledger/Debtor], the Pledger/Debtor, delivers to and pledges with [name of person who is receiving the property], the Pledgee, as collateral security in the following property,

[describe property being pledged], Collateral.

The Pledger/Debtor and Pledgee warrant that or agree to:

1. He/She is the owner of the collateral and that it is free of any liens, encumbrances, security interests, or mortgages except as noted herein.

2. The Pledgee may assign, sell, or transfer his/her interest in the Debt and may transfer the pledged property to any third party who is assigned, sold, or transferred interest in the Debt.

3. On a default of any obligation for which the security interest is granted, or the breach of any term of this security agreement, the secured party may declare all obligations immediately due and payable and shall have all the remedies of a secured party as set forth in the Uniform Commercial Code as enacted in Debtor's state. These rights are to be considered as cumulative and not necessarily successive with any other right or remedy.

4. Debtor will maintain insurance on the collateral as the secured party may require, with the secured party named as loss payee. In addition the Debtor will pay any personal property tax, excise, or other tax or levy that may be imposed on the collateral during the life of this agreement.

5. In the event of default, Debtor shall be responsible to pay attorney fees, collection costs, and other fees associated with enforcement of this agreement.

6. This agreement is binding upon and inures to the benefit of the parties, their successors, assigns, and personal representatives.

7. This agreement shall also be in default upon the death, insolvency, or bankruptcy of any party who is obligated under this agreement or on the material decrease in the value of the collateral.

8. Pledgor understands that upon foreclosure the pledged property may be sold at public auction or private sale. In the event that sale of the property is less than the amount owing, after expenses of sale, the Pledger shall be liable for any deficiency.

Signed under seal this _____ day of _____, 19_____.

_____

Pledger/Debtor

_____

Pledgee

State of   )
County of   )
    On this date, [list names of person(s) who signed above] personally appeared before me and acknowledged that the above signature(s) are valid and binding.

_____

Notary Public

My Commission expires:

11-12 PLEDGE OF STOCK

For good and valuable consideration of [describe the debt, e.g. the loan of $1,000], [name of Pledger/Debtor], the Pledger/Debtor, delivers to and pledges with [name of person who is receiving the shares of stock], the Pledgee, as collateral security in the following property, _____ shares of stock in the _____ corporation, Collateral.

The Pledger/Debtor and Pledgee warrant that or agree to:

1. He/She is the owner of the shares of stock and that it is free of any liens, encumbrances, security interests, or mortgages except as noted herein.

2. The Pledgee may assign, sell, or transfer his/her interest in the Debt and may transfer the pledged property to any third party who is assigned, sold, or transferred interest in the Debt. The Pledger shall retain the right to vote the shares and dividend income, except that stock dividends shall also be pledged.

3. On a default of any obligation for which the security interest is granted, or the breach of any term of this security agreement, the secured party may declare all obligations immediately due and payable and shall have all the remedies of a secured party as set forth in the Uniform Commercial Code as enacted in Debtor's state. These rights are to be considered as cumulative and not necessarily successive with any other right or remedy.

4. Debtor will pay any personal property tax, excise, or other tax or levy that may be imposed on the collateral during the life of this agreement.

5. In the event of default, Debtor shall be responsible to pay attorney fees, collection costs, and other fees associated with enforcement of this agreement.

6. This agreement is binding upon and inures to the benefit of the parties, their successors, assigns, and personal representatives.

7. This agreement shall also be in default upon the death, insolvency, or bankruptcy of any party who is obligated under this agreement or on the material decrease in the value of the collateral.

8. Pledger understands that upon foreclosure the pledged property may be sold at public auction or private sale. In the event that sale of the property is less than the amount owing, after expenses of sale, the Pledger shall be liable for any deficiency.

Signed under seal this _____day of _____, 19_____.

_____
Pledger/Debtor

_____
Pledgee

11–13 INDEMNIFICATION AGREEMENT

Date:

This indemnification agreement is made and entered on [date] by and between [first party], First Party, and [second party], Second Party.

WHEREAS The undersigned parties have agreed to resolve certain disputes which have arisen between them; and

WHEREAS, each party wishes the other to indemnify and hold the first party harmless from any and all costs and expenses which have arisen or may arise as a result of their prior relationship;

NOW THEREFORE, in consideration of the premises set forth herein and intending to be legally bound, the parties hereto agree as follows:

[first party] and affiliates hereby jointly and severally agree to indemnify and hold harmless [second party] and any affiliate of his/hers from every liability, claim, action, cause of action, judgment, loss, expense, or cost whatsoever (including but not limited to reasonable attorney's fees and court costs) arising from or in any way related to or resulting from:

(A)   Any and all business relationships entered into between the Parties from the beginning of time to the date of these presents; and

(B)   Any materially inaccurate representation made by either Party pursuant to their recent agreement; and

(C)   [List any other items parties want to be indemnified from].

IN WITNESS WHEREOF the undersigned have hereunto set their hands this _____ day of _____, 19____.

_____

First Party

_____

Second Party

11–14 ASSIGNMENT OF NOTE

The undersigned, [person assigning the note], the "Assignor," for good and valuable consideration given by [person to whom the note is being assigned], the "Assignee," to Assigned Note Debtor including any renewals, extensions, or refinancing of all or any part thereof and any and all other liabilities of Assigned Note Debtor or Assignor to the Assignee, direct or indirect, absolute or contingent, due or to become due, now existing, or hereafter arising and howsoever evidenced (all herein called the "Liabilities") hereby assigns, pledges, transfers, and delivers to the Assignee the following:

1. All of its right, title, and interest along with any and all profits, money, or funds due or to become due to Assignor of whatsoever description or character presently or hereafter derived from the certain promissory note, executed on or about [date note executed] by [name of person who is the debtor on the note], the Assigned Note Debtor and any extensions or renewals thereof (herein called the "assigned note"), wherein the Assigned Note Debtor agrees to pay to the Assignor the sum of _____ Dollars ($_____), pursuant to the terms and conditions as are more specifically set forth therein.

2. All damages, money, and consideration of any kind or character to which Assignor may now or hereafter be entitled and arising out of or derived from proceedings now or hereafter instituted by or against the Assigned Note Debtor in any Federal or State Court, under any bankruptcy or insolvency laws or under any laws relating to assignments for the benefit of creditors, to compositions, extensions, or adjustments of indebtedness, or to any other relief of debtors or otherwise.

Assignor further represents, warrants, and agrees as follows:

1. That he/she has full legal right and authority to execute and carry out the terms of this instrument; and that as of the date of the execution of this instrument, Assignor is not in default in the performance of any of the obligations existing with respect to the Assigned Note.

2. That the Assignee shall not be liable to any person or persons for damages sustained in connection with the Assigned Note or such other contract into which the Assignor may have entered in connection therewith.

3. That Assignor will execute and deliver any additional instruments which the Assignee deems necessary to carry out the purport and tenor of this instrument and to better secure the payment of the Liabilities.

This Assignment is binding upon and inures to the benefit of Assignee and any holder of any of the Liabilities and is binding upon the Assignor.

IN WITNESS WHEREOF, Assignor has executed this Assignment of Note on _____, 19_____ at [place where signed].

Signed and acknowledged
in the presence of:

_____   _____
Assignor   Assignee

ACKNOWLEDGMENT

The undersigned, the Assigned Note Debtor, hereby acknowledges receipt of a copy of the foregoing Assignment of Note and agrees to pay all income, issues, and profits from the Assigned Note directly to the Assignee.

_____
Assigned Note Debtor

_____
Date

11–15   SUBORDINATION AGREEMENT (FULL)

For good and valuable consideration, the Undersigned hereby subordinates any and all claims or other rights to monies due as now or hereinafter owed the Undersigned from [debtor], Debtor, to any and all claims as may now or hereinafter be due [other creditor], Creditor.

This subordination shall be unconditional, irrevocable, and unlimited both as to the amount or duration and notwithstanding whether the respective claims against Debtor are now or hereinafter secured or unsecured in whole or in part, and notwithstanding any other rights to priority as may exist. In addition, the Undersigned shall forbear from collecting any monies due on its claim until all claims due Creditor from Debtor have been fully paid.

This agreement is binding upon and inures to the benefit of the parties, their successors, assigns, and personal representatives.

IN WITNESS WHEREOF the undersigned have hereunto set their hands this _____ day of _____, 19_____.

_____
Undersigned

_____
Creditor

11–16 SUBORDINATION AGREEMENT (PARTIAL)

For good and valuable consideration, the Undersigned hereby subordinates the only below listed claims or other rights to monies due as now or hereinafter owed the Undersigned from [Debtor], Debtor, to any and all claims listed below as may now or hereinafter be due [other creditor], Creditor.

Claims or other rights subordinated by this agreement are as follows:

This subordination, only as to the above listed claims and rights, secured or unsecured in whole or in part, and notwithstanding any other rights to priority as may exist. In addition, the Undersigned shall forbear from collecting any monies due on the above claims until those above listed claims due Creditor from Debtor have been fully paid.

This agreement is binding upon and inures to the benefit of the parties, their successors, assigns, and personal representatives.

IN WITNESS WHEREOF the undersigned have hereunto set their hands this _____ day of _____, 19_____.

_____
Undersigned

_____
Creditor

11–17 CHECKLIST FOR NEGOTIATING A LOAN

The Loan Agreement

Most banks and finance companies have their own loan agreements or letters of understanding that contain their financial arrangements. Before you sign them, read all of the agreements carefully. Make sure you understand them and that you have no questions about them. Some of the essential terms you should know and that should be clearly set forth in the agreements are the following:

1. When will the loan proceeds be available?
2. When is the interest payable?
3. When is the principal payable?
4. How is the interest rate calculated?
5. Is there a penalty if you repay the loan early?
6. Are there provisions to extend the term of the loan, to renew the loan, or to convert the loan to a different type?
7. What are the reporting requirements?
8. What are the restrictions on the use of the loan proceeds?
9. What are the restrictions on incurring other debts, selling major assets, or changing business lines?
10. Under what circumstances can the bank or finance company declare the loan in default and demand immediate payment?
11. What events can trigger a default?
12. What are the insurance provisions?
13. Who is required to insure any collateral?
14. What are the restrictions on the use of any property used as collateral?
15. Can the financial institution accelerate the due date of the loan payments or principle?

And above all else,

16. What is the total cost of the loan?
17. Are there other loan fees, commitment fees, placement fees, points, and so on, that will be charged in addition to the interest rate?

11–18　NOTIFICATION OF DEBT ASSIGNMENT

Date:

To: [debtor]

Dear Madam/Sir:

Your creditor, [name of creditor], has assigned and conveyed your account to our company. Attached is a copy of the assignment. To insure that you receive proper credit, all future payments should be sent directly to us at the following address:

Include the following account number on all your checks: _____.
According to our records, your outstanding balance is $_____. If this is not correct, please notify us as soon as possible.

Sincerely,

Chapter 12

Partnership Forms and Agreements

This chapter contains a discussion on partnerships and all the forms and agreements that are used in forming and operating general, limited and special partnerships. Other forms and agreements in this chapter include those concerning joint ventures and business trusts.

Legal Aspects of Partnerships

The Uniform Partnership Act defines a *partnership* as two or more persons who carry on a business for profit. One law expert defines a *partnership* as an association based on the expressed or implied contract of two or more competent persons to unite their property, skills, and labor to carry on a lawful business as principals for joint profit.

Because partnership agreements are considered to be contractual in nature, they are governed by the law of contracts. And because one partner may enter into agreements that are binding on other partners, the law of agency also applies. Generally, anyone capable of entering into a binding contract may be a partner in a partnership. In most states, a corporation may enter into a partnership agreement with persons or other corporations. In a few states, corporation acts or laws prohibit corporations from being a partner in a partnership. Except in those cases when the court has implied a partnership to prevent fraud, no one may become a partner in the partnership without the expressed or implied consent of all the other partners involved.

As a general rule, no formal agreement is necessary to constitute a partnership. Unless prohibited by state law, a partnership may be established solely from the actions of the parties involved, without the need for an expressed contract. However, a prudent businessperson should always require an expressed written contract setting the terms and conditions of the partnership before entering into it. The partnership agreement is discussed in greater detail later in this chapter.

Unlike a corporation, a partnership is not a legal entity. It is an unincorporated association. Accordingly, in some states a partnership may not bring suit in its own name but must instead bring suit in the names of the partners. For some purposes, however, a partnership is treated as an entity. In most states, for example, title to land may be taken in the partnership name.

More than 40 states have adopted the Uniform Partnership Act. The act restates the common laws regarding partnerships and provides a certain degree of legal uniformity. Accordingly, when most states adopted the Uniform Partnership Act, no substantial changes were made in this area of the law.

The two basic types of partnerships are the *general partnership* and the *limited partnership*. Limited partnerships are discussed later in this chapter. Most partnerships are of the general type. General partnerships are classified as commercial or professional, with the main distinction between the two involving the implied powers of each partner.

A professional partnership is an association of professionals such as doctors or lawyers. Unlike a general partner, a partner in a professional partnership has only limited authority to bind the other partners. A joint venture is a partnership established for a single or limited enterprise.

Partnership Existence

To determine if the business is a partnership, the courts usually look at the parties' intentions when they formed the association. If there was an agreement and the partners intended the business to be a partnership, then clearly a partnership existed. Making the determination becomes difficult when the intentions of the parties are unclear. The courts use several tests to determine if a partnership exists. Merely taking property in the joint names of several persons does not establish a partnership. As a general rule, a partnership is presumed if the parties share in the profits of a business. However, this rule does not apply in situations in which the share of profits goes toward the payment of debt, wages, rent to a property owner, interest on a loan, or consideration for the sale of the business by a former owner.

There is no general rule that all partners must share the burden of any losses. The lack of an agreement to share any losses is, however, evidence that the parties did not intend to form a partnership.

Partnership by Estoppel

There are several situations in which the courts infer a partnership to prevent fraud, even though the parties involved did not intend to create one. For example, if a person by word or conduct represents himself as a partner or allows others to represent him as partner, the courts will hold him liable as a partner to persons who extend credit to the partnership.

In most states, two or more persons who conduct business under an apparent corporate form of ownership without completing the necessary legal requirements to incorporate are held liable by the courts as general partners.

Partnership Agreements

As noted earlier, a formal, written agreement is not necessary to constitute a partnership. However, partnership agreements that cannot be completed within a year or those in which real property is to be taken in the partnership name are exceptions to the rule. Most state statutes of fraud require that all other partnership agreements be in writing.

All partnerships should be established by written contract. The contract should include the principal duties of each partner, the division of profits or losses, the distribution of partnership property on dissolution of the partnership, any buy-out agreements, and the rights of each partner. The contract should also state whether the partners are to be paid for any work they do for the business and how much pay they are to receive. Any other agreements or understandings between the parties should also be included.

The forms included in this chapter are typical partnership agreements that can be used as guides in drafting your own agreement. Make sure that all the parties involved understand each clause in your agreement.

Limited Partnership

In a general partnership, each partner has a role in the management of the business and thus is subject to the financial liability discussed earlier. In a limited partnership, a partner's liability is limited to his or her investment in the business. A partner may lose the investment but will not be liable for debts of the partnership exceeding the investment.

There must be at least one general partner in all limited partnerships. Because a limited partnership was unknown at common law, one can be formed only under the specific authority of a statute. Most states have adopted the Limited Partnership Act, which provides for limited partnerships. The act allows persons to contribute to the business and enjoy the profits (if any) without being liable as a general partner. A limited partner is really only an investor in the business and not one of the managers.

A limited partner may not take part in the management of the business. On taking part in the management, a limited partner becomes a general partner and thus becomes subject to the financial liability. The limited partner's investment in the business must be in cash or property but not in personal services. In addition, a limited partner's last name may not be used in the partnership name. In most states a limited partnership must indicate in its name that it is a limited partnership by using the abbreviation "Ltd."

Powers of Partners

In carrying on the business of the partnership, each general partner is an agent of the other partners. Each partner has the same rights and duties regarding the partnership business as does a general agent. If a general agent of the business can bind the partnership in a particular situation, a general partner may do the same. Each general partner is authorized to carry on the whole business of the partnership. For a definition of a general partner, refer to the discussion on "Liabilities of Partners," page 447.

Under agency law, partners are not bound by the unauthorized acts of their other partners in situations outside the apparent scope of the business. This provision may be modified by placing specific provisions in the partnership agreement. If the partner's acts are within the apparent scope of the business but are prohibited by the partnership agreement, the other partners are still bound by his or her acts, especially if blameless third persons may be defrauded. In this situation, the other partners may sue the wrong-dealing partner for any losses they suffer as a result of his or her acts.

If a partner commits an act beyond the scope of his or her authority, the other partners may ratify the act to take advantage of its benefits. In this case, the partnership is bound on the unauthorized act.

Secret provisions do not bind persons dealing with the partnership unless they know about them.

A partner is authorized to pay the debts of the partnership and to enter into contracts in the name of the partnership. However, a partner has no apparent authority to dispose of the capital assets of the business or to sell the business.

Rights of Partners

The Uniform Partnership Act sets forth in detail some of the rights and duties of general partners, which include the following:

- The right to share equally in the profits of the business.
- The right to receive a repayment of her or his contribution.
- The right to receive payment for any personal funds used to pay partnership debts.
- The right to share in the management and conduct of the business.
- The right of access to the partnership's records and books.
- The right to a formal accounting of the partnership's affairs.

Duties of Partners

The Uniform Partnership Act imposes the following duties on partners:

- To contribute toward any losses suffered by the partnership.
- To work for the partnership without compensation except for a share of the profits (unless otherwise agreed to by all the partners.)
- To abide by a majority vote when differences occur in the conduct of the business.
- To account to the other partners for any profit derived from the partnership.
- To share with other partners any essential information regarding the partnership business.

Liabilities of Partners

To consider the extent of a partner's financial liability, first determine if the partner is a *general partner*. A general partner is any partner who takes an active role in the management of the business. In most states, *limited partners* are liable only to the extent of their investment in the business. Limited partners may be held liable as general partners if they hold themselves out as other than limited partners to creditors or if they take an active role in the management of the business. Generally, limited partners are considered only as investors in the partnership. To be protected, the business must hold itself out as a limited partnership—for example, The Arrow Company, A Limited Partnership, or The Arrow Company, Ltd.

General partners are liable for contracts made by the business and for any contracts expressly authorized by its parties. Each general partner is personally liable for debts arising from the partnership entity. If legal proceedings or threats of legal proceedings force a partner to pay the debts of the partnership out of personal funds, the partner has a right to require the other general partners to contribute their pro rata shares of the debt if the firm cannot pay the debt.

General partners are also liable for torts committed by any partner or employee of the business in the course of the partnership's business. *Tort* is a legal term that refers to a civil wrong for which a person may be sued. An example is when the reckless operation of a company truck results in the injury of a person.

A partner usually is not liable for any criminal act committed by other partners or employees unless the partner either knew of the criminal act or should have known it was going to be committed. Those cases involving the conduct of a business without a license or the violation of the pure food and drug acts are exceptions.

Dissolution of the Partnership

The lack of flexibility in the ownership of the business is one disadvantage of a partnership. Any change in the makeup of the ownership, such as the death of one partner or the selling of a partner's share to a third person, in effect dissolves the partnership. This does not mean the business ends. It means that a new legal relationship for it has to be established. If the business continues after a change in ownership, then a new partnership (a construcive partnership) is considered to be in existence.

Former partners are still liable for the outstanding debts of the partnership when a dissolution occurs. In addition, there is a question of liability when third persons, without knowledge of the change in partnership, extend credit to the partnership. A former partner may be liable if the third party does not know about the withdrawal. A partner who withdraws must notify third persons who have extended credit to the partnership of the discontinued association and the resulting lack of responsibility for any additional credit the partnership receives.

Limited Partnerships

A limited partnership arrangement is another financing method that permits a businessowner to obtain needed funds. This arrangement offers investors the advantages of current tax deductions and potential capital gains. Yet, limited partners do not have a voice in the management of the partnership. A limited partnership is sometimes used in the takeover of an existing business. The new businessowner forms a limited partnership with the previous business owner. Once the business gains financial strength under the new owner, the new owner buys out the previous owner. The previous owner's share in the business diminishes with each payment until eventually the investment retained in the business has been fully purchased by the new owner.

Tax Considerations

Partnerships are considered to be entities by the federal tax code and are therefore required to submit an annual tax return. A partnership, however, does not pay federal income taxes. The partnership's tax return is for information purposes only; the partners must include in their individual tax return their share of the partnership profits. If the partnership loses money, however, the net operating loss usually cannot be a deduction on an individual partner's tax return until the partnership is dissolved. Then the loss can be deducted as a capital loss on investment.

Any distribution of property or cash made to individual partners is considered taxable income if the distribution represents profits made by the partnership. If distribution of the assets is part of the partnership capital, the distributions are then considered to be a return of capital and are not taxable until the distributed assets exceed the partner's adjusted basis (investment less write-offs). The partners are usually required to include their share of the partnership's profits in their personal income tax returns even though the profits are retained and reinvested by the business.

Forms in This Chapter

- FORM 12–1: PARTNERSHIP AGREEMENT (GENERAL). Used to form a general partnership.

- FORM 12–2: PARTNERSHIP AGREEMENT (LIMITED). Forms a limited partnership.

- FORM 12–3: PARTNERSHIP ACKNOWLEDGMENT. Acknowledges a document by a partnership.

- FORM 12–4: ATTORNEY-IN-FACT ACKNOWLEDGMENT. Acknowledges a document by an attorney-in-fact.

- FORM 12–5: OFFER TO PARTCIPATE IN JOINT VENTURE. An invitation to join a joint venture.

- FORM 12–6: ACCEPTANCE OF JOINT VENTURE OFFER. An acknowledgment the acceptance of a joint venture offer.

- FORM 12–7: JOINT VENTURE AGREEMENT. An agreement to join a joint venture.

12-1　PARTNERSHIP AGREEMENT (GENERAL)

On this date [date], at the City of [city], County of [county], State of [state] this partnership agreement is hereby entered into, by and between the below listed partners:

Names   Addresses

_____   _____

_____   _____

_____   _____

In consideration of the mutual promises contained in this agreement, the above named persons agree to and do hereby form a partnership under the Uniform Partnership Act of the State of [state] and the terms of this agreement.

The name of the partnership shall be [name]. Its principal place of business shall be at [address] or any other place as mutually agreed on by the partners. Other places of business of the partnership shall be mutually agreed to by the partners.

The business to be carried on by the partnership is that of [state type of business].

The partnership shall commence on [date] and shall continue until dissolved by mutual agreement of the partners.

The initial capital of the partnership will be [state total value in dollars and cents including value of noncash assets invested]. Of this amount invested [amount of cash invested] is in cash and [value of noncash property] is in property.

The below listed partners will contribute the following amounts of cash:

Names   Amounts

_____   _____

_____   _____

_____   _____

The below listed partners will contribute the following noncash assets:

Name   Description of property

_____   _____

_____   _____

_____   _____

The contributions and transfer to the partnership of all noncash assets must be made on or before [date], or this agreement is null and void.

Each of the partners shall share in the profits and losses of the partnership in the following manner: [set out in detail the agreement as to sharing profits and losses].

Each of the partners will give his or her undivided time and attention to the partnership business and shall to the best of his or her ability promote the interests of the partnership. [If one or more partners will not devote full-time employment to the partnership, include that fact in this paragraph.]

Partners [will not receive] or [will receive the following] salary for work devoted to the partnership business.

Partners [may not draw any advances of expected profits] or [may draw the following advances of expected profits for living expenses every [time period]. These advances will be charged against their share of the profits of the partnership.If profits are not as expected, partners may be required to reimburse the partnership for any advances they have taken.

The books of the partnership shall be kept at [location] and shall be open for inspection by any partner during normal business hours. The fiscal year of the partnership shall be the normal tax year of all the partners.

All partners shall have equal rights in the management of the partnership and the conduct of the business of the partnership. Decisions shall be by majority vote of the partners, except as noted below. [Note any special situations below.]

No partner will, without the consent of all the partners, sell or dispose of the capital assets or property of the partnership.

On the death of a partner or the withdrawal of any partner, the partners desiring to continue the business shall pay to the estate of the dead partner or to the withdrawing partner the cash value of his or her interest in the partnership. If necessary to prevent economic strain on the business, the partners desiring to continue the business may delay the distribution of assets for a period of not longer than 180 days. If there is a dispute as to the value of the withdrawing or deceased partner's share in the partnership, an independent and neutral appraiser will be appointed.

In the event that the majority of partners shall agree to dissolve the partnership, the business shall be wound up, debts paid, and the surplus divided among the partners in accordance with the ratio of their share of the investment in the partnership at the time the dissolution is started.

This agreement may be amended by the two-thirds vote of the partners as measured by their interest in the sharing of the profits and losses.

Executed at [place] on the date first above written.

[signatures of all partners]

12-2   PARTNERSHIP AGREEMENT (LIMITED)

On this date [date], at the City of [city], County of [county], State of [state] this partnership limited agreement is hereby entered into, by and between the below listed general partners:

Names   Addresses

_____   _____

_____   _____

_____   _____

AND the following LIMITED Partners:

Names   Addresses

_____   _____

_____   _____

_____   _____

In consideration of the mutual promises contained in this agreement, the above named persons agree to and do hereby form a limited partnership under the Uniform Partnership Act of the State of [state] and the terms of this agreement.

The name of the partnership shall be [name].Its principal place of business shall be at [address] or any other place as mutually agreed on by the general partners. Other places of business of the partnership shall be mutually agreed to by the general partners.

The business to be carried on by the partnership is that of [state type of business]:

The partnership shall commence on [date] and shall continue until dissolved by mutual agreement of the general partners.

The initial capital of the partnership will be [state total value in dollars and cents including value of noncash assets invested]. Of this amount invested [amount of cash invested] is in cash and [value of noncash property] is in property.

The below listed partners will contribute the following amounts of cash:

Names   Addresses

_____   _____

_____   _____

_____   _____

The below listed partners will contribute the following noncash assets:

Names   Addresses

_____   _____

_____   _____

_____   _____

The contributions and transfer to the partnership of all noncash assets must be made on or before [date], or this agreement is null and void.

Each of the general and limited partners shall share in the profits and losses of the partnership in the following manner: [set out in detail the agreement as to sharing profits and losses].

Each of the general partners will give his/her undivided time and attention to the partnership business and shall to the best of his/her ability promote the interests of the partnership. [If one or more general partners will not devote full-time employment to the partnership, include that fact in this paragraph.]

General Partners [will not receive] or [will receive] the following salary for work devoted to the partnership business.

General Partners [may not draw any advances of expected profits] or [may draw the following advances of expected profits for living expenses every [time period]. These advances will be charged against their share of the profits of the partnership. If profits are not as expected, general partners may be required to reimburse the partnership for any advances they have taken.

The books of the partnership shall be kept at [location] and shall be open for inspection by any partner during normal business hours.The fiscal year of the partnership shall be the normal tax year of all the general partners.

All general partners shall have equal rights in the management of the partnership and the conduct of the business of the partnership.Decisions shall be by majority vote of the general partners, except as noted below. [Note any special situations below.]

No general partner shall, without the consent of all the partners, sell or dispose of the capital assets or property of the partnership.

On the death of a general partner or the withdrawal of any general partner, the general partners desiring to continue the business shall pay to the estate of the dead partner or to the withdrawing partner the cash value of his/her interest in the partnership. If necessary to prevent economic strain on the business, the general partners desiring to continue the business may delay the distribution of assets for a period of not longer than 180 days. If there is a dispute as to the value of the withdrawing or deceased partner's share in the partnership, an independent and neutral appraiser will be appointed.

In the event that the majority of general partners shall agree to dissolve the partnership, the business shall be wound up, debts paid, and the surplus divided among the partners in accordance with ratio of their share of the investment in the partnership at the time the dissolution is started.

This agreement may be amended by the two-thirds vote of the general partners as measured by their interest in the sharing of the profits and losses.

Executed at [place] on the date first above written.

[signatures of all partners]

12-3   PARTNERSHIP ACKNOWLEDGMENT

State of   )
County of   )

   On this _____ day of _____ , 19_____, before me personally appeared [one of the partners], known to me or proved to me on the basis of satisfactory evidence to be one of the general partners that executed the within instrument, and acknowledged to me that the said partnership executed the same.

_____
Notary Public

My Commission expires:

12-4   ATTORNEY-IN-FACT ACKNOWLEDGMENT

State of   )
County of   )

   On this _____ day of _____ , 19_____, before me personally appeared [name of person signing acknowledgment], known to me or proved to me on the basis of satisfactory evidence to be the attorney-in-fact who executed the within instrument, and acknowledged to me that he/she subscribed the name thereto as principal, and his/her own name as authorized attorney-in-fact executed the same.

_____
Notary Public

My Commission expires:

12–5

OFFER TO PARTICIPATE IN JOINT VENTURE

Date:

To: [name of person to whom the offer is made}

We, the below signed individuals, are in the process of forming a joint venture for the purposes of [describe purpose] and hereby extend an offer to you to become a party to this joint venture under the below conditions:

1. Each party shall be required to contribute the sum of $_____ as that party's share in the joint venture.
2. The required contribution must be made not later than [date].
3. You must notify our attorney of record of your acceptance of this offer not later than [date].
4. The attorney of record for the joint venture is [name and address].
5. The joint venture shall be jointly managed by all parties. Each party shall have the authority to obligate the joint venture only on the approval of the remaining parties.
6. Nothing in this venture shall be deemed to constitute a partnership.
7. A party may withdraw from the joint venture only with the approval of the majority of the parties involved. Any withdrawing party forfeits any future profits of the venture.
8. In addition to you, the below listed persons have also been invited to become a party in the venture:

Dated: _____

[names and signatures of parties
forming venture]

12–6   ACCEPTANCE OF JOINT VENTURE OFFER

Certified Mail, Return Receipt Requested

Date:

To:

Re: Joint Venture; Acceptance of Offer

I, [name], hereby accept the offer of [date] to join the joint venture. I agree to the terms set forth in the offer and will deposit with the attorney of record the sum of $_____ as my total investment on or before [date].

Your offer was conditioned upon my notification of acceptance by [date], which condition is hereby met with this acceptance.

_____

[signature]

12-7　JOINT VENTURE AGREEMENT

The parties of [names of all parties] by this agreement mutually agree to engage in and carry on as joint ventures for profit motives the below described activities:

[list activities]

Each party shall contribute on or before [date] the below listed contributions:

Party Name   Total Contribution

_____   _____

_____   _____

If any party fails to make a contribution as required on the date required, that party may be expelled by the remaining majority of the parties and shall be liable for any damages caused to the venture as the direct result of the default.

The duties and assignments of the venture required of the parties are listed below:

Party Name   Party's Duty or Assignment

_____   _____

_____   _____

The division of profits and losses of the venture shall be as follows: [describe how the profits or losses shall be distributed].

The effective date that the venture shall commence operation is [date]. The venture shall continue until [date] unless sooner terminated by a majority of the parties involved.

WITNESSED the hands of said parties this _____ day of _____, 19_____.

_____

_____

State of   )
County of   ) SS

On this date, [list names of person(s) who signed above] personally appeared before me and acknowledged that the above signature(s) are valid and binding.

_____
Notary Public

My Commission expires:

Chapter 13

Powers of Attorney

This chapter discusses the legal aspects of powers of attorney and the law of agency. Also included are various sample powers of attorney and sample agency agreements.

Powers of Attorney

Powers of attorney are written authorizations for individuals to perform specific acts on behalf of another person, who is the principal. A person who has the power to act under a power of attorney is called an *attorney-in-fact*. An attorney-in-fact differs from an agent in that an agent is a representative of a principal, whereas an attorney-in-fact is one whose authority derives from a formal written instrument.

In many cases, the laws that govern an attorney-in-fact are similar to those that govern agents. The greatest differences are that the powers of an attorney-in-fact are created by the formal document (power of attorney) and that the courts limit the powers of the attorney-in-fact to only those powers set forth in the document. An agent, however, may have implied powers.

To create a power of attorney to perform certain acts involving real estate, there must be a written instrument. For example, to execute a trust deed, an attorney-in-fact must have a written, notarized power of attorney.

Powers of attorney are subject to strict interpretation by the courts. For this reason, care must be taken in drafting any power of attorney.

In most states, a person must be 18 years old or older in order to execute a power of attorney. To execute a power of attorney, the principal (i.e., the person who gives the power) must have the ability to enter into a binding contract. A minor, however, may be appointed as the attorney-in-fact. Any minor appointed would have the same powers as any other attorney-in-fact, including the power to sign contracts.

Except for durable powers of attorney, the death or incapacity of a principal (i.e., the person who executes the document) terminates the power. Durable powers of attorney extend beyond the death or incapacity of the principal. Many states have special warning that must be included in a durable power of attorney for it to be effective.

For a power of attorney to be effective, not only must there be a properly executed document; it must also be delivered to the attorney-in-fact or someone who accepts it on his or her behalf.

Law of Agency

Agency is the legal status of a person, the agent, who is authorized to conduct business for another party, the principal. Except in the very smallest of businesses, a businessowner must rely to some extent on others to conduct portions of the business. Because of this necessity, the owner needs to be familiar with the laws of agency.

Creation of the Agency

As a general rule, any person who can legally enter into a contract may be a principal in the agency relationship. However, a person may be an agent even though the person cannot enter into a binding contract. Thus, although a minor cannot be a principal in the agency relationship, the minor can be an agent. In most cases, because unincorporated associations may not enter into contracts, they cannot be principals. Individual members, acting on behalf of the associations, may in most states be principals; in which case the individuals are personally liable on the contract.

A person is usually disqualified from being an agent if the law requires that he or she be licensed and the proposed agent is not, i.e., a real estate broker must be licensed as a broker or he/she is disqualified by law. An agent cannot represent both parties unless they are informed of the facts and approve the relationship. In addition, the agent cannot act secretly for personal gain. These last two restrictions on an agent's actions are designed to ensure that the agent owes undivided loyalty to the principal.

The agency relationship may be created by either the acts of the parties or by operation of law. The usual method of creating a relationship is for the principal to appoint the agent to act on the principal's behalf by communicating with the agent either verbally or in writing. This is considered *actual authority*. The relationship may be established by an act of *apparent (or implied) authority*, in which the principal through a third person authorizes the agent to act for the principal. The relationship can also be established by the concept of *inherent authority*. With inherent authority, the agent has the authority to act on the behalf of the principal because of the agent's position in relation to the principal. For example, your business manager or supervisor has the inherent authority to act in your name because of her or his position of authority. The agency relationship in this situation is created by operation of law to prevent fraud or injustice.

Agent's Authority

As has been said earlier, an agent's authority to act on behalf of a principal may be actual, apparent, or inherent. *Actual authority* is that authority an agent has because the principal has given it to the agent and the agent has accepted it. For the agent to have actual authority, both the agent and the principal must consent to the relationship. No consideration or payments to the agent are necessary. If the agency relationship involves buying or selling land, the agreement usually must be in writing. In most other cases, no written agreement is necessary to establish the relationship.

Apparent, or *implied,* authority of an agent is the result of authority implied by reason of the agent's relationship with the principal or the principal's business, by reason of custom and use, and by acquiescence. To have implied authority by custom and use, the agent must know the general custom and act in accordance with it. Implied authority by acquiescence occurs when the principal fails to object to the agent's actions or has ratified previous similar acts the agent has taken.

Unless specifically authorized to do so by the principal, the agent cannot delegate authority to a third person. The rationale is that the relationship between agent and principal is consensual in nature and that the principal has not consented to others' performing the agent's functions. Exceptions to this general rule are when the acts the agent gives to a third person are purely mechanical or ministerial, when circumstances indicate that at the time the delegation was made to the agent a subagent would be necessary, and when it is a general custom of a particular business to delegate an agent's duties to a subagent.

An agent with actual authority to purchase on the principals behalf has the implied authority to pay for the goods either out of any of the principal's funds in the agent's control or on credit. There is also the implied authority to accept the delivery of any goods that the agent has the authority to purchase.

An agent who has the authority to sell the principal's property has the implied authority to give general warranties regarding the property. If the agent possesses the property, then the agent has the implied authority to collect payment. The agent must accept payment only in cash unless some other means are approved by the principal. An agent does not have the implied power to accept a check as payment for the property or to sell on credit unless the principal has previously approved it. An agent with the authority to sell usually has the authority to deliver the property on receipt of payment.

Termination of the Agency

An agency relationship can be canceled in several ways. If the agency relationship is for a specific period, it will automatically terminate at the end of that period. If no period is agreed upon between the agent and the principal, then the courts will imply termination within a reasonable time unless the agent's acts are ongoing. In many cases, the agency terminates when a certain event occurs. For example, if you hire an agent to sell property for you, the agency terminates when the property is sold.

A change of circumstances that materially changes the relationship also terminates the agency. The following changes of circumstances are sufficient to terminate the agency:

Destruction of the property that is the subject matter of the agency.

Closing of the business associated with the agency.

A drastic change in business conditions.

A change in laws that substantially modifies the business relationship.

Insolvency of either the principal or the agent.

A major breach of an agent's fiduciary duty terminates the relationship. The agency relationship terminates when a party either dies or loses the capacity to enter into a contract (e.g., becomes insane). When corporations or partnerships are involved, their dissolution also terminates the agency. Either party may terminate the agency by informing the other party. The power to terminate exists even in those cases when there is a contractual agreement not to terminate. In this case, the party breaching the contract may be liable for breach of contract, but the party still has the right to cancel the agency.

There are two exceptions to the unilateral right of either party to cancel the relationship. The first exception is an agency "coupled with an interest—that is, when the agent has an interest in the property involved. For example, a principal borrows $50,000 from an agent and gives the agent the authority to sell a certain piece of property and to subtract the $50,000 from the proceeds of the sale. Because the agency is "coupled with an interest," the principal may not cancel the agency until the principal first repays the amount borrowed. The second exception occurs when the grant of authority is given to the agent or to a third person to protect a debt or other obligation.

Apparent Authority

A person is usually not responsible for a second person's acts unless that second person is authorized to act on behalf of the first person. An exception is the apparent authority concept used by the courts to prevent injustice to third persons. The mere statement by a person that he or she is an agent of a certain person is insufficient to establish the agency. The third person has a duty to ascertain whether an agent has the authority to act in a particular situation. If the principal has led others to believe that the agency relationship exists, the principal is bound by the acts that an agent in that situation would customarily have the authority to do.

The agency relationship is used by the courts when the principal has a duty to deny the relationship but fails to do so. For example, if John in Joe's presence tells others that he is Joe's agent, Joe has a duty to deny the relationship. If he fails to, then any third persons present may consider that John is in fact an agent of Joe.

One may also be held to be an agent when the principal negligently allows another person to act as his or her agent. For example, a stranger comes into the business place and no one is present. The stranger then waits on a customer, sells a product, and pockets the money. Because it is reasonable for the customer to have assumed that the stranger was a clerk, the businessowner cannot force the customer to pay for the merchandise a second time.

If the agent's authority is stated in writing and if the writing is still in the possession of the agent, a third person may reasonably assume that the agency relationship is ongoing. However, if the document has an expiration date, it is not be reasonable for a person to act on the assumption that an agency exists after that date.

A similar situation exists when an individual dies after writing some checks. Until the bank receives notice of the death, it may continue to honor the transactions pursuant to its agreement with the individual.

Inherent Authority

In some situations, to protect innocent third persons, the courts find an inherent authority for an agent to act. Under this concept, a principal is liable for the wrongdoing committed by his or her employees if the acts are within the scope of the employees' duties. For example, a car salesperson is instructed by the employer not to warrant the fitness of any of the automobiles being offered for sale. In violation of these orders, the salesperson warrants the correctness of the indicated mileage on an automobile. The employer will be held to the warranty. In this regard, *scope of employment* means that the employee is engaged in the furtherance of the employer's business.

If the agent possesses the merchandise and is either a regular dealer in that type of merchandise or has indicia of ownership, it is assumed that the agent is authorized to sell the merchandise. Mere possession of the goods is insufficient to establish the right to sell.

Ratification

If an unauthorized person acts as a businessowner's agent, the owner may ratify the unauthorized transaction. An owner who does this is bound by the act of the unauthorized agent. To ratify the act, the principal must know the material facts involved in the transaction and accept the entire transaction. The owner cannot approve the part that is favorable and deny the unfavorable part. A principal may ratify only legal acts.

The ratification of an agent's unauthorized acts may be by expressed approval, by acceptance of the benefits of the act, or by silence when the principal had a duty to speak. The third person may withdraw from the transaction upon notification to the principal before the principal ratifies the transaction.

Parties to an Agency Relationship

Generally, the third person may not sue an agent because her or his contract was with the principal and not with the agent. Exceptions to this general rule occur when the agent fails to disclose that he or she is acting on behalf of a principal or when there is a clear intent to bind the agent in the terms of the contract.

If the third person knows the principal, and if the agent acts within his or her authority, the principal will be bound on the contract. If the principal's identity is unknown when the contract is entered into, then both the agent and the principal will be bound on the contract and the third person may sue either or both.

An agent who acts on the principal's behalf without the principal's authorization is liable for breach of warranty. In stating that he or she is acting on someone's behalf, the agent warrants the existence of the principal, that the principal has the capacity to enter into contracts, and that the agent has the authority to act.

If the agent fails to disclose that he or she is acting on behalf of a principal (undisclosed principal), the third person may sue either the agent or the principal if default occurs. The third person may sue both, but the third party can collect from only one. For example, if the third person sues the agent and gets a judgment against the agent, the third person can still attempt to collect from the undisclosed principal until the judgment is paid.

Because the transaction between the agent and the third person is for the principal's benefit, the agent usually cannot sue for breach of the contract. The principal may sue in such a situation unless it involves a case in which the principal has fraudulently concealed his or her identity.

Rights and Duties of Agent and Principal

The agent also has the duty of undivided loyalty toward the principal. A person cannot act as an agent for more than one party and cannot self-deal with the principal's property without the principal's expressed permission. If the agent has any interests that are adverse to those of the principal, the agent has a duty to disclose them.

The agent is liable for any loss the principal suffer as the result of failure to complete the agent's duties or to follow the reasonable directions of the principal. The agent is also obligated to perform his or her duties in a reasonable and prudent manner. This duty applies even to those situations in which the agent is gratuitously acting on behalf of the principal.

If the agent breaches his or her duties, the principal may sue the agent for either breach of contract or in tort. *Tort* refers to a suit brought because of negligent or wrongful acts that cause injuries to others. Under a breach of contract suit, the agent may be held liable for any reasonably foreseeable damages that the principal suffers as the result of the agent's failure to fulfill the agency contract. In a suit in tort, the principal may recover for any damages suffered because of the agent's wrongful or negligent act. In some cases, the principal may also collect punitive damages. *Punitive* damages are those damages assessed by a court that are in excess of the actual damages and that are imposed as punishment.

If the agent makes a secret profit from the relationship, the principal may bring suit to recover it. In some situations, the principal may bring a court action to force the agent to account for any funds that the agent receives as the result of the relationship. In some cases involving agent misconduct, the principal may withhold any compensation owed to the agent.

The principal owes a duty to reasonably compensate the agent for the agent's time and effort, unless the agent has agreed to act without pay. In addition, the principal must reimburse the agent for any reasonable expenses that were expended by the agent in the furtherance of the relationship. Additional duties may be imposed by the contract. In most situations, the agent has a lien against the property of the principal for any monies owed to him or her.

Liability

Under the doctrine of *respondeat superior,* the principal may be liable for certain acts of the agent. For there to be liability there must be an agency relationship, and the conduct must be within the scope of employment. For conduct be within the scope of employment, an employment situation must exist. If the agent is an independent contractor, the duties of whom the principal has no right to control, no employment situation exists and the principal is not usually liable for the acts of the agent.

To determine if an employment situation exists, the courts not only look at the degree of control that the principal has over the agent but also whether the agent is engaged in a distinct business, the degree of skill involved in the duties, and the period of employment. If the court determines that the agent is in fact an employee and not an independent contractor, the employer (i.e., principal) will be liable for the torts (i.e., the misconduct and negligent acts) the agent committed that injured others or damaged property belonging to others.

To determine if the employee was within the scope of employment, many courts use the test, "Was the employee about the employer's business when the injury or damage occurred?" Another test commonly used is, "Were the acts of the employee motivated by a desire to serve the purposes of the employer?"

Forms in This Chapter

- FORM 13-1: GENERAL POWER OF ATTORNEY (LONG FORM). Gives a general power of attorney. General powers of attorney should be used rarely, since they give the attorney-in-fact the authority to take any legal action in name of the principal. If a general power of attorney is given, it should have a definite expiration date.

- FORM 13-2: GENERAL POWER OF ATTORNEY (SHORT FORM). May be used to give someone a general power of attorney. As noted early, general powers of attorney should be used rarely, since they give the attorney-in-fact the authority to take any legal action in name of the principal. If a general power of attorney is given, it should have a definite expiration date. The short form is acceptable in most cases, but if real estate is involved it may be better to use the long form.

- FORM 13-3: SPECIAL POWER OF ATTORNEY. Used by an individual to give someone the power of attorney to do some special acts.

- FORM 13-4: SPECIAL POWER OF ATTORNEY (CORPORATION). Used by a corporation to give someone the power of attorney to do some special acts.

- FORM 13-5: SPECIAL POWER OF ATTORNEY (FROM ONE SPOUSE TO ANOTHER). Used by one spouse to give the other spouse the authority to take action on behalf of the other.

- FORM 13-6: SPECIAL POWER OF ATTORNEY (FROM HUSBAND AND WIFE TO ANOTHER). Used by husband and wife to give another person the authority to take action on behalf of them.

- FORM 13-7: RENUNCIATION OF POWER OF ATTORNEY. Renounces a power of attorney.

- FORM 13-8: DURABLE POWER OF ATTORNEY. This power of attorney is not revoked by the incapacity of the principal. A durable power of attorney is created in most states by using words that clearly show an intent for the power to continue even during the subsequent incapacity of the principal.

- FORM 13-9: NOTIFICATION OF REVOCATION OF POWER OF ATTORNEY. Notifies individuals that a power of attorney is being revoked. Persons and companies who have been relying on the power of attorney must be personally notified of the revocation.

GENERAL POWER OF ATTORNEY (LONG FORM)

I

I, [name of person giving the power of attorney] of [city and state] hereby appoint [name of person to whom the power is given] of [city and state], as my true and lawful attorney-in-fact for me and in my name, place, and stead for my use and benefit:

> To perform or exercise any act, right, power, duty, or obligation that I have or may acquire the right, power, duty, and capacity to exercise or perform;

> To engage in and transact any lawful business for me and in my name;

> To sign, endorse, execute, acknowledge, deliver, receive, and possess any contracts, agreements, notes, options, covenants, deeds, bills of sale, trust deeds, leases, mortgages, assignments, insurance policies, bonds, checks, drafts, any commercial paper, receipts, evidences of debt, warehouse receipts, security agreements, liens, and any other such instrument in writing whatsoever and kind as may be necessary in the exercise of the rights and powers granted herein;

> To lease, purchase, trade, exchange and acquire, to bargain for, contract, and agree to lease, purchase, acquire and take, possess any real or personal property whether tangible or intangible, on any terms and conditions as such attorney-in-fact shall deem proper;

> To improve, repair, maintain, manage, insure, rent, lease, sell, release, convey, mortgage, subject to lien, and in any manner deal with all or any part of any real or personal property, intangible and tangible, whatsoever, or any interest which I may own or may hereafter acquire for me and in my name under such terms and conditions as the attorney-in-fact deems appropriate and proper;

II

I grant to my attorney-in-fact the full power and authority to do and perform all and every act and thing required and proper to be done in the exercise of any of the rights and powers granted herein as fully as I might do.

III

This instrument is to be construed and interpreted as a general power of attorney. The failure to enumerate a specific item, power, or authority does not restrict nor limit my attorney-in-fact from doing them.

IV

The rights, powers, and authority granted to my attorney-in-fact shall be effective on the date this document is signed and delivered to the attorney-in-fact and shall remain in effect unless sooner canceled by me until [date].

Dated: _____

_____
[signature]

[acknowledgment]

13-2 GENERAL POWER OF ATTORNEY (SHORT FORM)

I, [name of person giving the power of attorney], of [city and state] hereby appoint [name of person to whom the power is given] of [city and state], as my true and lawful attorney-in-fact for me and in my name, place, and stead for my use and benefit:

> To perform or exercise any act, right, power, duty or obligation that I have or may acquire the right, power, duty, and capacity to exercise or perform.

I grant to my attorney-in-fact the full power and authority to do and perform all and every act and thing required and proper to be done in the exercise of any of the rights and powers granted herein as fully as I might do.

This instrument is to be construed and interpreted as a general power of attorney. The failure to enumerate a specific item, power, or authority does not restrict nor limit my attorney-in-fact from doing them.

The rights, powers, and authority granted to my attorney-in-fact shall be effective on the date this document is signed and delivered to the attorney-in-fact and shall remain in effect unless sooner canceled by me until [date].

Dated: _____

_____
[signature]

[acknowledgment]

13-3   SPECIAL POWER OF ATTORNEY

I, [name of person giving the power of attorney], of [city and state] hereby appoint [name of person to whom the power is given] of [city and state], as my true and lawful attorney-in-fact for me and in my name to act in my capacity to do any and all of the following:

[list special duties or powers that the attorney-in-fact is empowered to do on behalf of the principal]

This instrument is to be construed and interpreted as a special power of attorney.

The rights, powers, and authority granted to my attorney-in-fact shall be effective on the date this document is signed and delivered to the attorney-in-fact and shall remain in effect unless sooner canceled by me until [date].

Dated: _____

_____
[signature]

[acknowledgment]

13-4 SPECIAL POWER OF ATTORNEY (CORPORATION)

_____, [name of corporation giving the power of attorney], a corporation organized under the laws of the State of _____ hereby appoint [name of person to whom the power is given] of [city and state], as its true and lawful attorney-in-fact for the corporation and in its name to act in its capacity to do any and all of the following:

[list special duties or powers that the attorney-in-fact
is empowered to do on behalf of the principal]

This instrument is to be construed and interpreted as a special power of attorney. The authority to grant this power was conferred by resolution of the board of directors of the corporation dated: [date of resolution]. A copy of such resolution is attached.

The rights, powers, and authority granted to the attorney-in-fact shall be effective on the date this document is signed and delivered to the attorney-in-fact and shall remain in effect unless sooner canceled by the corporation until [date].

Dated: _____

_____
[signature]

[corporate seal]

[acknowledgment]

13-5 SPECIAL POWER OF ATTORNEY (FROM ONE SPOUSE TO ANOTHER)

I, [name of person giving the power of attorney], of [city and state] hereby appoint by [husband or wife], [name of person to whom the power is given] of [city and state], as my true and lawful attorney-in-fact for me and in my name to act in my capacity to do any and all of the following:

[list special duties or powers that the attorney-in-fact
is empowered to do on behalf of the principal]

This instrument is to be construed and interpreted as a special power of attorney.

The rights, powers, and authority granted to my attorney-in-fact shall be effective on the date this document is signed and delivered to the attorney-in-fact and shall remain in effect unless sooner canceled by me until [date].

Dated: _____

_____
[signature]

[acknowledgment]

13-6 SPECIAL POWER OF ATTORNEY (FROM HUSBAND AND WIFE TO ANOTHER)

We, [name of one spouse], and [name of other spouse], husband and wife of [city and state], hereby appoint [name of person to whom the power is given] of [city and state], as our true and lawful attorney-in-fact for us and in our names to act in our capacity to do any and all of the following:

[list special duties or powers that the attorney-in-fact
is empowered to do on behalf of the principal]

This instrument is to be construed and interpreted as a special power of attorney.

The rights, powers, and authority granted to our attorney-in-fact shall be effective on the date this document is signed and delivered to the attorney-in-fact and shall remain in effect unless sooner canceled by us until [date].

Dated: _____

_____
[signed by one spouse]

Dated: _____

_____
[signed by other spouse]

[acknowledgment]

13-7 RENUNCIATION OF POWER OF ATTORNEY

To: All persons

The power of attorney in which I, [name] was appointed as the attorney-in-fact for _____ is hereby renounced. I renounce all right and claim to act as attorney-in-fact for [name of principal].

Dated: _____

_____
Signature

13-8   DURABLE POWER OF ATTORNEY

Warning to person executing this document

This document is an important legal document. It creates a durable power of attorney. Before executing this document, you should know the below information:

1. This document may provide the person you designate as your attorney-in-fact with broad powers to dispose, sell, convey, and encumber your real and personal property.
2. These powers will exist for an indefinite period of time unless you limit their duration in this document. These powers will continue to exist notwithstanding your subsequent disability or incapacity.
3. You have the right to revoke or terminate this durable power of attorney at any time.

I, [name of person giving the power of attorney], of [city and state] hereby appoint [name of person to whom the power is given] of [city and state], as my true and lawful attorney-in-fact for me and in my name to act in my capacity to do any and all of the following:

[list special duties or powers that the attorney-in-fact is empowered to do on behalf of the principal]

This instrument is to be construed and interpreted as a durable power of attorney and any subsequent incapacity of the principal shall not affect this power of attorney.

The rights, powers, and authority granted to my attorney-in-fact shall be effective on the date this document is signed and delivered to the attorney-in-fact and shall remain in effect unless sooner canceled by me until [date].

Dated: _____

_____
[signature]

[acknowledgment]

13–9   NOTIFICATION OF REVOCATION OF POWER OF ATTORNEY

To: All persons

The power of attorney in which I, [name] appointed _____ as the attorney-in-fact for me on [date] is hereby revoked. I have revoked all rights and claims of _____ to act as attorney-in-fact for me.

Dated: _____

_____
[signature]

Chapter 14

Professional Services

Professional advice is like medicine in many ways. You can take it to cure problems or to prevent them. Sometimes the problems are aggravated by either failing to consult an attorney, tax accountant, or other consultant or waiting too long to seek their advice and assistance. In this chapter, both the text and forms look at professional services from two aspects. The first is from the aspect of providing professional services to clients. If you are a provider of professional services, the discussion and the forms associated with providing professional services are directed to you. The bulk of the chapter, however, deals with the problems of obtaining professional services. This part of the chapter pertains to everyone. Even a professional must at times hire other professionals. The second part of the chapter discusses selecting attorneys, accountants, or professional assistants, your relationship with professional advisors, reducing your professional fees, and firing your advisors.

Selecting the Attorney

It is very difficult to evaluate an attorney and the attorney's ability to give you the legal advice and assistance you need in specific situations.

The world's greatest criminal lawyer probably is not a competent business attorney, so seek an attorney who is competent in the field of law in which you need assistance. Many people wrongly believe that gray hair or maturity indicates an attorney's experience and ability to handle their cases. This belief could be a grave mistake. Although it is nice to have an attorney with 20 years of experience in the issues involved in your situation, it is also important to have an attorney who is abreast of the current status of the law. Many attorneys fail to keep their knowledge current and may not know as much as an attorney fresh out of law school. In addition, many attorneys have one year's experience repeated 20 times rather than having 20 years of varied experience.

Selecting an attorney is like selecting a family doctor. An attorney's ability to handle your affairs and the fees she or he charges may have little relationship to each other. There are many good attorneys who have very reasonable fees, and unfortunately there are some inept attorneys who charge high fees. It is difficult for the average person to know what is the best legal advice and assistance for the money. The best guarantee of competent legal advice for a reasonable price is selecting the right attorney.

It pays to do some comparison shopping for an attorney. The promise of lower fees isn't an important factor the client should consider, because an incompetent attorney is too expensive at any cost. Like other professionals, attorneys vary in their abilities and in the amount of time they need to provide the necessary services. An attorney who charges $75 an hour is more expensive than an experienced attorney who charges $125 an hour but completes the job in half the time.

The usual areas of expertise for attorneys are bankruptcy, probate and estate planning, criminal, corporate, commercial, and trade law. Attorneys who specialize in commercial or trade law are more appropriate for business-related problems.

In many states, attorneys can get their bar certification in selected areas and thus hold themselves out as "certified specialists." In most situations, the businessperson doesn't need to pay the extra cost of getting a certified specialist to handle routine business problems.

Attorneys also specialize in certain areas or limit their practice to selected areas, which usually means that they accept cases in those areas only. They may be the best type of attorney to retain because they should be fairly competent in the needed area and usually not as expensive as a certified specialist.

Finding the Attorney

Using common sense in hunting for an attorney is important. It is not something that you should rush into. As in selecting a family physician, professional referral is the best method. If you know an attorney whose opinion you value, ask for a referral. An attorney working for the government or for a corporation may be able to recommend a competent attorney for you. A second preferred method is to ask your banker, accountant, and business associates for their recommendations.

Another approach is to check with other businesspersons in your area for the names of attorneys who have assisted them. If that is still unproductive, check with the referral services of the local bar association. Their numbers are in the telephone book under the bar association. Most county bar associations operate a referral service through which an individual can get a free or low-cost 15-minute consultation with an attorney.

Usually, any attorney who wants to be listed by the bar referral service can do so by agreeing to give a free initial consultation to persons referred to her or him and by providing proof of malpractice insurance. Attorneys list several areas of law they want to practice. They are then referred to clients in rotating order by the referral service. Fees for services beyond the initial consultation are determined by an agreement between the lawyer and the client. During this initial consultation, the attorney should determine the complexity of the client's problem and give an estimate of the legal fees involved.

The major problem with referral services is that bar associations do not evaluate the competence of the attorneys on their lists. Any local attorney who has malpractice insurance and agrees to provide the initial free consultation is usually listed. Many people wrongly believe that, in referring them to a specific attorney, the bar association is also recommending that attorney. A positive factor in using referral services is that most of them have procedures to informally settle conflicts between the referred attorney and the client.

Another way to find an attorney is to ask local public interest groups or trade and business associations for their recommendations. Using a prepaid legal plan is another way to select an attorney. Prepaid legal plans are discussed later.

A less reliable source is to ask your neighbors or relatives for recommendations. If you do this, make sure they are not basing their recommendation on a divorce case, for example, when you need help on a commercial matter.

Attorneys Who Advertise

Attorneys have been allowed to advertise since 1976. This method of selecting an attorney is not recommended and should be your last alternative. Although many good attorneys advertise, unfortunately an unusual number of incompetent attorneys hire good public relations firms. An attorney who advertises may not be getting enough new clients from referrals by former clients who were happy with her or his performance. In addition, the quality of legal services varies so greatly that there is no way to evaluate an attorney by merely looking at an ad. I would rather select an attorney from the telephone book than to select one from a newspaper or a television commercial. A competent, affordable attorney more often than not gets more referral business than she or he can handle, without resorting to advertising.

Law Directories

To get information on attorneys, such as their experience and the schools they attended, check in a law directory at your local public library. The most popular and complete directory is the *Martindale-Hubbell Law Directory*, consisting of seven volumes, each about five inches thick. Attorneys are listed alphabetically by cities.

Legal Clinics

Legal clinics are generally storefront-type law offices located in shopping centers and are designed to provide cheap legal services for simple legal problems. If your problem is relatively simple, it may be advantageous to use a legal clinic, but if your legal need is something more than the preparation of a simple will, beware of getting cut-rate legal advice.

Prepaid Legal Plans

Prepaid legal plans are new to the legal profession. They were first used by labor unions as a benefit to union members. Now the plans have grown in both numbers and types. Today many of them resemble medical plans. If you buy a prepaid legal plan, make sure that you understand the services that you will obtain for the basic fee and under what circumstances additional will be fees charged. One major disadvantage of prepaid legal plans is the inability to establish a confidential relationship with one attorney; most plans use several attorneys and rotate them.

Initial Consultation with an Attorney

Having made an initial appointment with the attorney you have selected, continue to consider whether you have made the choice that is the right one for you. The initial appointment should be a screening process for both of you to decide if you want to continue the association. Prepare for your appointment much as you would prepare for a job interview. Be on time. Take all your papers with you. Above all else, do not take your children. You and the attorney should be free from unnecessary distractions so that you can concentrate on the legal problem.

At the first meeting, clearly and concisely tell the kind of help you need. This is not the time to gossip, because you are usually billed by the clock. Find out if that attorney or an associate will handle your case. If the attorney promises you the world, be wary. In most legal situations, there are no clear answers to problems. If you are uneasy about the attorney, end the association before it starts. Above all, make sure you understand what the attorney's fees are and what that money will buy for you. Attorney fees are discussed more in detail later in this chapter.

Before you retain an attorney, get a commitment about accessibility and willingness to handle your problems. A busy attorney usually indicates competence. But if the attorney is too busy to handle your problems, go elsewhere. If, during the initial interview, the attorney is being interrupted by staff or telephone calls, you can expect similar problems later in your association.

Many attorneys tend to nitpick and get bogged down in details. Such an attorney will cause you unnecessary expense in dealing with your problems. In your initial consultation, look for this fault in the attorney. Look for someone who does not spend a lot of time on minutiae.

Look for personal compatibility, good judgment, legal expertise, a habit of thorough preparation, prompt response to your needs, and reasonable fees in the attorney you eventually select.

Relationship with Your Attorney

Try to maintain a professional relationship with your attorney. Never enter into an attorney–client relationship with a friend; it only causes problems. Convince the attorney that you are important and that you can be the source of future business and references in the community.

Attorneys are generally conservative in nature in their advice. Their theme is to prevent problems before they begin. Although this is usually the most prudent course of action to take, be aware of this conservative trend when dealing with an attorney. If you are willing to take certain legal risks to save money, make sure your attorney is aware of the level of risk that you can accept.

A second factor to be aware of is that most attorneys have a very high opinion of themselves and may tend to oversell their abilities. Because of this attitude, they often try to give advice in other than legal areas. If this happens, remember that you have latitude to disregard it.

In all appointments with your attorney, be on time, be prepared, be concise and don't waste his time. The attorney may be too polite to say that you are wasting his or her time but will not be too polite to bill you for it. To accomplish the most in the shortest period, do your homework before you meet with your attorney. Have your papers and records complete and in a form the attorney can readily understand.

Reducing Your Legal Fees

A famous person once said, "In law, nothing is certain but the expense." With this in mind, never, never, hire an attorney without a clear understanding of the fees that will be charged, when they will be due, and how the attorney will earn them. Attorneys generally use three methods to set legal fees: by the hour, by a flat fee, and on a contingency basis. When the latter method is used, the attorney receives a percentage of any recovery you receive. In some cases, the attorney may combine any of the three methods.

Legal fees are negotiable. If you feel the attorney's quoted fees are unacceptable, ask for a modification. Do so before your relationship is established but after your attorney has an idea of the nature and complexity of your problem. Do not give your attorney an unlimited budget to work with.

If your problem will require only a few hours of legal work, an hourly rate may be your best choice. In most cases, this is the most economical way to employ an attorney. It may be to your advantage, though, to use a combination of an hourly fee with a maximum fee—for example, $100 an hour, not to exceed $500.

In many situations the attorney may ask for a retainer fee. A retainer fee is merely an employment fee that the attorney charges to handle your case. It usually is not a payment for any time the attorney expends on your behalf. If you can guarantee the attorney a minimum number of hours each month or year, he or she may forgo the retainer fee or reduce the hourly rate.

In most states attorneys are not permitted to pay court fees or costs. Therefore, any fee an attorney quotes does not include court fees or costs. In lengthy or prolonged cases, make sure that at specific times the attorney submits an itemized bill that includes a progress report.

Because the attorney's time is the standard measurement of the fee, do as much as you can on the case to reduce the time the attorney needs to spend. If certain records are needed from a government office, get them yourself. If possible, give draft contracts to your attorney for review rather than having the attorney draft them.

If your attorney uses an hourly rate, find out if there is a minimum billing time. For example, if the attorney has a minimum billing time of 15 minutes, plan your calls to take full advantage of the 15 minutes you will be charged for. Call the attorney instead of visiting; telephone calls inevitably take less of the attorney's time than do personal visits. Before you make the visit or call, have your records and all other pertinent information ready so that you can accomplish your objective in the minimum of time. *Note:* It is not unusual for a client to make the attorney wait while the client hunts for records or information. This is a waste of legal fees.

Firing Your Attorney

The attorney and the client have certain basic rights that each should honor. The client has the right to be treated fairly, honestly, and courteously, to be charged only reasonable fees as agreed upon, to receive prompt responses to inquiries regarding the case, to be informed of the status of the case, and to have his or her legal problems handled diligently and competently. The attorney is also under a duty to keep the client's confidences.

If you feel that your attorney isn't handling your case properly or respecting your rights as a client, you may want to end the relationship. When you change attorneys, it usually costs you extra time and money to establish a relationship with a new attorney. You usually lose any money you paid to the first attorney, and the new attorney will need time to get current on the case. If possible, try to settle any conflicts and retain the original attorney. Many times, the only problem is a failure to communicate. If all else fails, however, consider firing your attorney.

You always have the right to terminate the attorney–client relationship. However, there may be a problem with your right to any legal fees that you have already paid. If a problem occurs, check with another attorney about your right to get the fees back.

If the conflict results from a serious breach of duty by the attorney, consider filing a complaint with the state bar association. This can be done by explaining the problem to the association in writing. The association's address is in your telephone book. Do not write to the bar association until you have ended your relationship with the attorney.

Most conflicts between attorneys and clients are over time and the money billed to the client. Keep an accurate record of what your attorney does for you and the time spent. If you feel that the bill is too high, ask the attorney to explain why the bill is higher than you feel it should be. If this does not settle the matter satisfactorily, check with the bar association. Many state bar associations have fee arbitration panels. Usually, the dispute is referred to an arbitration panel of one or more persons who listen to both sides and then decide the fee the attorney should have charged. In some states, such as California, the attorney has to arbitrate if the client chooses to.

The case files belong to the client, not the attorney. Accordingly, when the relationship has terminated, you have a right to the files in your case. In most cases, the attorney keeps the files because the client fails to demand them. In most states, the attorney may not withhold your files even if you owe the attorney money.

Accountant

An accountant is more than the individual who prepares your income taxes. This professional should be a part of your decision-making process. Businesses often find out too late that their management decisions have unnecessarily increased their tax liability or that they have failed to maintain the proper records in order to achieve maximum tax advantages.

Selecting an Accountant

The process of selecting an accountant is similar to that of selecting an attorney. In selecting an accountant, consider the following criteria:

    Experience and skill
    Reputation
    Time and motivation to handle your accounts
    Reasonable fees

The Certified Public Accountant

The designation, Certified Public Accountant (CPA), is reserved for only those accountants who have demonstrated to the state licensing agency a sufficient degree of expertise in accounting, legal, and auditing principles. Only a CPA can certify a financial statement. When a CPA certifies your financial statement, it means that the accounting records of your business are being maintained in accordance with accepted accounting practices and that in the CPA's judgment the financial statement is proper and correct.

The fees of a CPA are normally higher than those of an accountant who is not a CPA. If you need a certified financial statement, then you must use a CPA. If there are no requirements for certified financial statements, then consider the use of an accountant who is not a CPA. If you only occasionally need a certified financial statement, use a good uncertified accountant and for those special occasions hire a CPA to check the statements and certify them.

Accountant's Work Product

Your accountant should help you to establish an accounting system and maintain it, and should conduct periodic reviews of the system to ensure that it is being properly maintained. The accountant should provide advice to help you to identify the true costs of your products and to determine those products that are not making a profit. The accountant should assist you in raising capital and provide tax management.

Banker

You need to establish a relationship with a banker who can provide guidance and can work with you as a member of your professional team. *Note:* There are still bankers who provide you assistance and guidance. In selecting a bank, find one that is not too large, that specializes in small businesses, that is familiar with your type of business, and that is willing to provide you with assistance.

Bankers, like other professionals, like to be associated with winners. Accordingly, portray a winning attitude and have facts and figures to back up your confidence. If there are negatives in your business situation, don't attempt to hide them but don't put them up front. Always explain how you are going to overcome the negatives.

Insurance Agent

To some extent, the selection of an insurance agent depends on the type of coverage you need and the types of policies provided by the agent. Once you select an agent by using tactics similar to those you used in selecting an attorney and an accountant, use the agent as part of your decision-making team. Remember that although the agent is the expert in insurance, he or she makes a living selling insurance.

Forms in This Chapter

- FORM 14–1: LETTER REQUESTING INFORMATION FROM A CLIENT. Obtains additional information regarding a client. This example is drafted for an employment problem. For other types of problems, modify the the request appropriately.

- FORM 14–2: COMPROMISE OF PROFESSIONAL SERVICES FEES. Used to compromise fees when there is a dispute as to the correct amount due.

- FORM 14–3: RELEASE OF ALL CLAIMS. Settles a claim.

- FORM 14–4: JOINT RELEASE (HUSBAND AND WIFE). Obtains a release of liability from a husband and wife.

- FORM 14–5: CONSULTATION AGREEMENT (TELEPHONE). Used by a professional to provide consultation services over the telephone at an hourly rate.

- FORM 14–6: LETTER FIRING AN ATTORNEY. A guide for drafting a letter firing an attorney.

- FORM 14–7: LETTER TO THE BAR ASSOCIATION REGARDING ATTORNEY. A guide for drafting a letter to the bar association regarding attorney misconduct.

- FORM 14–8: LETTER REGARDING ATTORNEY FEES. Notifies your attorney that you intend to submit his fees to bar arbitration process.

- FORM 14–9: LETTER TO LOCATE LICENSED REAL ESTATE AGENT. Locates a real estate agent when you have no current address.
- FORM 14–10: LETTER TO SECRETARY OF STATE REGARDING A CORPORATION. Determines the registered agent of a corporation.

14-1

LETTER REQUESTING INFORMATION FROM A CLIENT

[date]

[name and address of client]

Dear [name]:

Thank you for contacting us about your _____ problem. If you wish us to evaluate your case, please provide our office with the following materials:

1. A typed narrative statement of your complaint, including a chronology of events, your performance appraisals, the identity of witnesses, what each witness is likely to say, and whether the witness is friendly, hostile or something in between;

2. A recent job résumé and/or curriculum vitae;

3. Copies of all written job performance appraisals;

4. Any state or federal charges you may have filed; and

5. All documents regarding the alleged wrongful termination or discrimination (such as interoffice memos, correspondence, job descriptions, etc.).

If you have any questions regarding these documents or other matters, do not hesitate to call us.

Very truly yours,

[signature of attorney; typed name below]

14-2 COMPROMISE OF PROFESSIONAL SERVICES FEES

[name of client or patient]

[address of client or patient]

[date]

Dear [client or patient's name]:

This letter is to confirm our agreement we reached in our telephone conversation of [date] concerning the amount due for professional services rendered by my office.

As we discussed in the telephone conversation, you were billed $_____ for the following services:

[list services]

You expressed concern over the amount due. Since there can be a valid difference of opinion regarding the value of professional services and because you are a valued [client or patient], I agreed to accept $_____ in full settlement of the account if that amount is received on or before [payment date].

Please note that this agreement is conditioned on receiving payment of the agreed amount by the above date. If I have not received payment by that date, then our agreement is canceled and the original amount billed will be due.

Please date and sign the attached copy of this letter in the place provided and return the copy to me.

Sincerely,

_____

Signature

- -

Date: _____

I agree to pay the compromised amount of $_____ by [date].

_____

Signature of patient or client

14–3 RELEASE OF ALL CLAIMS

In consideration of the payment of $_____, I [name of individual with a claim], hereby expressly release and discharge [your name] from all claims and causes of action that I ever had, now have, or may have in the future, known or unknown, or that of any person claiming through me may have or have against [your name] that was caused by or arising out of [describe incident].

I hereby acknowledge receipt of the payment of $_____.

It is my intent that this release be binding on my heirs, legal representatives, assigns, and my wife.

Dated: _____

_____

[signature of person with claim]

14–4 JOINT RELEASE (HUSBAND AND WIFE)

We,_____ and _____, husband and wife, of [city and state], hereby execute this release of liability with the express intention and specific purpose to extinguish the obligations as herein set forth.

In consideration of $_____ [spell out amount] dollars, receipt of which is hereby acknowledged, we, for ourselves, our assigns, legal representatives, and anyone claiming through us release and discharge [name of person being released], of [city and state], and his/her heirs, assigns, legal representatives, from all claims and causes of action that we or either of us ever had, now have, or may have in the future, known or unknown, or that any person claiming through us or either of us may have or claim to have against [person being released] or his/her heirs, assigns, or legal representatives created or caused by or arising out of [description of incident].

We have read this release, understand its terms and their legal significance, and have voluntarily executed the release.

Dated: _____   _____
                           Husband

Dated: _____   _____
                           Wife

14–5 CONSULTATION AGREEMENT (TELEPHONE)

Date:

[name of professional] agrees to provide telephonic consultation services regarding questions on [describe services] to selected clients pursuant to the below terms:

Charges for consultation will be $_____ for any call less than 10 minutes. Calls in excess of 10 minutes will be charged at the rate of $_____ per minute. Clients will be billed monthly. There are no minimum monthly charges. If client is not satisfied with consultant services provided, the bill will be canceled if this office is notified in writing by client within 10 days after receipt of the bill by the client.

If I am not available at time of initial call, then I will normally return the call within two hours. This agreement may be canceled by either party without advance notice.

The charges for any services other than telephonic consultations will be established by agreement between client and me prior to performing subject services.

_____   _____
Provider   Client

                                                      _____
                                                      Address

14–6   LETTER FIRING AN ATTORNEY

Certified Mail, Return Receipt Requested

[date]

[name and address of attorney]

Dear [name]:

As I stated over the telephone, I am unhappy regarding the manner in which you have handled my case. Accordingly, your services are hereby terminated. You are not authorized to take any further actions on my behalf.

As you are aware, my file belongs to me, not to you. Please provide me with instructions on when and where I can pick up the file.

Sincerely,

14-7 LETTER TO THE BAR ASSOCIATION REGARDING ATTORNEY

Certified Mail, Return Receipt Requested

[date]

[name and address of bar association]

Attn: Section on Attorney Misconduct

Dear Madam/Sir:

The purpose of this letter is to inform the Bar Association that I am unhappy regarding the manner in which Attorney [name] has handled my case. The circumstances are as follows:

[include a brief statement of the problem]

It is requested that your committee conduct an investigation into the actions of Mr./Ms. [name], since it appears that his/her conduct is not in accordance with the state requirement for the conduct of the practice of law. I will be happy to provide additional information or to testify before your committee regarding this case.

Please keep me advised as to the status of this complaint.

Sincerely,

14-8 LETTER REGARDING ATTORNEY FEES

Certified Mail, Return Receipt Requested

[date]

[name and address of attorney]

Dear [name]:

As I stated over the telephone, I am unhappy regarding the statement of attorney fees which you have presented to me. Your original estimate was less than 50 percent of the amount billed.

Accordingly, I hereby request that you submit this dispute to the Bar Association for Arbitration of Fees.

Sincerely,

14–9 LETTER TO LOCATE LICENSED REAL ESTATE AGENT

Certified Mail, Return Receipt Requested

[date]

[name and address of state board of real estate]

Re: [agent's name and license number]

Dear Madam/Sir:

I have a claim against the above listed real estate agent in connection with the sale of our home in _____, 19____. I have been unable to locate the individual. Accordingly, please provide the most recent listed address for the above named person.

If there is a charge for this service, please advise so that payment can be forwarded.

Sincerely,

14–10 LETTER TO SECRETARY OF STATE REGARDING A CORPORATION

Certified Mail, Return Receipt Requested

[date]

[Name and address of secretary of state]

Re: [corporation's name and address]

Dear Madam/Sir:

Please provide me with the name of the registered agent of the above named corporation and the registered agent's address for the purpose of service of court papers.

If there is a charge for this service, please advise so that payment can be forwarded.

Sincerely,

Chapter 15

Bankruptcy

This chapter briefly discusses bankruptcy and forms that may be used by a business if a debtor files for bankruptcy. For the official forms needed for a business to file for bankruptcy, check with your local bankruptcy court.

Bankruptcy is an unpleasant subject to talk about, but because approximately 50 percent of new businesses fail in their first year of operation, it is an important subject. Only one of three businesses lasts five years. It is necessary to consider the aspects and the possibility of bankruptcy. The Supreme Court in one famous case in 1934 stated that the primary purposes of the Federal Bankruptcy Act are to relieve the honest debtor from the weight of oppressive indebtedness and to permit a fresh start. Pursuant to a provision in the Constitution, bankruptcy is controlled almost exclusively by the federal government. The primary source of statutory authority for bankruptcy is the Bankruptcy Reform Act of 1978 (BRA). It is Title XI of the United States Code. That act also provides the Supreme Court with the authority to make rules for situations the statutes don't cover.

There are two popular types of bankruptcy proceedings: liquidation under Chapter 7 and reorganization under Chapters 11 and 13. In liquidation proceedings, the trustee collects the nonexempt property of the debtor, converts the property to cash, and distributes the cash to the creditors. The debtor gives up all nonexempt property in return for a discharge of the debts. Most bankruptcy proceedings are Chapter 7 liquidation cases.

Chapters 11 and 13 deal with the reorganization of a debtors' debts. In reorganization proceedings, the creditors usually look to the future earnings of the debtor, not to the property or to the beginning of the proceedings to satisfy their claims began. Under reorganization, the debtor retains all assets and makes payments to the creditor, usually from post-petition earnings pursuant to a court-approved plan.

Bankruptcy proceedings begin with the filing of a petition with a federal bankruptcy court. In most cases the debtor files the petition. Such debtor-initiated proceedings are referred to as *voluntary proceedings*. In certain cases, creditors have the right to initiate *involuntary bankruptcy* proceedings against a debtor under either Chapter 7 or 11.

Voluntary Bankruptcy

For a debtor to apply for voluntary bankruptcy under Chapter 7, the debtor must be a person. A *person,* as defined under the act, includes partnerships and corporations. A sole proprietorship is not considered to be a person and therefore cannot commence voluntary bankruptcy proceedings unless its owner files bankruptcy as to total assets.

Railroads, insurance companies, and banking institutions may not initiate voluntary bankruptcy proceedings under Chapter 7. Any person eligible to file a petition under Chapter 7 may also file a petition for reorganization under Chapter 11, with the exception of stockbrokers and commodity brokers.

To file for reorganization under Chapter 13, the debtor must be an individual and must have an income that is sufficiently stable and regular to make individual payments under a Chapter 13 plan. Thus, Chapter 13's primary purpose is to cover wage earners, whereas it is mainly businesses that are covered under Chapter 11. An additional limitation under Chapter 13 is that the debtor must have unsecured debts totaling less than $100,000 and secured debts totaling less than $350,000. If the debtor does not meet the requirements under Chapter 13, he or she still may be eligible for bankruptcy under Chapter 11.

Insolvency is not a requirement prior to petitioning for voluntary bankruptcy. In the case of a husband and wife, they may file a single petition for voluntary relief under any chapter available to each spouse. If the husband and wife file together under Chapter 13, their aggregate debts are subject to the monetary limitations of $100,000 for unsecured debts and $350,000 for secured debts. A voluntary bankruptcy case is started with the filing of a petition by an eligible debtor. No formal adjudication is necessary to start the proceedings.

Involuntary Bankruptcy

Under certain conditions creditors may file involuntary petitions for bankruptcy against a debtor under either Chapter 7 or 11 but not under Chapter 13. Certain debtors, such as railroads, insurance companies, banking institutions, and farmers, are protected from involuntary petitions. For a creditor to file a petition in bankruptcy, three (generally) creditors with unsecured claims totaling at least $5,000 must join in the petition. If, however, the debtor has fewer than 12 unsecured creditors, a single creditor with an unsecured claim of $5,000 is sufficient to file the petition.

The basis for involuntary relief is that the debtor is generally not paying debts as they become due. This is often referred to as *equitable insolvency.* An alternate basis for involuntary proceedings is that within 120 days before the petition was filed, a receiver, assignee, or custodian took possession of virtually all the debtor's property or was appointed to take charge of a substantial part of the debtor's property.

Unlike a voluntary petition, an involuntary petition does not operate as adjudication or as an order for relief. The debtor has a right to file an answer contesting the involuntary proceedings.

If the judge dismisses the petition on the request of the debtor, the court may grant judgment for the debtor against the petitioning creditors for all costs and reasonable attorney fees. If the creditor's petition was filed in bad faith, the court may also award punitive damages.

Stays in Debt Collection Proceedings

When a debtor files a bankruptcy petition or when a court sustains an involuntary petition, an automatic stay is issued. The stay virtually bars all debt collection efforts and gives the bankruptcy trustee time to collect the property of the estate. The stay acts to restrain creditors from taking any further action to enforce their claims or liens during the period of the stay. The creditors cannot foreclose on any property in the hands of the debtor during the period of the stay, except where permitted by a court order. The bankruptcy court may order an end to the stay. And the stay automatically terminates when the bankruptcy proceedings are closed or dismissed, or the debtor receives or is denied a discharge.

A creditor who has a secured interest in a debtor's property may, under certain circumstances, request that the court grant relief from the stay and allow the property to be attached.

Property of the Estate

Property of the estate includes all the debtor's property as of the time the petition was filed. The property of the estate includes both real and personal property, tangible property, and intangible property either in the debtor's possession or any property the debtor has an interest in. Property acquired after the petition was filed remains the debtor's property with the exception of that acquired by inheritance, settlement of a divorce degree, or being a beneficiary of a life insurance policy if the benefits were received within 180 days after the filing of the petition.

Fraudulent Conveyances

Section 5 of the Uniform Fraudulent Conveyance Act provides that every conveyance a businessperson makes that does not leave enough capital to pay the debts as they mature is fraudulent to both present and future creditors and that any such conveyance can therefore be set aside. The purpose behind the Uniform Fraudulent Conveyance Act is to prevent debtors from giving away or selling their property at a lower than market price and thereby defrauding creditors. Any creditor who can establish that a transfer of property was made by a debtor without fair consideration may take judicial action to have the transfer set aside. The creditor may also disregard the transfer and attach a levy on the property conveyed.

The Uniform Fraudulent Conveyance Act does not apply if fair consideration is given for the property. *Fair consideration* is defined as the exchange for such property, obligations, or monetary amounts as the fair equivalent thereof. Therefore, the selling of property by a debtor for a reasonable market price would not be considered in the Uniform Fraudulent Conveyance Act.

Forms in This Chapter

- FORM 15–1: REAFFIRMATION AGREEMENT. Used when the debtor agrees to reaffirm the debt (i.e., to pay the debt despite the fact that the debt could be discharged in bankruptcy). *Note:* This form must be filed with the bankruptcy court.
- FORM 15–2: PROOF OF CLAIM. Used to file a proof of claim against a debtor. Normally, this claim should be filed in only those cases where there are assets to be distributed by the court.
- FORM 15–3: SUMMONS. Summons a debtor or other party to appear at a hearing before the bankruptcy court.
- FORM 15–4: LETTER TO FILE CLAIM. Files a claim (Form 15–2) with the clerk of the court.

15-1 REAFFIRMATION AGREEMENT

B 240
(1/88)

REAFFIRMATION AGREEMENT

Debtor's Name	Bankruptcy Case No.

INSTRUCTIONS:

1) Write debtor's name and bankruptcy case number above.
2) Part A — Must be signed by both the debtor and the creditor.
3) Part B — Must be signed by the attorney who represents the debtor in this bankruptcy case.
4) Part C — Must be completed by the debtor if the debtor is **not** represented by an attorney in this bankruptcy case.
5) File the completed form by mailing or delivering to the Bankruptcy Clerk.
6) Attach written agreement, if any.

COURT USE ONLY

PART A — AGREEMENT

Creditor's Name and Address

Summary of Terms of the New Agreement

a) Principal Amount $ _____
   Interest Rate (APR) _____
   Monthly Payments $ _____
b) Description of Security: _____

Date Set for Discharge Hearing (If any)

Present Market Value $ _____

The parties understand that this agreement is purely voluntary and that the debtor may rescind the agreement at any time prior to discharge or within 60 days after such agreement is filed with the court, whichever occurs later, by giving notice of recission to the creditor.

_____   _____
Date   *Signature of Debtor*

_____   _____
Signature of Creditor   *Signature of Joint Debtor*

PART B — ATTORNEY'S DECLARATION

This agreement represents a fully informed and voluntary agreement that does not impose an undue hardship on the debtor or any dependent of the debtor.

_____   _____
Date   *Signature of Debtor's Attorney*

PART C — MOTION FOR COURT APPROVAL OF AGREEMENT — Complete only where debtor is not represented by an attorney.

I (we), the debtor, affirm the following to be true and correct:

1) I am not represented by an attorney in connection with this bankruptcy case.
2) My current monthly net income is $ _____
3) My current monthly expenses total $ _____, including any payment due under this agreement.
4) I believe that this agreement is in my best interest because _____
_____
_____

Therefore, I ask the court for an order approving this reaffirmation agreement.

_____   _____
Date   *Signature of Debtor*

                               _____
                               Signature of Joint Debtor

PART D — COURT ORDER

The court grants the debtor's motion and approves the voluntary agreement upon the terms specified above.

_____   _____
Date   *Bankruptcy Judge*

B10 (Official Form 10)
(Rev. 5 92)

United States Bankruptcy Court _____ District of _____	PROOF OF CLAIM
In re (Name of Debtor)	Case Number

NOTE: This form should not be used to make a claim for an administrative expense arising after the commencement of the case. A "request" for payment of an administrative expense may be filed pursuant to 11 U.S.C. § 503.

Name of Creditor *(The person or other entity to whom the debtor owes money or property)*	☐ Check box if you are aware that anyone else has filed a proof of claim relating to your claim. Attach copy of statement giving particulars.	
Name and Address Where Notices Should be Sent	☐ Check box if you have never received any notices from the bankruptcy court in this case.	THIS SPACE IS FOR COURT USE ONLY
Telephone No.	☐ Check box if the address differs from the address on the envelope sent to you by the court.	CHAPTER OF BANKRUPTCY CODE UNDER WHICH CASE IS PROCEEDING: Chapter _____

ACCOUNT OR OTHER NUMBER BY WHICH CREDITOR IDENTIFIES DEBTOR: Check here if this claim ☐ replaces / ☐ amends   a previously filed claim, dated: _____

1. BASIS FOR CLAIM

   Goods sold   ☐ Retiree benefits as defined in 11 U.S.C. § 1114(a)
   Services performed   Wages, salaries, and compensations (Fill out below)
   Money loaned   Your social security number _____
   Personal injury/wrongful death   Unpaid compensations for services performed
   Taxes   from _____ to _____
   Other (Describe briefly)   (date)   (date)

2. DATE DEBT WAS INCURRED	3. IF COURT JUDGMENT, DATE OBTAINED:

4. CLASSIFICATION OF CLAIM. Under the Bankruptcy Code all claims are classified as one or more of the following: (1) Unsecured nonpriority, (2) Unsecured Priority, (3) Secured. It is possible for part of a claim to be in one category and part in another. CHECK THE APPROPRIATE BOX OR BOXES that best describe your claim and STATE THE AMOUNT OF THE CLAIM AT TIME CASE FILED.

SECURED CLAIM $ _____
Attach evidence of perfection of security interest
Brief Description of Collateral:
   Real Estate   Motor Vehicle   Other (Describe briefly)

Amount of arrearage and other charges at time case filed included in secured claim above, if any $ _____

UNSECURED NONPRIORITY CLAIM $ _____
A claim is unsecured if there is no collateral or lien on property of the debtor securing the claim or to the extent that the value of such property is less than the amount of the claim.

☐ UNSECURED PRIORITY CLAIM $ _____

Specify the priority of the claim.

☐ Wages, salaries, or commissions (up to $2000), earned not more than 90 days before filing of the bankruptcy petition or cessation of the debtor's business, whichever is earlier—11 U.S.C. § 507(a)(3)

☐ Contributions to an employee benefit plan—U.S.C. § 507(a)(4)

☐ Up to $900 of deposits toward purchase, lease, or rental of property or services for personal, family, or household use—11 U.S.C. § 507(a)(6)

☐ Taxes or penalties of governmental units—11 U.S.C. § 507(a)(7)

☐ Other—11 U.S.C. § 507(a)(2), (a)(5), (a)(8)—(Circle applicable §)

5. TOTAL AMOUNT OF CLAIM AT TIME CASE FILED: $ _____ (Unsecured) $ _____ (Secured) $ _____ (Priority) $ _____ (Total)

☐ Check this box if claim includes charges in addition to the principal amount of the claim. Attach itemized statement of all additional charges.

6. CREDITS AND SETOFFS: The amount of all payments on this claim has been credited and deducted for the purpose of making this proof of claim. In filing this claim, claimant has deducted all amounts that claimant owes to debtor.	THIS SPACE IS FOR COURT USE ONLY
7. SUPPORTING DOCUMENTS: *Attach copies of supporting documents,* such as promissory notes, purchase orders, invoices, itemized statements of running accounts, contracts, court judgments, or evidence of security interests. If the documents are not available, explain. If the documents are voluminous, attach a summary.	
8. TIME-STAMPED COPY: To receive an acknowledgement of the filing of your claim, enclose a stamped, self-addressed envelope and copy of this proof of claim.	
Date Sign and print the name and title, if any, of the creditor or other person authorized to file this claim (attach copy of power of attorney, if any)	

Penalty for presenting fraudulent claim: Fine of up to $500,000 or imprisonment for up to 5 years, or both. 18 U.S.C. §§ 152 and 3571.

15-3 SUMMONS

B 250-A
(1 88)

United States Bankruptcy Court

_____ District of _____

In re

Bankruptcy Case No.

Debtor

Plaintiff

Adversary Proceeding No.

Defendant

SUMMONS IN AN ADVERSARY PROCEEDING

YOU ARE SUMMONED and required to submit a motion or answer to the complaint which is attached to this summons to the clerk of the bankruptcy court within 30 days after the date of issuance of this summons, except that the United States and its offices and agencies shall submit a motion or answer to the complaint within 35 days.

> Address of Clerk

At the same time, you must also serve a copy of the motion or answer upon the plaintiff's attorney.

> Name and Address of Plaintiff's Attorney

If you make a motion, your time to answer is governed by Bankruptcy Rule 7012.

IF YOU FAIL TO RESPOND TO THIS SUMMONS, YOUR FAILURE WILL BE DEEMED TO BE YOUR CONSENT TO ENTRY OF A JUDGMENT BY THE BANKRUPTCY COURT AND JUDGMENT BY DEFAULT MAY BE TAKEN AGAINST YOU FOR THE RELIEF DEMANDED IN THE COMPLAINT.

_____
Clerk of the Bankruptcy Court

_____   By: _____
Date   _Deputy Clerk_

CERTIFICATE OF SERVICE

I, _____ , certify that I am, and at all times during the service
            (name)

of process was, not less than 18 years of age and not a party to the matter concerning which service of process was made. I further certify that the service of this summons and a copy of the complaint was made _____ by:
        (date)

☐ Mail service: Regular, first class United States mail, postage fully pre-paid, addressed to:

☐ Personal Service: By leaving the process with defendant or with an officer or agent of defendant at:

☐ Residence Service: By leaving the process with the following adult at:

☐ Publication: The defendant was served as follows: [Describe briefly]

☐ State Law: The defendant was served pursuant to the laws of the State of _____ ,
  as follows: [Describe briefly]   (name of state)

Under penalty of perjury, I declare that the foregoing is true and correct.

_____   _____
           Date   *Signature*

Print Name		
Busines. Address		
City	State	Zip

15-4   LETTER TO FILE CLAIM

Clerk, Bankruptcy Court

[address]

Re: No. [case number of debtor's case]; [debtor's name]

Dear Madam/Sir:

Enclosed is a Proof of Claim with supporting documentation. Please file the subject claim. Enclosed is a stamped self-addressed envelope. Please return one copy of the claim form after it has been stamped with your filing stamp.

Sincerely,

Legal Glossary

Note: For legal terms not listed in this glossary, refer to Black's Law Dictionary or Cochran's Law Dictionary in the reference section of most libraries.

Adverse impact. Disadvantage to members of the protected class due to a substantially different rate of selection in hiring, firing, promotion, or other employment decisions.

Affidavit. A written statement of facts, signed and sworn to before an official with the authority to administer oaths.

Affirm. To ratify or approve the judgment of a lower court or an administrative decision.

Agent. A person with the authority to do an act for another.

Appeal. A request or application to a higher court to set aside or modify the decision or ruling of a lower court.

Appellant. The party who initiates the appeal.

Appellee. The party to a lawsuit against whom an appeal is taken.

Arbitration. The submission of a dispute to the nonjudicial judgment of one or more disinterested persons, called arbitrators.

Assign. To transfer rights to another party, called the assignee. The party who assigns the rights is called the *assignor*.

Bona fide. In good faith, honestly, and without fraud.

Bona fide occupational qualification (BFOQ). A good faith, honest, and without fraud preemployment qualification that is essential to establish the ability of the applicant to perform the necessary and required duties of the position in question.Book value. The net worth of a business's assets, minus liabilities, without considering any value for goodwill.

Brief. A prepared statement of a party's position in a legal proceeding.

Burden of proof. The duty of a party to present the evidence to establish that party's contentions or version of the facts. Failure to meet the burden of proof will result in a decision for the opposing party.

Case law. Judicial precedent set forth in prior court opinions that will bind parties in future lawsuits.

Caveat. A warning.

Circumstantial evidence. Evidence not directly proving the existence of a fact in question but tending to imply its existence.

Civil Rights Act of 1964. The civil rights act that forms the basis of most equal opportunity requirements. Title 42, U.S. Code, section 1447 et seq.

Civil service commissions.   Various groups of local, state, or federal officials that supervise public employees.

Claimant.   A person who makes a claim for benefits.

Clayton Act.   The act that amended the Sherman Antitrust Act and that prohibits unlawful restraints on trade.

Collective bargaining.   The bargaining between management and labor unions regarding the terms and conditions of employment.

Commerce clause.   Article I, section VIII of the U.S. Constitution, which gives the U.S. Congress the authority to regulate trade between the states.

Common law.   An ambiguous term used to describe the concept of law that relies on precedent (i.e., previous court opinions) and traditions.

Compensatory damages.   The measure of actual damages or losses.

Concurrent jurisdiction.   The authority of two or more courts to entertain a particular lawsuit.

Consequential damages.   A measure of damages referring to the indirect injuries or losses that a party suffers.

Defendant.   The party against whom a lawsuit is initiated.

De novo.   A new, fresh start.

Deposition.   Oral questions and answers reduced to writing for possible use in a legal proceeding.

Dictum.   Statement in a judicial opinion that is not necessary to support the decision in that case and therefore not considered as precedence.

Equal Employment Opportunity Commission (EEOC).   A commission established under the Civil Rights Act of 1964 to administer the act.

Et seq.   Latin term meaning "and following parts."

Fair Labor Standards Act of 1938.   An act designed to establish fair labor standards in employment involved in interstate commerce. (See Chapter 5 and Title 29 U.S. Code, section 201 et seq.)

Good faith.   An honest and fair purpose without the intent to commit an unjust act.

Hearsay evidence.   Statements made by witnesses in legal proceedings regarding information obtained from a third person.

Injunction.   A court order directing a party to refrain from certain activity.

Interstate commerce.   Any trade, transportation, or communication among the several states or with the District of Columbia. *Affecting* interstate commerce means "involved in," "having an impact on," "burdening," or "obstructing it."

Job analysis. A detailed statement of work behaviors and other information relevant to a job.

Job description. A general statement of the duties and responsibilities entailed in a job.

Jurisdiction. The authority for a court or administrative body to hear and decide a dispute.

Labor arbitration. A nonjudicial settlement of disputes between labor and management.

Labor dispute. Any dispute under a labor contract between the employer and the labor union concerning the terms, conditions, or tenure of employment or concerning the representation of persons in negotiating, maintaining, or changing the terms or conditions of employment.

Labor–Management Relations Act of 1947 (LMRA). The Taft–Hartley Act, which amended the National Labor Relations Act, to provide additional facilities for mediation of labor disputes and place obligations on labor organizations similar to those earlier placed on management.

Labor–Management Reporting and Disclosure Act of 1959 (LMRDA). An act designed to ensure democratic procedures in labor unions and to establish a bill of rights for union members.

Labor organization. Any labor organization, committee, or group that is organized for the benefit of employees and subject to the provisions of the Civil Rights Act of 1964 or the federal labor management acts.

National Labor Relations Act of 1935 (NLRA). The Wagner Act, which established the NLRB and was designed to support unionism and collective bargaining.

National Labor Relations Board (NLRB). A commission established by the NLRA to enforce the rights of employees under the act.

Nationality. The status acquired by belonging to or being associated with a nation or state. It arises by birth or nationalization.

Norris–LaGuardia Act. An act passed by U.S. Congress in 1932, designed to stop federal courts from issuing injunctions in labor strikes.

Original jurisdiction. The court with the authority to hear the case first. The trial court.

Plaintiff. The party who initiates a lawsuit.

Pleadings. The formal written statements of parties to a lawsuit that establish the basis of each party's contentions before the court.

Prejudice. A bias that interferes with a person's impartiality and sense of fairness.

Right-to-work laws. State antiunion laws that prohibit labor contracts that require all employees to join a union.

Sherman Antitrust Act. An act passed in 1890 that was designed to protect trade and commerce by prohibiting certain restraints of trade and monopolies.

Strike. An organized refusal to work by the employees that is designed to place economic pressure on the employer.

Total disability. A physical disability that prevents a person from performing all of the substantial acts necessary for the person's job or occupation.

Index